THE LIGHTED PATH

THE LIGHTED PATH

A JOURNEY OF TRANSFORMATION AND TRANSCENDENCE

Risha Henrique

B

BERKLEY BOOKS, NEW YORK

THE LIGHTED PATH

A Berkley Book / published by arrangement with
the author

PRINTING HISTORY
Berkley trade paperback edition / December 1996

The Putnam Berkley World Wide Web site address is
http://www.berkley.com/berkley

ISBN: 0-425-15456-4

BERKLEY®
Berkley Books are published by The Berkley Publishing Group,
200 Madison Avenue, New York, New York 10016.
BERKLEY and the "B" design
are trademarks belonging to Berkley Publishing Corporation.

PRINTED IN THE UNITED STATES OF AMERICA

10 9 8 7 6 5 4 3 2 1

CONTENTS

PROLOGUE:

THE SACRED CHANT

On the evening of August 16, 1987, an event occurred on our planet that reverberated throughout the universe.

There was not a drop of rain, yet the sky was alive with lightning when Hawk on the Wind, a medicine woman, spoke a sacred word for the first time in tens of thousands of years.

So began the fulfillment of prophecies passed down to Hawk on the Wind by her ancestors. One prophecy stated that at a specific time on the evening of August 16 she was to perform a ceremony and dance with those who gathered with her on a plateau in the land south of the Great Lakes where it is said that Creator's hand touched the Earth. She was to release upon the wind a sacred word for the first time in 28,860 years, a word so sacred that it was not to be spoken again for another 30,000 years.

Between August 16 and August 17, an unusual alignment of planets caused a cosmic door to stay open for twenty-two hours. Our galaxy provided a wave of vital energy to enhance the evolution of all life-forms on Earth. Many people gathered at sacred sites throughout the world to celebrate the event known as the Harmonic Convergence, which was initiated by the Mayan people, one of the great civilizations of our planet.

The celebration drew like-minded individuals into a united force to show the rest of the universe that we were prepared and worthy to enter into the next stage of the evolution of our planet.

According to the Mayan calendar, 1987 marks the beginning of the final twenty-five years of a major historical cycle. The end of this cycle, approximately in the year A.D. 2012, indicates that great change is expected to occur within ourselves and on the planet. Over this next two and one half decades, from 1987 to 2012, humanity will be forced into a significant period of reckoning and growth.

Many prophets of various cultures, from Christian and Hebrew to Hopi and Tibetan, have predicted that we have entered a time in which there will be a great spiritual transformation on Earth.

The ceremony that took place on August 16, 1987, represented the beginning of the transformation of our world, and for me it also signified the beginning of a dramatic personal journey.

Hawk stood on a hill and proclaimed the sacred word that could be heard throughout the valley, but I believe it was heard throughout the world. This momentous occasion took place where the Creator originally placed His palm, in what is recognized today as Ohio, "the heart of it all." Humanity originated here in the area south of where His fingers of fire scorched the land and created the five great lakes of North America.

The people on the hill chanted and drummed. They danced a movement that reflected the way the planets were aligned. They all felt that a fire had been lit inside them, a fire that warmed them and illuminated their very being. They saw themselves and others with brilliant clarity. The hill had been charged with energy and great healing power; and since then many extraordinary experiences have happened there.

It was also in the prophecies that the Thunderbeings would come to Earth at this time. Thunderbeings were present on the hill that day. In current terminology, they are referred to as illuminated ones, healers, avatars, buffalo hearts, starseeds, rainbow children, planetary servers, wizards. They are beings and keepers of the light and guardians of the knowledge of the universe. Thunderbeings come from the Pleiades star system. They come from a planet that has four suns. Their goal is to help humankind take a quantum leap into a new age of global harmony. Thunderbeings are the bringers of the final transformation; their lightning-quick energy brings instantaneous change. They are spirit creatures whose creative power can make thunder and bring the rain. They turn hate and anger into caring and harmony. Nature trusts them because their hearts are true. Wherever they go they create the kind of thunder that has universal effects not just upon this Earth, but throughout all the galaxies.

The Pleiades look like a cluster of seven stars. Hawk says that as long as all the Thunderbeings are on Earth, no one will be able to see the light of the seventh star; only six stars will be visible. The seventh star will not be seen again until the Thunderbeings return home.

Beneath the surface, Thunderbeings are beautiful creatures with misty faces and large, liquid eyes. They are visionary beings from the stars who inhabit human forms. Their aura emanates lavender and pink, like the colors of the northern lights. They are recognized by the heavens as the trusted keepers of the gateway that will lead to the transformation of this planet. They are the Creator's dream team!

The Thunderbeings are here to do battle with the forces of darkness and ignorance. They are sacred warriors with the galactic mission of transforming the planet, and they won't rest until the final transformation is under way. I was given the opportunity to be a part of this; I am here to participate in the most exciting drama in the history of Earth: the Great Awakening and the enlightenment of the human mind. Many beings from other planetary systems have chosen to become incarnate at this time to witness and participate in the accelerated spiritual evolution.

The awakening is about recognizing that separate nations and separate peoples are an illusion, for we are all part of the same cosmic dance. It is about realizing that an overly materialistic civilization, which neglects the instinct for spiritual growth, produces a society that destroys the planetary immune system. It is about the need for a new phase in human development in which we step beyond anger and violence and establish higher spiritual goals. It is about recognizing that suffering has no purpose. It is about giving up our addiction to unhappiness. In the new world there will be no suffering and no disease, for we will live in perfect harmony with ourselves and everything around us.

Hawk on the Wind informed us that on August 30, 1987, we began a new cycle of a new world. She said that humanity has been through five evolutions of five worlds, or stages of development. We were at our purest and most spiritual in the First World. Then with each successive world we decreased in purity of consciousness until the recent Fifth World, where we've reached our lowest point with an uncontrolled expression of ruthless materialism and the use of force to achieve dominance over others.

The Hopi prophecies also refer to worlds of evolution. As each world turned away from spirituality, it ended in catastrophe; at the end of each world Spirit called for a cleansing. One world ended in volcanic eruptions, the next, in powerful winds, and the third, in a great flood. The final cleansing would see all the natural forces being called into action, which is happening right now.

The time has arrived in which we must take action. Our current problems, which range from overpopulation and nuclear threat to pollution and the collapse of governmental institutions, are getting worse. We're consuming billions of tons of resources, and we're also spewing out billions of tons of pollutants into the environment every year. This cannot continue on a planet with limited resources. The planet is already overcrowded. Statistics show that *within* our lifetime there will be four people on Earth for every one alive today. Humankind needs to decide whether to live within the limits of Earth's resources or to keep on growing until stopped by nature, which will most likely be a much harsher fate. It is as though humankind has become the illness of the Earth, and because she is a living entity, just like our bodies, the Earth Mother is sending out white blood cells to fight and attack the illness within. It seems almost ironic that one of the major diseases facing our society, AIDS, resembles this particular scenario.

Many of the prophecies of a great upheaval at the end of the millennium are coming true. We are experiencing an increased number of disasters as all the natural forces are being called to restore the balance of creation.

Human beings will have to undergo a period of great turmoil and calamity, and possibly massive destruction, before they are ready for the new world. Those who do not choose to participate in awakening to a more spiritual consciousness will have the most difficult time. Life for them will be an uphill battle, for they will not be in flow with the universal forces.

The Thunderbeings are also here to help the Earth avert a major cataclysm that threatens to bring total destruction sometime before the year 2012.

We are headed either for planetary catastrophe or for the birthing of a new world, depending on whether or not we elevate our consciousness.

Hawk said that if humans do not expand to a greater consciousness by 2012 they will cease to exist.

The Thunderbeings themselves faced a major hurdle that had to be overcome. If they did not succeed in jumping this hurdle, Earth might very well be doomed. Although they are enlightened beings who have assisted many planets in their evolution, they agreed to come to Earth under the same pretext as every other human: *they agreed to forget who they really are.* They came to Earth under the same veil of forgetfulness, of not seeing the divine essence of their being. They arrived almost in a state of amnesia, having forgotten the very purpose for which they had come: to help humankind ascend to its next evolutionary stage. In choosing to be here they also took a tremendous risk: if they do not succeed, they will have to continue to be reincarnated until full consciousness is realized.

If the Thunderbeings are to succeed in their mission, they must first transform themselves. They must awaken into levels of being and knowing undreamed of in present-day society. They must travel on Hawk's wing, creating change wherever they go. They must journey into the subterranean chambers of inner earth. They will have to *become* one with the wind; they will have to *become* one with the fire—and not burn—and one with the Earth. They will have to become one consciousness: one heart, one mind, and one soul. They will have to experience an extraordinary intimacy with nature, just as our ancestors did.

Their success in these endeavors will accelerate the advancement of humanity. It will facilitate the passage to a more exalted consciousness needed to reverse our global challenges. We have reached a critical juncture on Earth, a point of no return. Humans will either self-destruct or become pure again. If we become pure, we will be able to experience all of our potential, all of the gifts originally given to us, the natural powers that we have lost and forgotten. We will once again find ourselves in the paradise that existed at the beginning of time.

CHAPTER 1

IN THE BEGINNING

There was a great earthquake; and the sun became
black as sackcloth of hair, and the moon became as
blood; and the stars fell unto the earth . . . and the
heaven departed as a scroll when it is rolled together;
and every mountain and the islands were moved out of
their places.

—Revelation 6:12–14

INDEED, THE THUNDERBEINGS WERE up against a deadline. The end of the millennium was fast approaching. The disintegration of the social fabric was affecting the consciousness of entire nations and cultures, producing confusion, chaos, and extremes of behavior. Many signs have appeared indicating the breakdown of human civilization, such as the conjunction of two powerful planets, Neptune and Uranus, in 1993. (Uranus-Neptune changes are said to be connected with the dissolution of empires and kingdoms.) This conjunction, which happens once every 171 years, was accompanied by devastating storms, droughts, and floods. *Life* magazine, in September 1993, reported it was "the year of killer weather."

As the 1990s unfold, every day brings new stories of weather disturbances, ecological disasters, irrational swings in the economy, tragedies, scandals, and crimes. We are seeing people in power finally being exposed for their deceptions.

We can expect some of these events in the coming years: a shift of the polar axis; a new climate being established; major disturbances on both coasts of the United States; major sections of the United States falling into the sea; some parts of the British Isles being submerged; land rising in the North Sea, as Norway, Sweden, Denmark, and Finland experience repeated coastal innundations; and most of Hawaii and Japan breaking away. These projections correspond very closely with the entire range of prophecies for the millennium made by prophets as far back as biblical times.[1]

We have already faced many natural disasters because of environmental changes wrought by humans. Deforestation and intensive farming have caused floods and landslides while global warming is suspected of altering weather patterns and producing more killer storms and typhoons. The biggest hole ever in the Earth's protective ozone layers is forming over the Antarctic. Geologists warn that the rise of big cities along seismic fault lines could cause unprecedented catastrophes in the next several decades.

As Mother Earth rejuvenates her body, things are expected to get worse before they get better. The world cycle of topsy-turvy temperatures and record-breaking storms will continue probably until 2005, according to climatologists. We may have to face increasingly vicious and destructive natural phenomena, with earthquakes possibly reaching readings of 10.0 and 12.0 on the Richter scale. The chain of events will rearrange the land masses of the planet, according to the Hopi, Mayan, and Tibetan prophecies, which foresee a different geography after the year 2012.

Overpopulation and industrialization have severely depleted the natural resources of the planet. Our species already consumes more food than all other land vertebrates combined. We have stripped and altered most of the forests and grasslands. Our nonrenewable resources, such as minerals and fossil-fuel deposits, are being depleted. The world supply of crude oil and natural gas will be exhausted within a few decades. We have been extravagant and wasteful, we have poisoned the soil and the waterways, we have destroyed tropical forests, and we have driven many species to extinction.

What does it say about our determination and will if we're not able to save the black rhino and countless other creatures from extinction? Imagine how lonely a world without animals would be. The destruction of any creature on our planet is a foreshadowing of our own demise. If we are not willing to allocate our resources to save even one animal, how can we possibly save ourselves? Our wildlife should be a top priority.

Every other consciousness on Earth understands the changes. The animals seem to know already. A place like California does not have a huge population of animals because nature has prepared them for catastrophe. Drought, forest fires, and earthquakes have driven them away, and they're not eager to come back. People, on the other hand, continue to disregard the danger signals. But deep down inside, they *know* there is a quickening; they can *feel* it. That is why we're more jittery; we are all reacting to the earthquakes.

Hawk advised the Thunderbeings to stay tuned in to nature for warning signs; there are many to watch for. The feathered beings and the animals and the water spirits will communicate with us. A shift in the Earth's axis is a great probability. And we are in the path of meteorite activity, with meteors moving rapidly toward Earth. The indigenous peoples say that meteors have been speaking through the mountains and the stones for a long time.

As storms, floods, and earthquakes accelerate, Hawk and the Thunderbeings will attempt to do whatever they can. They will use ancient dances and chants to minimize or ease the effect of the destructive forces, or at least to delay some of the devastation.

The area around the Great Lakes was in danger of a buildup of pressures. Hawk led the Thunderbeings gathered there in prayer and song for the release of this energy. Afterward she was given a vision that they were successful and able to defuse the buildup of energy.

When a cycle of severe storms began at the end of the 1980s, the Thunderbeings worked at reducing the impact; it could have been much worse. Hurricane Gilbert had the highest winds ever recorded in the Northern Hemisphere—200 mph. Then Hurricane Hugo devastated the Caribbean and the Carolina coast. When another hurricane ripped apart south Florida, followed by a blizzard that swept up from that state to Maine, it was called the biggest storm of the century.

After an earthquake rocked Los Angeles, Hawk and the Thunderbeings focused their thoughts to assist the victims. They sent their prayers across the country in the hope that the victims of the quake would understand the message of the Earth Mother: *move!*

In the years to come they would also continue to pray and work their medicines to help curtail the spread of certain deadly diseases.

There was only so much that Hawk and the Thunderbeings, including myself, could do. In fact, we struggled to decide how much we should interfere with the Earth Mother's need to cleanse herself. She needs to get on with her growth; she is under a tremendous amount of stress because of poisons and chemicals in her body. She feels the vibrations of hatred and anger—and of our total disregard for one another and for her. We continue to value our economies and technological advances more than her well-being when in fact her well-being is our survival. As a people if we do not choose to change our path, then the path will be changed for us.

In her need to protect herself, the Earth Mother will unleash her floods, her winds, and her quakes, which will certainly tear down our human-made structures and force us to return to what is truly important. It is not a punishment—if people were helping one another in a spirit of caring and respect, the disasters wouldn't have to happen. We need more people around the world, including positive-thinking people in major positions of power, to insist on peace and harmony. As Hawk said, we have the ability to circumvent disaster, just as our ancestors did, by knowing future events and being a part of the solution, not the problem.

Meanwhile we wondered, is it our place to try to prevent destruction? Or are we an instrument for what needs to be done? We knew that the purification was necessary and yet we felt that we could minimize or eliminate some of the cleansings. The outlook didn't have to be all doom and gloom. If people woke up from their stupor and all collectively made a change, we wouldn't have to run around trying to defuse calamities. There were times when I didn't understand what power we really had to do this. What could twenty or thirty people do? Who heard our chants and prayers? Who saw our dances?

My anxious questions were answered one cold sunny day in January toward the end of the 1980s when we had gathered on the shores of Lake Erie. I was thinking to myself, What am I doing here? Are you telling me that ten women and five men are going to make a change? And almost at that very moment a thick ice-crystal rainbow, colored brilliantly beyond anything I'd ever seen, appeared. It arose out of the lake and extended all the way south of Cleveland. It cleared away all my doubts. It was as though the Earth were smiling at me and thanking me. I had a big wide grin on my face, and I knew from this moment on that I was truly making a change.

We have to try our best, but we also need to be joined by other Thunderbeings around the planet. All of these events are in line with our ancestors' prophecies that describe a great purification, also known as earth changes, which would prepare the way for a new world.

It has been said that during the time of the Thunderbeings there will be a great wind and fire on the face of the Earth. The Thunderbeings will be the breath of new life that will bring humanity back into oneness again. They will build the new fire of wisdom that will illuminate the world. This new fire will burn away the restrictions of the mind and reveal the deeper, more spiritual aspects of our nature.

Another prophecy states that the Thunderbeings, once they have completed their mission, will return to their home in the Pleiades. Hawk on the Wind has said to them: "I will not leave you. Wherever there is God, so will I go on; and I will gather the Thunderbeings who have moved into form."

Hawk was told to watch for signs that will fulfill the prophecy of the great purification. One of these signs consisted of the discovery of a doorway to the other home through the black hole behind the Milky Way. This doorway is the place called "the Lighted Path to other worlds." In 1988 scientists discovered that a massive black hole exists at the center of the Milky Way galaxy. This has been spoken of in the ancient teachings for more than 100,000 years.

And another prophecy states that "When the time of the heavens begins they will see the great light from the star moving toward them, bringing the universal song. And there shall be a great light amongst the Earth people."

Some time ago it was reported in several journals that scientists in North America are greatly concerned because particles of light, called photons, are bombarding our atmosphere. A photon belt was first detected with satellites in 1961. Later there arose speculation that this light is emanating from the center of our galaxy. The Mayans refer to it as *la luz*, the light.

Hunbatz Men, a Mayan elder and daykeeper,[2] once told me that we are starting to experience different influences of energy from other solar systems. "That energy," he said, "will begin to wake us up to understand more about our existence on Earth." He mentioned a Mayan calendar called the Tzolkin, which is based on the cycle of the Pleiades. It takes 26,000 years for all the planets in our solar system to complete one cycle around the Pleiades. He noted that one cycle is now close to completion, and this indicates "big changes in the mentality of the human race when we will again receive the old cosmic knowledge."

We have moved so far away from our original full consciousness that we no longer understand or accept it. In fact we've made our psychic ability something supernatural that's *outside* us. We don't realize how far we have wandered from being a part of the great circle of creation. Let us put things into perspective. . . .

Although the first people on Earth were of different colors and spoke different languages, they still understood one another; people and animals all felt as one. There was peace, friendship, and harmony; there were fields of plenty. People were so pure that in the first and original languages there was no word for "lie."

In the First World everything was all light and energy. We were created as love. From the center of all creation came the experience of life. We lived as sacred beings and as part of God, in a complete state of trust. We reflected the beauty and love of nature with one consciousness. We were the great council of humans and there was no government. In the original nation, the two-legged was known as the brother to the tree. That was the time before the civilization of Atlantis. That was the time before separation, when all the creations were in communication with one another. We were the most trusted of all the creations. We followed the original instructions on how to live in balance and harmony, instructions that were given to humans long before the existence of religion or government.

But with the passage of time, we grew further away from our intimate connection with the Earth; we discarded the original instructions. The animals started to draw away from us. And then things got worse when some humans wanted to control other humans and started religions that did not tolerate contrary beliefs. In their quest for domination and control, they insisted that the Earth was a place of suffering. They invented horror stories about hell and the devil, which even intelligent people believed! They insisted that those who practiced the old ways of ceremony—who did not need cathedrals or priests—were pagans! And the ultimate deception happened before our very eyes when a group of humans declared that the Earth was just a lifeless ball of matter!

And so we became disconnected from the cycles of nature. We moved away from following the natural cyclical patterns of the sun and the moon to the linear and abstract fragmentation of time into hours, minutes, and seconds. We stopped following the thirteen-moon calendar, which reflects the Earth's orbit around the sun; each moon of twenty-eight days corresponds approximately to the female menstrual cycle. Thirteen moons is the annual biological rhythm of the human species in one orbit around the sun.

In our arrogance, in our desire to be of ourselves and separate from Creation, we instituted our own timekeeping system: the twelve-month year and sixty-minute hour. It is said that the twelve-month calendar was created in Babylon and then picked up by the Romans and Pope Gregory XIII, who then initiated the Gregorian calendar. It does not correspond to the natural cycles of time; it has no connection to the sacred numbers of the cosmos; there is no such thing as a cycle of thirty or thirty-one days. The thirteenth moon was distributed as extra days to the calendar of twelve. Thirteen is the number of God's cosmic wisdom; thirteen represents the strongest frequency of harmony, yet we've made it something to be feared. How can harmony come from buildings where we've refused to name the thirteenth floor?

Only in a few places around the world did people continue to follow the calendar of thirteen. Among them were Mayans, who were masters of time, as well as mystics who could escape time. The Mayans used several calendars because they worked with the larger cycles of time. Hunbatz Men told me they understood through their calendars that we carry millions of years of evolution in our body and our spirit is billions of years old. Their calendars were calculated to numbers that are harmonious with the movements of the stars and planets. When we follow this system, we are flowing with rather than against the cosmic order.

We are the only species that does not live as part of a biosphere of Earth that is all one web of life. We have refused to synchronize ourselves to the natural cycles of time, and as we have mechanized time, that is what has happened to our mind. The calendar and the clock have become icons of worship. We are imprisoned by the clock—it tells us when to wake up, when to eat, and when to work and play. We have given away our own power to something that is so cold and brutal and relentless that it ticks away no matter what; it controls and manipulates us. Meanwhile there's passion in the moon and the sun, which are true indicators of time—and yet we refuse to use them as our timekeepers.

We are trying to keep up with the technology we've created, which is going faster and faster. José Argüelles, a proponent of the thirteen-moon calendar, says that the biosphere is now carrying a species that is moving on its own time and we don't know how to stop it.[3]

The Thunderbeings, from their home in the Pleiades, watched in horror as the memory of the original order of Earth faded in increasing numbers of humans. By the time of the emergence of skyscrapers, X-rays, airplanes, the theory of relativity, psychoanalysis, and the detonation of the first atomic bomb in 1945, the planet was spinning out of control. There was a total disregard of the sun and moon and true principles of cosmic order. Loneliness and despair were born in us, feelings we had never experienced when we were a part of the rest of creation. With time winding down to the coming of the millennium, things seemed worse than ever before.

We were on a disaster course.

Fortunately, a few enlightened people have always stayed connected to the voices of the universe and nature. The peacekeepers and earthkeepers, for example. They held on to their vision, waiting for the time when Earth would return to her original pristine order. For five hundred years they waited for Hawk and the Thunderbeings to come back to Earth. They called out for the Thunderbeings in their sacred song. They showed their caring to all living beings through their dance. They spoke to the spirit world through the rhythm of their rattles. They touched upon the heart of the Earth Mother with the sound of their drums. Their ceremonies contained built-in codes, ensuring they would never forget the original instructions even when others had lost their way.

The arrival of great teachers, or avatars, such as the Buddha, Christ, and Quetzalcoatl, also helped to keep alive the memory of our true evolutionary purpose. Some say that the world would have fallen apart even sooner without these noble peacekeepers and teachers.

When the Thunderbeings and Hawk finally arrived, we had lived for many years like the rest of humanity, under a veil of forgetfulness, not knowing of one another. Yet with each passing year, a deep yearning stirred and grew within each of us.

Hawk saw many of our faces in visions and dreams long before she met us.

"I knew many of you were coming," she was to tell us. "I kept my fire burning, waiting for you."

Though we were scattered across the globe, unseen forces—or, as Hawk would say, Spirit—worked to bring us together. Initially, those who gathered lived mostly within the region that stretched from the Great Lakes to the southeastern portion of the United States. Some encountered "the right person," who led them to Hawk. Others felt compelled to do something without knowing why, and this impulse ultimately led them to an encounter with Hawk. One Thunderbeing by the name of Tonya said she was inexplicably drawn "to go to the other side" of her hometown, and when she did, she found information that led her to Hawk. Others received visions of what was to come. A huge hawk flew into Katherine's backyard and perched outside the door of her kitchen.

Each situation was unique enough to seem beyond mere coincidence.

By the mid-1980s we Thunderbeings had started to gather. During that first encounter with Hawk, many felt an immediate attraction to her. They described seeing a "beautiful golden light" around her. Nora said she met Hawk at a weekend program on ancient methods of connecting to the Earth Mother: "We were doing a meditation around a medice wheel. There was a big crystal in the center, and the spirit of the crystal spoke to me loud and clear. It said, 'Your life will change!' For a total skeptic like me it was mind-boggling."

Liz recalled what a beautiful sunny day it was when she arrived at a celebration of cultural dancing, drumming, and singing: "Hawk called in the thunder, and you could hear it rumble, even though there was not a cloud in the sky. Within ten to twenty minutes the clouds piled up on the western horizon. Hawk had a beautiful golden light around her, and I had an urge to touch her face. She was so vibrant yet so tender."

Alison spoke of her unhappiness with her religion. She said she had searched long and hard for a medicine woman and had even set up a medicine wheel in her backyard. "I would dance and dance in circles. It helped me to contain my strong urges." One day she was dancing so furiously that a lightning bolt hit her roof—the thunder spirits had come into her living room!

And John said that he met Hawk at a seminar she was giving. He approached her: "After she hugged me I couldn't speak for twenty minutes. I pulled away and started to cry. I tried to express how I felt. 'I don't know what's come over me,' I said to her. And she replied, 'It's because you have never experienced unconditional love before.' "

And so it was that the Thunderbeings came together as part of a great plan. We had come in response to Earth's cry for help. Many of us bided our time waiting until we made that fateful connection with Hawk. We did not understand violence or malice, nor did we feel comfortable with the widespread disregard for Earth. When we finally connected with Hawk, we felt as though we had found a safe place to express our feelings. We felt accepted and empowered in being involved with liked-minded individuals. We felt embraced by a caring mother, nestled close to her bosom, protected from the world.

Hawk told us that one day we will be beautiful light beings that will fly and bring beauty to everything. "Beloveds, I know what you are capable of," she said again and again. "You don't know how magnificent you are yet. Your ability will come back. It didn't go anywhere. You will awaken!" She talked about the beauty of being human and the magnitude of activity that is in just one little cell of the body.

"Your fire is the wisdom of the world," she told us. "It is time to start embracing Spirit. Spirit is the only real thing. The body makes you desperate. Are you this body? Is that your totality? Look at how it wears you out. We are Spirit. When you make this third-dimensional existence your whole focus, you remain fragile and vulnerable."

She encouraged us to bring spirituality into our everyday lives. She said that spirituality is not an occasion; it is not something reserved for one day of the week. It is in the way we think and speak and act. For too long we have viewed the spiritual as something apart from our everyday self.

We got together and spent time in meditation and prayer. We burned sage, cedar, and sweet grass and, through the smoke, sent out our prayers for the Earth, for peace and harmony, for humankind. We concentrated on creating a halo of love around the planet.

As we started to awaken and remember who we really were, something significant started to happen.

With our prayers we were creating another force on Earth, a counterforce to ignorance and destructiveness. We were extending past our individual boundaries and assisting the Earth. We did not have that much time—the great cosmic moment of the millennial year was around the corner. Many new lethal diseases had begun their dance of death across the planet, and medical science was helpless to cure them.

Hawk advised us to keep our energy up and watch our thoughts.

As we emerge into the last twenty years before 2012, we have come to the gateway of a new world; this is the time to establish the patterns for the future. Everything will move so fast and occur so spontaneously that time will seem to be shrinking; increasingly we will experience time lapse, time warps, and timelessness. Stability will no longer be a part of the global scene. The way we used to analyze life will no longer work. We will feel frustrated if we try to grasp what is happening with the mind; there will be no place for the mind. Instead we are being forced to look within ourselves. We are being forced to examine how we habitually disengage from the feeling part of our nature, for modern man has much knowledge but little feeling.

The tremendous infusion of cosmic light reaching us will cause erratic behavior. Many will experience physical fatigue as well as increased mental and emotional stress: headaches, tightness in the neck and shoulders, nausea, vertigo, and other chronic undiagnosable problems. (A doctor once pointed out to me that "stress" is actually a fear of what is happening around us. It is a modern word coined to denote a true feeling, which is fear of such things as losing control and not having the answers.)

As the changes quicken, many will doubt their own sanity. Those who harbor negative attitudes such as despair and mistrust will have the most difficult time. The best way to ride the wave of change is to realize that we are not in control—only the great mystery is in control. As Hawk says, "I am never crazy enough to think that I am controlling anything or anybody." In this regard, we can learn much by watching nature. A bird opens its wings to catch the wind and flows with it in whatever direction it's going. The bird knows enough to allow itself to be directed by the wind and doesn't battle with it.

As we approach the year A.D. 2000, we will accelerate through changes we can't even begin to fathom. If the new world dawns, we will return to peace and a harmonious existence. We will come again into a knowledge of our sacred beginnings, and we shall awaken to the true meaning of life. At this very moment we stand at the doorstep of a new world. The Great Awakening has already begun; there will be nowhere to run or hide from it. We are walking into the uncharted space between two worlds, and for many the experience will be frightening and painful and fraught with upheaval.

NOTES

1. A.T. Mann, *Millennium Prophecies* (Element Books, Inc., Rockport, Mass: 1992.), p. 113.
2. A daykeeper is an authority on the history, chronology, and calendars of Mayan civilization. Humbatz lectures on the teachings of the traditional Maya and is the author of several books, including *Secrets of Mayan Science/Religion*.
3. José Argüelles is also the author of a number of books, including *The Mayan Factor* (Bear & Company, Santa Fe, NM: 1987).

CHAPTER 2

CHANCE MEETINGS

Our deepest fear is not that we are inadequate. Our deepest
fear is that we are powerful beyond measure. It is our light,
not our darkness, that frightens us. We ask ourselves, who am
I to be brilliant, gorgeous, talented, and fabulous? Actually,
who are you not to be? You are a child of God. Your playing
small doesn't serve the world. There's nothing enlightened
about shrinking so that other people won't feel insecure
around you. We were born to manifest the glory of God within
us. It's not just in some of us; it's in everyone. And as we let
our own light shine, we unconsciously give other people
permission to do the same. As we are liberated from our own
fear, our presence automatically liberates others.

—NELSON MANDELA, *1994 Inaugural Speech*

LONG BEFORE I MET Hawk I contemplated my existence on Earth.
What was my purpose? What had happened to the sacredness and
value of life? Where was the bliss reported by the mystics who had
reached Nirvana? Where had it gone? I was in search of a deeper
reality, and so far I hadn't found it. I felt myself drowning in the masses
of people, feeling lonelier instead of more connected with them. What
I had been taught about God did not ring true—I felt no resonance

in my soul with it. My image of God was that "He" was high above me and outside me. I had to send my prayers "up" in the hopes that "He" would answer them. The Supreme Being was more of a stern parent than a deep mystical experience. I had no sense of a powerful connection with the great divine Spirit. I experienced no divine bliss or oneness. My existence was defined by the constraints of time, space, and a body that would eventually meet its demise. I felt isolated and guilty for reasons I did not understand. At times I felt like an outsider, trapped in a bubble.

These feelings intensified when I was in my early twenties. I was living in Toronto and attending university. I dabbled in the theater and dreamed of pursuing a career as a playwright or journalist. At this time I became further immersed in the life of the mind and intellect. God was out of style with twentieth-century philosophers—Camus, Sartre, and Nietzsche. And I identified with them: it was a natural progression for me. The universe was a bleak place in which heroic ideals had collapsed. Existence was perceived as a kind of limbo, and nature was either indifferent or hostile. I soon found that I no longer had a strong belief; my questioning became the very basis of my life. I grew disillusioned, wondering why I had been abandoned in such a strange place.

I felt most strongly in tune with British novelist D. H. Lawrence, a relentless spiritual quester. In the early 1900s Lawrence was already reacting to what he called the modern disease of consciousness. He traveled around the world, including Mexico and New Mexico, in pursuit of a primitive consciousness. Civilized humans, he felt, were caught at a mental level, disconnected from the creative spontaneous soul; the deep self had to be reawakened. He felt that the cerebral mind was the dead-end street of consciousness. Civilized man's problem was in viewing the cosmos as matter that had to be conquered. Lawrence preferred the aboriginal societies for whom the cosmos was alive. In his words: "The American-Indian sees no division into Spirit and Matter, God and not-God. Everything is alive, though not personally so . . . Everything lives. Thunder lives, and rain lives, and sunshine lives."[1]

In those days and for a long time afterwards I felt caught, to use Lawrence's term, at the mental level. I did not even think to look at the universe as if everything were alive and had spirit. I tended to view everything from the logic of my head and not the knowing of my heart. I analyzed everything, as if I could understand reality through the power of linear thinking. I did not look at the rocks, trees, and mountains as beings that could communicate. I was part of a world in which the scientific conquest of the natural forces had become all-important. As Lawrence wrote, man sought to conquer "the cosmic monsters of living thunder and live rain"—and erected dams and reservoirs and windmills—whereas the aboriginal strove to live in harmony with the cosmos.[2]

I knew there was more to reality than the physical world, and I had a strong yearning for something other than what I saw around me. Perhaps I was a piece of a puzzle that didn't fit anywhere? At times I became despondent because I sensed that a deeper reality existed, but I didn't know how to get there. On the surface I looked normal—I had a career, friends, my travels—yet I knew there was something greater waiting for me, if I could only find the path that would lead me there.

And without my knowing it, all of the events of my life were taking me to the right path, and once I stepped on it everything would finally become clear. A voyage that seemed to be in darkness was soon to come to an end. Finally, as I was getting into my mid thirties, I met Hawk and the other Thunderbeings and I embarked on a new voyage.

The incident that led me to them occurred one Sunday, on what must have been the coldest day of 1987. I decided to take a stroll in a quaint little town just north of Toronto. There were several interesting shops, including a bookstore; I walked into it and, browsing, I noticed an advertisement offering a course on dreams which I decided to take. Katherine was the instructor; she was in her early forties with long shimmering silver-blond hair and haunting blue eyes.

Katherine had recently met Hawk and when she spoke about this medicine woman my curiosity was instantly aroused. After a few classes, Katherine and I struck up a friendship and she invited me to a celebration of traditional dancing and drumming.

On a rainy day in the spring of 1987, I arrived at a charming country location just south of Buffalo. I found my way to a room filled with people where Hawk was talking. I was immediately struck by her charisma and natural warmth. Like her name, she was intriguing and mystical yet very down-to-earth. Accompanying her were a couple of people who, I later found out, were Thunderbeings.

As I learned more about Hawk I discovered that she had spent the first twenty years of her life living in the forest, learning survival and healing at the side of her grandparents. They had passed on to her the original instructions, which are currently held by only a small number of people around the globe. With her insatiable curiosity about life she went on to accumulate knowledge on a wide range of subjects, from physics and ancient astrology to psychology and the workings of the mind to metaphysics and parapsychology.

A few months later I saw Hawk again, this time at her home near the Pocono Mountains of Pennsylvania. I arrived by car with three other Thunderbeings. As we neared our destination the road became full of sharp, winding curves cutting a path through lush rolling hills and forested valleys. We stopped in front of a white two-story house with green shutters and red-tiled roof. In the background a deep valley extended all the way to the horizon, glistening in the sunlight. It was a beautiful and peaceful setting, which would be the site of many of our gatherings.

We opened the gate and walked up to a veranda. The sound of wind chimes greeted us as the door opened. About fifteen people were gathered inside. I sat down on the floor in front of a fireplace. It was a cozy and welcoming room with a wicker love seat, a rocking chair, and a wood-burning stove. The mantelpiece held a collection of gleaming quartz crystal and a wood carving of an eagle.

Hawk was burning sage and cedar leaves in a carved stone bowl etched with mysterious symbols. As the fresh woody aroma wafted around the room, she explained that the sage represents female energy while the cedar is male energy, and burning them together creates a balance of energies. She called it "smudging": we hold a flame to the sage and cedar until it burns and produces a good amount of smoke; then we fan it with a feather.

As I studied her, I observed a woman about five feet six inches tall, whose robust size conveyed the volume of her power. Her mass of curly strawberry-blond hair looked like tumbleweed in the desert. She was wearing a sky-blue tunic with a blue-and-white shawl draped over one shoulder; a small bird's feather dangled from one ear. While I knew she was in her fifties, she appeared extremely youthful. I was fascinated, for she embodied so many different features. Sometimes she looked Native Indian, especially with those piercing eyes and high cheekbones. At other times you would look at her blond hair and pale skin and swear she was of Scandinavian descent. Then there were moments when her small hands and large arms conveyed the image of a nurturing African-American mother. Yet again her facial expressions and the way she smiled suggested she might be Inuit or Tibetan.

At first she seemed so familiar. Had I seen her in a dream? When I looked into her astonishingly clear amber eyes, I saw compassion. When she looked at me, I felt that she was looking into my very soul. Her first words to me were: "You're different; you're beautiful. . . . At some time between the ages of three and seven, the seeds of loneliness were planted in you . . . but you don't need to worry—you're not really that way." These words were like a new breath of life that had been breathed into my being.

Over the course of time, as I got to know Hawk, I realized how difficult it was to describe or define her. She cannot be reduced to fit into any title or category, because she is a galactic being whose family includes all of the Earth and all of the celestial bodies. Her universe is vibrational; there is no place she cannot be or go. She adapts completely to the moment, whatever the situation might be: she can be ancient or childlike, spiritual or earthy, fiery or gentle, strong but permissive, serious or zany. I have seen her be a fierce warrior who never quits once she has determined a course of action. I have experienced her tenderness. And I have laughed at her many stories until my sides split. Life with her becomes a playful dance, full of intensity and excitement. She lives completely in the moment, fully trusting where that might take her. She sees no limits to what she is capable of and would say, "My humanness is not my limitation." She constantly supports and encourages our dreams until they become a reality.

In my travels and time with Hawk I have begun to see that there are no walls between races, religions, or countries. People of different colors are all from the family called human. When I hear a Tibetan chant or study a Mayan glyph or watch Buddhist monks do ceremony, I feel a part of it; I feel connected. I have come to realize that the fundamental teachings of all of the world's religions are curiously similar. Perhaps this is because they've all been birthed from the same need?

Hawk would say to me: "If you want to understand people, you must walk in their shoes. Walk as they walk and live as they live. Live among them without judgment." And wherever we traveled, she encouraged me to *become* that place, to *become* those people—not to copy or take from them, but to *become* all of the possibilities on this planet and to accept all of the different ways of acknowledging the great mystery. At the same time she has taught me that I have a celestial family and that the heavens and stars are as much a part of me as the trees and the stones and the grasses.

However, the greatest and most profound revelation for me—the one that irrevocably changed my life and put me on a new path—was the discovery that I too am a Thunderbeing.

In those first days when we gathered, we all felt limited and restricted and disillusioned. Many of our weekends were crammed with teachings, often taking us very late into the night. Initially, Hawk helped us to understand that true spirituality is an experience of joy, not the fear of damnation that many of our religions have taught us. We learned that her word for God is "Creator" or "Great Spirit"—and that term encompasses all the various parts that make up nature's magnificence as well as the endless heavens about us. All of this is our family. And so I have come to understand that our concept of a punishing God does not make sense. If God is a punishing being, why are we still here? God *is* all allowing and forgiving. The Creator does not torture or damn us—this concept exists in the illusionary world that we've created. The punishment is within us; we create it and we choose it. As Hawk said: "Many of our religions want to control so they teach through fear and damnation. No child learns through fear. Fear chokes the light, and then bitterness, rigidity, prejudice, and hate take over. Light and growth come with love, appreciation, respect, kindness, acceptance, encouragement, and faith."

After she said that, we heard a great clap of thunder as though God were agreeing with her. When we looked out the window, the moon was shining and the skies were thundering.

A month later when we gathered at Hawk's home, there was a

foot of snow on the ground. We could hear the voice of a weather reporter emanating from a television in another room. The voice was saying there could be no snow without cloud cover. It asked if everyone was seeing the moon and the stars in a clear sky during a snow blizzard. And then it said: "Oh, my heavens, it is now thundering folks! Does anyone know what is going on here?" Alison laughed and said, "It's called medicine." Then Katherine remarked, "The weatherman is not having an easy time with all this."

We would see more unusual weather whenever we were with Hawk. Most of us were still fascinated with how the elements responded to her. But she said it is always like that for people who live close to nature and experience a oneness with creation.

Hawk could talk for hours on just about any subject, from spirituality to UFOs and the cosmos, from principles of prosperity and nature to relationships and sexuality. The information just flowed effortlessly through her, as though she were plugged into the universal Internet. We learned about her travels and her experiences with healers and shamans around the world. Nothing stood in the way of her search for ultimate truth. She went everywhere; she even disguised herself to get into an all-male order of monks!

From the beginning she explained to us the importance of tuning in to the Earth. She said that once we get back in touch with nature all of our confusion will clear. When we are in harmony with the Earth we will be in harmony with ourselves. She said that the Earth is like the human body: her breath is air; her circulatory system is the arteries of water and oil; and her skeletal system is the mountains. She spoke with such deep emotion that we could feel her profound love for the Earth: "Mother Earth has given us our bodily form while we are on this planet; and she provides us with complete nourishment: water, air, the winds, and the trees. Life within her body is a gift. She is the divine mother. Give thanks every day for your time with her. She hungers for your attention. Your love and respect are her nourishment; your song and dance are her smile; and your laughter is her sunshine."

She said that the birds and the animals have much to teach us. The pattern of the wolf, for example, is the true pattern of evolution to the highest good. "Only the most capable male and female wolf are the leaders of the pack. Wolves feed upon only the weak and sick, and by weeding out the herds they stay strong, their numbers remain balanced, and the land is not overgrazed. All members of the wolf pack are given full respect and love; they are a true family. They are not man's predator, yet he fears them and kills them. Could it be the pattern of the wolf that man fears in his own imbalance?"

After a few hours in Hawk's presence, we started to feel an intimacy. Our hearts opened up; we let her into the deepest part of our being. Whenever she hugged us we could feel that her love was larger than anything of a personal nature. "Allow your heart to be open, and your mind will catch up," she said to us. We then started to remember who we were and why we had come to Earth. The emotions we felt reverberated beyond the walls of that house. We rocked with laughter one moment, and in the next we held our breath in rapt attention. With Hawk sitting on the floor next to us, eye to eye and shoulder to shoulder, any preconceived notions we had about spiritual masters being on some loftier plane were quickly dispelled. She exuded a plea for us to elevate ourselves rather than to put her on a pedestal—it was an invitation to join her.

We quickly discovered that she is as earthy as she is spiritual. She was never shy when it came to speaking about a sensitive subject, whether it was death or sexuality or her own personal life. Her stories kept us up for hours.

She spoke often of her husband and their marriage. "I am in a relationship because it's important for my soul to have that growth," she explained. "I don't want a weak man—I couldn't stomach it. My husband keeps his identity." She said that loving oneself is the key to a successful relationship: "A man looks for a woman who will be a goddess to him. She must develop her own strengths in a relationship. She should not compete with him by being masculine."

And so our love for each other grew. In our shared laughter and tears, we felt the excitement of having embarked on a long and great journey together. The most important thing now was helping one another survive in a world of spiritual darkness. Perhaps our outer lives were different, but our hearts were the same. Thunderbeings are from the stars—Earth is not our real home—and so there was a comfort in having found one another.

In those first days and months we had to transform ourselves before we could tackle the job of transforming the planet. Hawk helped us to see the vastness of our potential—our inner fire, as she called it. She helped us to see how limited we had allowed ourselves to become. She made us feel good; we felt a connection with her. We became a team. We had a shared goal. Many of us felt empowered; our beliefs and thoughts were confirmed and attainable. Hawk was the catalyst; she was the spark that lit the fire. She created a place for us to focus our energies. We were all very strong individuals. And now it was as though we had emerged from small streams and brooks into a raging river; we fed upon one another and strengthened each other's will and determination. We set a new course.

NOTES

1. D. H. Lawrence, *Mornings in Mexico and Etruscan Places* (Penguin Books, Ltd., Harmondsworth, Middlesex, England: 1960), page 75.
2. Ibid.

CHAPTER 3

ANCIENT PRACTICES

Come to the edge, he said. They said: We are afraid.
Come to the edge, he said. They came. He pushed . . .
and they flew.

—GUILLAUME APOLLINAIRE

ON DECEMBER 31, 1989, thirty Thunderbeings gathered in Pittsburgh to bring in the new year. Hawk shared with us her belief that the final decade of the millennium will be a time of great turmoil and change.

"The momentum has started," she said quietly as we passed around a bowl of burning sage and cedar. "At midnight Jupiter will be in direct alignment with the Earth. As the nineties unfold, we will see the beginning of a great movement toward spirituality."

I pictured in my mind this thirst for spirituality. It was like masses of people wandering through a barren and scorched desert. There were no mountains and no paths to lead them out of the desert. They had gone a long time without water, but now they craved it. They yearned to swallow it and to immerse themselves in it. They would even give up their prized material possessions for the opportunity to sip from the chalice of spirituality. Maybe we can go without spirituality for long stretches of time, but then as if an instinct has been denied, we begin to feel empty. Life becomes a daily struggle for survival instead of a joyful and adventuresome experience.

In order to help us through this final decade, Hawk gave us advice on eating and exercise. "Eat smaller meals more frequently. Do more stretching and breathing exercises. Get outdoors more often. Spend time near a tree. Listen to the wind." She told us that we would start to experience various aches and pains and that we might feel melancholy.

She said that our spirit and our mind were coming together: "Feel the beauty of being physical. Get into a nice oil bath. Spend time with your body and talk to it. Sit in the water and massage yourself. Give thanks to your body."

About relationships she said: "Respect people and really listen to what they are saying. Learn to forgive yourself and others very quickly."

She told us that the planets are an intelligence and consciousness "that will come forward to assist this part of the universe."

I had a glimpse of what this meant one night while I was walking through the park at the end of my street. I gazed up into the stars, the same stars I had gazed at countless times before, but this time I understood they were not merely specks of light. All of a sudden these stars came to life, and I appreciated that there is no calamity in the heavens because of the perfect balance and harmony among them; otherwise they would collide.

Meanwhile, we continued to work on our transformation. We began a thorough exploration in order that we might free ourselves of anger, despair, jealousy, resignation, and all of the other troublesome emotions that clutter our minds and obstruct our life force. This meant having to confront all of our fears. It was necessary to relieve the mind of undesirable thoughts before we could take charge of our lives and elevate ourselves to cosmic consciousness.

Hawk wanted so much for us to understand and see the beauty of ourselves. In our hearts we knew that she spoke the truth. And we yearned for the truth more than anything. We were drawn to her as a river is drawn to the sea. We adored her spirit of adventure. We were fascinated by her dominance over death and failure. There was nothing else for us to do until we transformed ourselves. But if Thunderbeings have one natural gift, it is their ability to emerge strong and intact from the utter chaos of a world in which the old order is collapsing by the moment.

She told us that the answers to all of our questions were within ourselves. She said that we were simply remembering what our souls already knew: "You are not some cosmic mishap, nor are you here to experience the torment of the mind." If we let the mind dominate, with all of the limitations that it is clever at tricking us into, we will surely feel confined. But it is doubly confining for the Thunderbeings whose lightning-quick energy and strong urges can become a torment if they're not fully expressed. It might be hard for others to understand, but imagine the anguish of a bird that can no longer fly.

Hawk encouraged us to accept ourselves: "Don't think about what is wrong. Simply change. You can change anything!" She said there was no connection between suffering and enlightenment: "You don't have to suffer to remember your enlightenment. Let it be a joyful experience. Start trusting your own abilities." She taught us the importance of having faith in the intelligence of our hearts: "Having faith does not mean handing your well-being over to someone else's care or becoming a slave to all sorts of demands that you cannot understand. It means following the inner voices of the true mind, which is the heart."

Over the next few months we focused our efforts on acquiring the tools of ancient ritual and grasping their significance. These included a drum, a rattle, and our very own rhythmical dance. At our gatherings Hawk taught us many chants and dances. All of this was intended to expand our consciousness into the spiritual dimensions. As well, it was preparing us for future assignments where we would be called to assist in minimizing or delaying great destruction and catastrophe.

At first the drum seemed to me nothing more than a skin stretched over a piece of wood. It had a pleasing tone, and on it I could create an interesting beat. But over the course of time, the more I learned, the more I was able to appreciate the drum's power. I could feel the rhythmic sound enter my being until it caused the inside of my body to vibrate. The sound filled every part of my being. It drew me deeper into myself until it became the beat of my heart. As the drum's pace increased, so did my own heart. I saw myself ever so clearly and envisioned in my own inner eye a space not limited by my body.

I remember one occasion when a dozen of us were drumming at Hawk's home. You could hear the echo of the drumbeat as it circulated around the hills. After about thirty minutes of this constant vibration, I was totally entranced by it. The rambling of my mind ceased, replaced by an exuberant sense of belonging.

Eventually I found my own drum. Hawk had obtained it, and several others like it, through one of the southwestern tribes. It has a stylized design of a snake with head and tail forming a circle and almost touching. The tail of the snake has the form of a fish while the body has four tiny legs. The head is that of a four-legged creature. The body of the snake is replete with ancient symbols and is encircled by a geometric design with more symbolism. I am still fascinated by the design—so simple, yet every time I look at it I find something different.

The rattle has also come to have a meaning for me. It is said that medicine people use rattles to call to the spirit world. One description I read called them "telephones to the spirit world." I found that the rattle draws my attention to a subtler realm of communication.

Johanna, one of the Thunderbeings who happens to be a massage therapist, uses a rattle to help relax and heal her clients. She tried this on me. While I was lying down, eyes closed, the gentle shaking of her rattle seemed to disperse any negative or troubling thoughts I was having. Within a few moments my breathing slowed down and I was journeying in my imagination. I felt a sense of boundlessness; I felt peaceful and calm. No wonder a rattle is effective in calming babies. Depending on the type of rattle and how it's played, it can also evoke passion, anxiety, or fear.

Someone once eloquently said that using a rattle is like holding the sands of time in your hands, and that the rattle seemed to take on the significance of a timekeeper for a universal clock.

These tools help us regain contact with the spirit realm; they represent our communion with the Earth Mother. When we combine the sounds of several drums and rattles—and then add dance—it becomes quite magical. It becomes a *ceremony*. You feel connected. You become part of the dance of the universe. You feel in flow with the rhythms that exist in nature.

Some of my friends thought it was bizarre when they noticed a drum in my living room. I explained to them some of the ancient rituals, but instead of making myself understood and accepted, I got more puzzled looks. So I pointed out that ancient rituals are no stranger than modern ones. We think we're so advanced, but we're not, really, maybe just more complex. We're the same, only with more frills, more bells and whistles. We think that because we're in control of our instincts and aggression that we're superior to primitive people, but our basic emotions have not changed. I asked my friends to explain the difference between the modern ritual of a birthday party and a dance around a fire or a rhythmic chant. Once a year at roughly the same time everyone gathers at someone's hut, bringing offerings. The hut is adorned with trinkets dangling from the ceiling; everyone wears ceremonial headgear; they tell stories of past events. They then gather around a fire that has been lit upon an offering of food and chant in unison in celebration of the life of one of their tribe. What's so different? When young people get together for a rock concert, perhaps without even knowing it, they're participating in a ritual that draws them into a unifying consciousness. A rock concert is really one huge cultural ritual, a gathering that puts everyone in the same frame of mind; they forget the monotony of their lives. Similarly, in a sporting event, people are drawn into the swell of emotion, the yells and cheers. They feel connected; they feel a sense of sharing and community.

On a deeper level, ritual puts our conscious mind to rest so that our subconscious can express itself. It connects us back to the pure knowledge hidden within our being. It brings us into the realization that we are much more than our individual identity. Ultimately, it fine-tunes our consciousness. This was very important if the other Thunderbeings and I were to succeed in our mission. By strengthening ourselves and reconnecting to the spiritual realms, we would be in a position to bring the strongest and most positive change to humanity.

Another significant part of my learning involved the spirit keepers. At first I was a little bewildered by this concept, but eventually it too helped me to understand my relationship to the Earth and the heavens.

The spirit keepers are the four primary whirling forces of our Earth, powerful forces that maintain the delicate balance of this plane. They are the four fiery faces of God that are recognized in all sacred circles; they are a light, an energy, a colour—they have no form. They are the keepers of the gateways at the four cardinal directions. Different tribes use different animals to symbolize these directions. For the

Thunderbeings, the eagle is a symbol for the east; the wolf is the symbol for the south; the bear is the west; and the buffalo is the north.

At certain times of the day we can feel the presence of the spirit keepers for that is when the veil between the physical and spirit worlds is thin. Briefly: at dawn, just as the rays of light begin to reach across the horizon, we can feel the energy of the spirit keeper of the east. We face the east and welcome our new day; we envision how we want our day to be. At high noon we sense the energy of the spirit keeper of the south. As we analyze how our day is progressing and see what still has to be done, we ask ourselves if we are being steadfast to our true path and cultivating our relationships. At sunset, as our day comes to a close, we acknowledge the spirit keeper of the west. This is a time for introspection and to reflect on what we have accomplished. If we have had a difficult day we might ask the Earth to take our woes and recycle them. And midnight, the time of the north spirit keeper, is when we plan and dream our tomorrows, affirming to ourselves that we have the potential to attain our goals and dreams.

"Learn how to get in touch with these four spirit keepers," Hawk suggested. "Don't just acknowledge them, but learn to feel them. The spirit keepers hear you."

After about two years of trying to get in touch with them, I started to feel their energy. One day at high noon I was in my kitchen and suddenly felt a spinning sensation in my head; I sat back in my chair wondering, What was that! Other Thunderbeings say they have had similar episodes.

The spirit keepers have become a part of my life. They are like a natural organizer, a great tool for organizing my day. I use it in my profession, to help me set goals and to create order out of a busy, chaotic schedule. It helps me to focus on what's important and eliminate what's unnecessary. In a fast-paced world, good organization is essential, and I've found that the spirit keepers lend an undertone of spirituality to the daily task of managing my life.

With these practices, my life was changing. I could navigate into the place that Hawk calls "between the worlds"—between the mundane and supersensible worlds. I was starting to understand that I was part of something significantly larger and mysterious, where words were not spoken. Nowhere was this more evident than in the pattern of the medicine wheel, which was another part of my new learning.

Our medicine wheel ceremonies were celebrations of life. I remember when we erected a wheel near Hawk's home. As she entered the east gate of the wheel and moved to the center to do her prayers, the wind stopped blowing and even the birds were quiet.

As we constructed the wheel, I realized we were establishing a kind of mini-universe. Within the pattern of a wheel with spokes, we used stones to represent various parts of the universe. We started by placing a stone in the center of the wheel, to represent the Creator. Then we established four primary gates around the wheel, representing north, east, south, and west. When it was all laid out, it was like having a bird's-eye view of the universe. Everything was contained in that one circle, from the smallest to the largest: a mere second, a day in my life, the entire progression of my life as well as that of the sun, the moon, the wind, the animals, the plants, and the seasons. The wheel gave me the opportunity to see that I am part of a much larger entity, that the cycles of my life are interconnected with the cycles of the universe.

As we move around the wheel, in the north our spirit is birthed into form. When it has made its way around the circle it returns here to go back into spirit. In the east, where the sun rises, we find the power of the eagle to teach us to soar above our limitations; here we find inspiration, illumination, and vision. In the south, the wolf teaches us humor and playfulness, the meaning of family, and the making of new paths—this is the place of our adolescence. And in the west we learn from the bear how to transform weakness and fear into strength and courage—it is here that we experience old age and death. When we have experienced everything that is available on the wheel, we are complete; we finally understand our relationship to the divine.

How can there be "accidents" when such an intelligent order underlies everything? The medicine wheel puts our lives into perspective; we realize that the smallest aspect is as important as the biggest aspect of the cosmos—the one comes from the other. The wheel dispels the illusion that I am a separate being. It makes me feel more comfortable with my own mortality. I know that my energy will continue in some other form. Life through the perspective of a medicine wheel becomes an adventure, always changing and evolving.

Hawk taught us that we can use the medicine wheel to seek solutions in our lives. With a few stones we can construct a wheel in our living room, dance around it, and talk to the spirit keepers. We can get into the right mood by tapping on our drum. We might take counsel from the eagle if we are starting a business or a new relationship. Or we might turn to the wolf for direction about where our loyalties lie. If we want to handle a confrontation or balance our ego, we would seek help from the bear.

The Thunderbeings spent many hours practicing ancient dances and chants. I remember one bitter cold weekend in February 1990 when we rented space at a hotel in Pittsburgh to practice the sundial dance. We arranged ourselves in the circular pattern of the medicine wheel, forming the perimeter, the spokes and the four spirit keepers. Our movement was constant, with two people veering into the center of the wheel, then circling each other, and finally, returning to opposite sides on the perimeter for twelve complete rotations. We used drums and rattles to keep the beat. At first the dance took great concentration and focus. But I was astonished to see how the pattern forced us out of our rational thinking processes and into an intuitive state. The dance ultimately took over and danced us!

After hours of dancing, exhausted, we returned to our hotel rooms. That night I dreamed I was in a magnificent house with exquisite furnishings. When I asked Hawk what it meant, she said that the house symbolized a state of mind and that my dream meant that great possibilities lay ahead for me. "The foundation is being laid for your spiritual journey," she said. Indeed, the movement of change in my life had become rapid. Through ancient healing techniques that Hawk taught me, such as working on my breathing, I was letting go of old pent-up emotions. Indeed, we were all changing faster than we could understand. After much whirlwind change, we grew more confused as to what we were becoming. But Hawk assured us that confusion is always the ego's last attempt to avoid the truth.

Many of our practices helped us understand how interconnected we are with everything. This understanding will be crucial for the success of our mission. In one of the chants that Hawk taught, we used to sing: "I move in all directions; I am all things, I am in every blade of grass; I am the teardrop which is the body of the ocean; I am the sun, the moon, and the wind." *I am in all these things, and they are in me.* This is an original principle of life. A thread of light weaves us all together, from the tiniest element to the endless universe. We are made from the same energy, and this energy, which cannot be destroyed, continuously changes form, from a blade of grass to the sands on the shore to snowflakes on a mountain to the very planets that surround us; it is forever changing and evolving.

Once we realized this, we could start to work with the elements to make rain in a cloudless sky, to bring the thunder and the lightning, and even to defuse a catastrophic force.

Before we were ready to work with such immense forces, however, there was much preparation to be done. We had to learn to discipline our minds and control our thoughts. We had to work together toward one harmonious thought, for it was the collective force of our thoughts that would empower us and enable us to accomplish our goal.

Our ancestors believed in the power of thought. Thoughts are energy. We all know that this is true, for we have seen how people can rearrange atoms with their minds by bending metal with their thoughts. Our minds are connected to the same force that causes everything to be. We are vibration, and our consciousness shapes what is around us. Our collective thoughts are extremely powerful; they become the things of our planet. All of our artwork, technological gadgets, skyscrapers, and pyramids existed first as thoughts.

"You have to be in charge of your thoughts," Hawk reminded us again and again. "You do not *create* every thought you have, but you are *responsible* for which thoughts you send out into the environment."

She explained that the more we connect with our subconscious thoughts, the more we will move with balance in the many dimensions of our world, because in the dream state we are not confined by the rules that determine form. Our thoughts can reach as far as any known universe; they can go beyond gravity.

As Thunderbeings, we cannot be casual about anything. Because of who we are, we have to be extremely vigilant about our thoughts. We almost have to become aware of our every thought. That is why it is very important to acknowledge unconscious habits and rid ourselves of mental clutter. Thunderbeings have the ability to generate an electromagnetic field of incredible intensity—our thoughts move with thunder. But in the early stages of our apprenticeship we still didn't know how to control this ability.

Mastery of our thoughts is the secret to how we can transform the planet. Thoughts become forces when they are focused. When two Thunderbeings are holding the same focused thought, it becomes a tremendous force. Ten Thunderbeings in a focused thought can change the galaxy. Their thunder resonates out to the other planets. The more perfectly we are able to unite our frequencies and become one consciousness, the greater our thunder. If our thoughts can resonate a clear message of harmony, then we have a better chance of overriding the prevailing thought-forms.

Indeed, collective consciousness is an endless source of power. I know this term is overused, but I can't think of a more accurate phrase. Imagine if all of the human beings on the planet experienced a crisis at the same time and realized the true value of their lives! It would completely change the world. Similarly a planetary catastrophe could overhaul the collective consciousness. This can be observed on a smaller scale, for example, when a tragic crime is committed, causing millions of people to think the same way at the same time. The process of change starts to happen immediately, and laws are enacted to control the crime. Unfortunately, a catastrophe may be the only event that will wake us up and make us realize that we've gone too far with our indulgences, that negative and destructive thoughts are raging out of control.

"Our atmosphere is gorged with thought-forms, and most of them are destructive," Hawk said. "They must be transmuted now, not with fear and rage, but with clear intent." It is like a thousand people in a small room breathing each other's stagnant thoughts, choking and confused. We need new thoughts, fresh air. Hawk was encouraging the Thunderbeings to be the first to open the window. She told us that we must never underestimate our ability and that our "inner fire" can transform a whole country. But first we must transform ourselves:

"When there is balance within you, there will be balance outside of you." She meant that establishing peace and harmony in the world begins with ourselves. When we feel at peace with ourselves, we will be tolerant and compassionate with our neighbor, and this tolerance will in turn ripple out to touch the rest of the world.

I remember the first time I felt the collective force of our thoughts. We had gathered at Hawk's home and were sitting on the grass to face the setting sun. All around us, the land sloped downward into a forested valley. Directly above us, two red-tailed hawks circled. The sun was a white-yellow ball with mile-long streaks of pink and purple.

"Look at that sunset!" Hawk exclaimed. Her eyes became distant and glazed as she held a dialogue with the elements, motioning with her hands in a symbolic language. Her voice vibrated with tenderness. The wind passed among us like a warm caress. She said it was speaking to us. "Wind spirit speaks to us. Spend time with the wind . . . she moves inside you. Listen to the voices on the wind. They are speaking to us from all over the galaxies."

And Hawk acknowledged the water spirit: "As humans, we are primarily composed of water and we need sunlight. The Earth Mother is organic and lives around the sun; most of her surface is water. We are the same, humans and the planet." She described the mineral kingdom as our record keepers, as old as the Earth. And she said that the plant and tree kingdoms "give us everything we need for our life; they are unconditionally loving." She went on to talk about the four-leggeds: "They teach us about ourselves; they are our companions on this earth. Without them the Earth would be a lonely place." She also spoke of the feathered beings and the other intelligences, the whales and the dolphins. She did not forget any human or creature or life-form.

After she finished her ceremony, the clouds became like great white wings while lightning danced and flashed all around. Raindrops gently kissed our faces—and Hawk told us it was a demonstration that we are being loved. "God speaks through all things. Even the clouds give you designs. Everything around us starts talking. See how much you are loved!" We were feeling intimate with the Creator and with one another. We had started to move within each other's being. Where do you begin and I end? Where do you end and I begin?

These were powerful moments for me; I derived strength and purpose from them. I felt the intensity of our love; I imagined it reaching out across the Earth, touching everything.

As the nineties unfold, we will want more of these moments together. We will want to be detached from the erratic behavior and tumult that will intensify as the millennium comes to a close. We are being forced to break through our illusory reality to a deeper and more spiritual understanding of life. The quickest way to achieve this goal is to enter the shaman's otherworld of death and rebirth.

Through initiations of fire our pathway would be opened. Only then would we become whole beings, having obtained our powers in a sacred way. Only then would we be ready to save the world from destruction and elevate humanity and ourselves to a higher consciousness.

CHAPTER 4

THE FIRE WALK

Nothing before, nothing behind;
The steps of faith fall on the
seeming void and find the rock beneath.
  —JOHN GREENLEAF WHITTIER

IN APRIL 1990 I set out with two other Thunderbeings on a long drive from Toronto. We were headed to a place south of Pittsburgh, to participate in a fire walk. I had heard about this ritual but I didn't really understand all that was involved. The very thought of walking on fire struck absolute fear in me. During the drive, I had several hours to think and reflect about what was waiting for me. I was sitting in the back seat, while Katherine and Daniel were in the front. I had recently met Daniel and found him to be a funny and playful person. He was in his early thirties, five feet nine, and slim, with thin blonde hair. He had the energy of a jackrabbit—gentle yet seeming to possess a streak of fear.

The three of us took turns driving; after a while it was like musical chairs in the car. At every rest stop we would rotate; the driver would be the passenger and the passenger would move to the back seat.

After we'd been surrounded by highways, trucks, noisy restaurants, and strange people of strange character for some time, the trip began to seem unreal. Time seemed to take on a different meaning. I felt as though I were stuck in an illusion when I thought that my next level of spiritual evolution lay at the end of the journey. Sitting in the back seat, I imagined what Neil Armstrong, one of our first astronauts, must have felt like. Did he feel this bewilderment? Did the journey become surreal for him? Is that why he was so moved when he stepped on the moon? My mind raced ahead trying to understand. I had learned so much since I met Hawk and the others. It was as though I were going through a second puberty. I was besieged by new information and knowledge and yet excited about the possibilities that lay ahead. I wondered what my friends were going to think. What about my family? I doubted that they would understand if I told them that the fire dance was a ceremony of purification! I imagined myself rolling on the ground, screaming in pain. *I don't even believe I'm doing this. What am I doing?* All of a sudden, the car didn't seem that inviting. I felt a panic. Fear surged through my body. I listened to the whir of the other cars on the highway, took a deep breath, and calmed myself down.

About seven hours later I wasn't sure where we were. All I knew was that we were south of Pittsburgh. At this point I suddenly realized how much trust I had put in Katherine and Daniel. The car stopped in front of a big red-brick house framed by about a dozen trees and surrounded by hilly fields, thickets, and woodlands. There was not another house in sight. Other people had arrived and continued to arrive. By late evening, twenty-five of us had gathered inside the house, which was sparsely furnished with antique oak furniture.

"The fire dance awakens our soul to divine order," Hawk started to explain.

All I could think of was that they expected me, with bare feet, to walk across a bed of scorching hot coals. I had terrible doubts; I was wondering why I had ever gotten involved in something like this. There I was in the middle of nowhere. If I burned my feet, who would help me? Where was I going to go?

Hawk was determined to change our views about fire. She told us that unflinching contact with excessive cold or extreme heat indicated that the shaman had gone beyond the ordinary human condition and was participating in the sacred world. Fire, she said, is a medium into which forms vanish and from which they are born. Fire purifies; it awakens the spiritual flame inside a person's soul. She said that scientists still cannot explain what fire is.

It was such a beautiful description that it really made me think.

I realized that my experience of fire had been limited to the flickering flame of a candle, the pleasing heat radiating from a fireplace, and the satisfying embers in a barbecue. Isn't that true for most people? We therefore think of fire as something we control, for our own use. Or we associate it with conflict and destruction, for the fire that lights our way in the dark is the same fire that burns the forest.

Hawk went on to say that fire was brought here from the stars at the same time that human existence began on Earth. "It was the winds of the Pleiades that ignited the first flame," she said.

Fire is the spirit deep within us; it is the *wisdom fire*. She also added: "The wisdom fire will not harm you, the flames will consume your dross and refine your gold. Fire intrigues us because at some level we are remembering the eternal flame of creation and our soul hungers to return to that state."

And so I began to understand fire from a more spiritual point of view.

Fire is what our soul looks like when we leave the body. Fire is the movement of thought. Our thought, when transformed into action, *is* fire. Fire is responsible for forming what we are. The fire that burns within the heart of the Earth Mother is in perfect balance with the waters of the ocean, the land, and the sky.

We *can* walk on fire and not burn. It all depends on our connection and approach to the fire. We have to *respect* the fire as an intelligence. Fire has its own spirit. Not respecting it will get us into trouble. Ego and power trips and thinking that we are greater than the fire, or thinking that there is nothing to it, is dangerous. It is important to approach the fire with respect and recognition of its power.

I still felt uneasy about the challenge that lay before me, but at least my intuition understood what my mind couldn't.

When we do the fire dance we break free of old, restrictive patterns. We come into the realization that anything is possible, that we shape our reality simply by what we think. Our reality has been based on a belief in the value of restriction, denial, and limitation. We have believed for too long that we are imperfect and unworthy.

"I've watched all of your personal programs," Hawk said to us. "You're far more than that. Spirit is the only thing that's real. You started in a state of perfection. You're remembering when you were just pure spirit. You *are* worthy simply because you occupy sacred space on the Earth Mother."

Fire became essential to our development as Thunderbeings. Coming into contact with fire would empower us faster than anything else we had ever experienced. It would be the most awesome challenge of our lives. Achieving fire mastery is a common practice of mystics and shamans all over the world. Hawk herself had been tempered in the hottest of fires. She said that nothing burned away the dross on our beings faster than fire. When we become one with the fire, we will reach heights we never dreamed possible.

The next day, in preparation for our fire dance, we gathered wood and made offerings of tobacco and cornmeal to our tree relations.

We headed out across the two-lane highway and arrived at a grassy knoll, where we would build our fire. A gentle breeze originated out of the north. Big puffy white clouds stood in the sky like little deities who had come to be a part of our fire walk. My eye followed the horizon of lush green valley that surrounded us. In spite of the hydro poles and an occasional passing vehicle, it was peaceful; I enjoyed the drone of cicadas.

We walked over to the logs, which were stacked up on the east side of the hill. We had used kindling from seven varieties of trees. It was explained to me that each tree is a keeper of a different kind of knowledge; we would therefore be able to experience the combined knowledge of these seven trees. Hawk described them as messengers between us and the great mystery.

She asked us to put our prayers into each log as we brought it over to her. First she smudged the area. Then she placed three logs in the center of the fire pit, saying that they represented flames of wisdom that ignite the illumination of humanity.

"Hand me four more logs," she said, placing them in a square, calling in the powers of the four directions.

We chanted softly while she placed logs across the ends of the first logs in the square to form an octagon.

We continued to bring more logs as she requested. She was silent, concentrating on creating this orderly arrangement of wood in respect of the spiritual forces. "As above, so below," she said. She wanted to show to the Above Beings that she was honoring the harmony of the universe.

"Now I need tall grasses to poke underneath there so this will burn," she said, pointing to the sun-dried grasses at the edge of the hill.

Just as she put a match to this harmoniously balanced tower of wood, a strong wind arose.

As the flames broke out into a bonfire, they turned into vivid colors of violet and blue, like spears shooting up into the sky. I closed my eyes, letting the brilliance play against my eyelids. I felt a longing that would only intensify as the day progressed.

After the fire died down, we raked the coals into a long layer of sizzling hot embers. I tried to envision myself walking across it, and old emotions suddenly returned. Serious doubts emerged about my ability to pass this first test of fire.

Even though I was afraid, I felt an excitement take hold of me.

Hawk started to shake her rattle in a slow, rhythmic movement. She invited us to join her with our drums and rattles. The powerful hypnotic beat drew us downward, deeper, away from the realm of our conscious minds, allowing thoughts and memories that had existed from the beginning of time to reveal themselves to us.

As we danced around the bed of coals, the surrounding hills reverberated with our sounds. We quickened our pace, agitated, pounding our drums louder and more furiously, our faces flushed with emotion. We worked ourselves up to a frenzy.

Together we opened our mouths wide and let out a primal scream from the very pit of our being. We were psyching ourselves up, rather like weight lifters who scream or grunt when approaching the challenge of a lift in order to muster from deep within themselves every ounce of strength.

As I stared at the bed of shimmering coals, I felt the heat establishing its godlike power over me. My heart started to beat faster. I can't do this, I thought. What mortal person could survive this heat without burning? And yet my longing became even more urgent. I was drawn by some irresistible force, as though the fire spirit were beckoning me closer. Hawk started to chant softly: "Release your mind. See what you find. Bring it on home to your people." We chanted these words over and over like a mantra. The chanting helped us relax; it brought us back to the center of our being so that we were not controlled by our fear.

Hawk approached the edge of the bed of coals. Suddenly there was a hush, and all eyes were fixed on her. She was utterly calm as she placed one foot, then the other, on the glowing coals; she walked on them slowly, without haste, completely surrendering to the experience.

We continued chanting. I was gripped with fear, and yet I knew I would have no peace until I experienced the fire. My body began to feel the strain of nervous anticipation with a pounding heart and sweaty palms. Something deep within me—something primal?—was taking over my being.

Hawk encouraged us to talk to the fire and become one with it. "Don't think you can beat the fire," she cautioned. "Don't go with the attitude that you're greater than the fire. Be at one with it."

We continued pacing around the fire, chanting and drumming, trying to overcome the nagging voice of self-doubt that wanted to defeat us. We could not let our conscious mind have power over us, nor could we give it the authority to mask and rule our instinctual path.

"Okay, Thunderbeings," Hawk said, positioning herself at the edge of the bed of coals. At the other end stood a bucket of water for us to dip our feet into after we had walked across.

This was the moment of truth. There was no turning back.

Johanna and Patty approached the red-hot coals while the rest of us maintained the momentum of the chant: "Release your mind. See what you find. Bring it on home to your people."

I held my breath as I watched them. They walked quickly, nervously. Their faces looked wrenched with anxiety. When they reached the other end of the bed of coals, they squealed, "Ah! We did it!" We hooted and hollered, banging on our drums and shaking our rattles, sharing the excitement of their personal triumph and liberation.

"I did it!" Johanna screamed, running over to hug Hawk.

I knew my time would come soon. A relentless fear took over

again, starting in the pit of my stomach and radiating through my body.

I found myself struggling with the old beliefs, society's accepted rationale. I was up against a way of thinking that was deeply entrenched in me. As I gazed at the glowing coals, I closed my eyes and imagined myself one with the spirit of the fire. I could feel myself relenting. And then I thought, But no! What am I doing! Those are burning embers! And another fear dominated my mind: the peril of scorching my feet.

Lynn and Phillip approached the bed of coals. Before stepping forward, they took a long, hard look into the distance, as though they were calling upon some heavenly force to take them across. I could see their chests heaving as they took that first step.

"Don't turn around. Don't stop!" Hawk demanded, in response to their trepidation.

Drums and rattles maintained a ritual beat as they walked quickly, anxious to make it across. "Release your mind," we chanted. "See what you find. Bring it on home to your people."

"You did it!" Hawk exclaimed.

Shouts of celebration. Each Thunderbeing who walked across the bed of coals was an inspiration for the rest of us. The momentum intensified; two more Thunderbeings stepped forward.

"If you are feeling afraid, grab somebody else's hand and walk with them," Hawk advised.

Marcelle walked to the edge of the coals and stopped; she turned to look at Hawk. Sensing her trepidation, Hawk grabbed her hand and walked her across. *She did it!* Another round of cheers and hollers.

Hawk approached Liz, who admitted she was petrified.

"Is the fire not speaking to you?"

"Yes, but I'm afraid," she replied nervously.

"Then you shouldn't walk the fire. Everyone has these times. Even I have had them," Hawk said softly.

Something was happening inside me. I could feel myself being *pulled* to the fire as if by an instinct. My feet moved hesitantly. I murmured abstractedly to myself, "I want to do it." Some hidden force was guiding me. My heart was pounding like a drum, and my mouth was clamped tight as I veered over to the glimmering heat, allowing this force to direct me. Poised near the edge, I was totally consumed in the same moment by fear of the unknown and by longing. Driven by the stronger desire, I decided to take that first step. I dared not look down at the coals. I sensed the heat, but it was not unbearable. In fact, I was astonished at the way it felt. I had a sensation of walking on hundreds of pebbles made of velvet. "Ooh! This is unbelievable!" I dashed across with the determination of a sprinter in a race; my survival instinct took over. I had one single thought in my head: I just want to make it to the other end. Please! The moment I stepped on the grass, exhilaration flooded my body. I had broken through my limitations! My mind quickly left this time and place and bounded to the future. I saw challenges in front of me that I had not yet been acquainted with, but I already knew I would succeed, for I had found a new power.

Shouts of celebration confirmed my personal triumph over fear.

"Release your mind. See what you find. Bring it on home to your people."

"Okay, Thunderbeings, this is your last chance to walk," Hawk challenged. "Who will walk with me?"

"I'm waiting for the coals to cool down," Nora admitted, embarrassed, as she walked over to take Hawk's hand.

By that time a layer of gray ash had formed on top of the coals, and one could indeed conclude that they had cooled down.

"You think the coals have cooled down?" Hawk dared Nora. Then, turning to Daniel, who was standing behind her, she said, "Get me a piece of a paper from that pile of papers on my blanket."

Daniel rushed over, grabbed some paper, and handed it to her.

The moment she placed it on the coals, it went up in flames.

"I guess it's not that cool after all," Nora said nervously, trying to make a joke of it.

Hawk saw that all Nora needed was a little moral support. So she asked one of the Thunderbeings to accompany her; together they walked, hand in hand.

When she reached the other side, she screamed with delight, like a child who has discovered something new and exciting.

"There was absolutely no way I was going to do it!" she said to me afterward, laughing as she recalled her fear. "But I had this deep yearning. Something was pulling me and saying, 'Come, walk!' I fought it and fought it until the last moment. As I was walking, I repeated over and over in a pleading tone, 'I acknowledge you Fire Spirit. I appreciate you. I respect you.' "

After our fire walk, we realized that we really are the limitless beings that Hawk keeps telling us we are.

Many of us participated in other fire walks held in New York, Pennsylvania, Arizona, and Canada. On one occasion several Thunderbeings fire-walked in the middle of winter in a parking lot in Toronto. A two-person crew from a local television program showed up to film the event. As they watched, their stone-faced professionalism gradually turned into wary disbelief. It was so cold that icicles formed on the cameraman's beard. They couldn't take their eyes off Hawk who moved barefoot in the snow wearing only a cotton dress. Not once did she shiver or react to the icy north wind that was blowing through her hair.

"If you really feel this is not a fire, then get out your hot dogs and roast them," she joked with the cameraman. "This is real stuff. It's not fake."

The topic turned to the increasing popularity of fire-walking among business people as a way to develop self-control and acquire absolute domain over their personalities. One woman who came to participate in our fire walk said she had fire-walked with one of those groups. She said it was different from the way we were doing it: they had programmed themselves to believe that the fire was not hot. But that contradicts the body's experience. We acknowledge instead that the fire is hot and try to join energies with it. We accept and work with it as a living entity.

I now looked at fire differently. I feel as though it has become my mentor. I can picture it inside me and around me, protecting me from negative outside influences and people. Fire taught me a balance between being warm and nurturing and taking power when necessary, to scorch a path for myself.

•   •   •

Eventually we also learned to embrace the other extreme: cold.

We started by taking cold showers; later, when we traveled with Hawk, we would find an icy stream and immerse ourselves in it. I was surprised to find how this experience recharged me. Cold water cleans our aural field. It gives a tremendous charge to our cardiovascular system and brings more oxygen to the brain.

As we merge with the fire and the icy waters, we realize that the experience is not so frightening. We realize that everything we are and will ever be is already within us. It was always there.

CHAPTER 5

SACRED WATERS

I live not in myself, but I become
Portion of that around me: and to me
High mountains are a feeling, but the hum
Of human cities torture.

—Lord Byron

In the summer of 1990 Hawk took us to Sedona: a red-rock paradise of canyons, creeks, and ancient Indian ruins in north central Arizona. Originally the home of several Native American tribes, including the Hohokam, the Sinagua, and the Yavapai Indians, Sedona is considered very sacred land by the natives, who spend time in silence and prayer before making a pilgrimage here. This is a place for ceremony and ritual. This is a place that enhances our vision and ability to awaken to the true meaning of our life. Now it has become a popular cultural mecca with millions of visitors each year. Rapid expansion has taken its toll, resulting in a proliferation of tourist shops, increased traffic, and congestion.

Many people are drawn to Sedona because of the high concentration of vortexes: natural power spots located within a few miles of each other in the midst of awe-inspiring red-rock country. The spirit of the Earth is very strong here. Earth energies can be seen, felt, and experienced, energies that reached beyond the five physical senses. The crimson rock formations are among the most soul-stirring sights I have ever seen, a perfect place to connect with the possibility of timelessness and ecstasy. As Hawk said: "It gets so quiet you can hear the Old Ones whispering through the mesas as the winds dance around you. Things here are caught in time and never change. The vibrations of the land start to awaken memories locked deep within our cellular being until we emerge into the consciousness of the wisdom of the Ancients."

When I asked, "Who, exactly, are the Ancients?" Hawk explained that indigenous people consider them "parts of Great Spirit who have never had a physical experience on Earth"—intelligences that can be tapped, like the natural elements. When Hawk refers to the Ancients she is usually talking about the inhabitants of original civilizations that existed before Atlantis. These beings were illuminated forms, not physical beings. As she explained: "We began to take on a more physical body as we moved through the waters and the various masses of the Earth. That is why mythology is a legitimate part of our history. It is a living period, not just a figment of somebody's imagination. Zeus and all the other mythological figures existed in a time when we were still atmospheric beings, almost ghostlike presences or shapes."

She said that Greek mythology gives us a true understanding of how godlike souls, like Zeus, can place a physical form on the Earth to act out a drama. "That is why my elders always equate the mind with theater. They speak of a theater of the mind." That is how the original peoples of this Earth translated the mind. Whatever you think is what you become; if you don't like your reality, you can change it as you would change a theatrical script. You're playing a role in the unfolding story of the world. "Our two-legged form is simply a probe of the soul that is working out a drama in the Earth," she explained.

Hawk's son, David, had arranged rental vehicles for us at the airport. About six feet two with a solid wiry physique, he moved with the swiftness of a gazelle, always seeming to be two steps ahead of everyone else. His eyes were clear and direct, his manner a pleasing balance of gentleness and strength.

From the Phoenix airport it was a two-hour drive across the desert. We passed barren mountains and mountains covered with giant saguaro cactus. We passed all manner of shrubs and small trees, including paloverde, ocotillo, and mesquite. At places along the way there was not a sign of human life, just black rock and arid plain. I could feel my ears pop as the elevation rose. After a point where our vehicles spun downward toward a panorama of mountains covered with semiarid vegetation, we turned onto another highway. What a dramatic change in scenery! The road was framed with a lush and impenetrable growth of bushes, shrubs, juniper, and pine.

Just south of Sedona, at a turn in the road, loomed the first of many fire-red rocks. As we approached closer, they towered in every direction in fascinating shapes, some flat-topped, others slender and shaped like steeples; geologists describe them as buttes, mesas, spires, and hoodoos. They are amazing! We neared a turret-shaped formation rising at least 500 feet and, right next to it, an imposing square butte. I could feel an energy radiating out of them; I felt excited and exhilarated. The road wound through mountainous terrain covered with juniper, piñon, and cypress, with more spectacular red rocks spiraling upward some 2,000 feet! They looked like mystical sculptures carved by the forces of nature over hundreds of millions of years. Had we entered through heaven's gate into a magical realm? Surely this must be a meeting place for otherworld beings.

As we drove into the town of Sedona, a sharp turn took us over a stream past a grove of sycamore and cottonwood trees. The road climbed into uptown Sedona, a thoroughfare of gift shops, art galleries, and motels, dwarfed by the surrounding canyon walls.

Then we descended into Oak Creek Canyon, a sixteen-mile-long cleft in the south edge of a huge plateau. What a spectacular drive through twists and turns, past huge chasms that plunge, I am told, as deep as 2,500 feet. A creek, fed by mountain springs, runs along the bottom of the canyon. As we drove through the steep-walled canyon, we felt as though we were in midair. We craned our necks to see the dramatic rock walls covered with dense forest. The canyon wall rose steeply above the treetops, disappeared amid luxuriant vegetation, and then rose again. We were soaring with these heights, and then we became completely submerged within them.

After several miles, a forest of ponderosa pine emerged and continued along the vertical slopes of the canyon. We veered off the road to our left. We had arrived at Junipine Resort, a group of two-story cabins tucked between massive canyon walls. Standing in the parking lot was a scenic thrill—we were surrounded by incredibly lush foliage, towering pines, aspens, and firs. After checking into the front office—we had rented four of the creek houses to accommodate all twenty of us—we settled in, unpacked, and gathered in Hawk's creek house.

"Let the land here go directly to your soul," she said to us. "This is one of the sacred fire places on this continent. This area was a great sea seventy million years ago. The fire of the universe is in these rocks."

With this trek to Arizona, as with all future travels with Hawk, we would make great strides in self-healing. At the same time we would fulfill our mission as Thunderbeings and work with the energies of the Earth to accelerate *her* healing in places where she cried out for attention. But before venturing out to these places, it was necessary for us to cultivate a pure frame of mind. We did that by maintaining silence—no talking, no interacting for certain periods of the day. Silence is golden. Hawk says that our aura actually turns gold when we're silent. She says that silence is how we tap the vast potential of our minds, our mind being the child of our soul.

The meaning and purpose of silence was to be our first lesson.

"You don't have the slightest idea of the potential of your mind-child until you've been silent for at least six months," she said. Hawk herself had once spent six months in total silence.

Even though we were paired up to share bedrooms we refrained from talking to each other. Silence also meant no body or hand signs and no notes. When we prepared meals and ate at the same table, we avoided looking into each other's eyes by focusing on the table or the walls.

"Silence is the only way to observe your thoughts," Hawk said. "You still have mind games to work through. Energy is lost and our focus is broken when we engage in nervous chatter."

It took us a few days to get used to the silence and the isolation from one another, but it turned out to be a wonderful experience that drew us closer. When we finally congregated, we yearned to hear what the others had to say; there was no frivolous conversation. We interacted on a different level because now there were no words to mislead or misunderstand.

This experience made me realize how much the city divides us. We become cold because we're overloaded with noise, people, images, and information constantly coming at us. Our minds and our bodies cannot sustain such an overload; we become nervous and anxious. If someone strikes up a conversation, we think they're crazy or that they might hurt us or con us into something. On the other hand, I've walked through the woods in the midst of wilderness and encountered complete strangers—and longed to learn about them; it was easy to strike up a conversation.

I discovered that I loved the silence, especially here in Oak Creek Canyon, where you *disappear* into the silence.

The day after our arrival, Hawk asked us to change into our cotton wraps and bring towels.

"You're going to the stream. Be ready in ten minutes."

I rushed to get ready and, while waiting for the others, enjoyed the intoxicating power of the sun and a perfectly clear azure sky. The creek houses looked like toy houses amid the canyon walls, which are capped by huge hexagonal columns of black basalt.

Once we had all gathered in the parking lot, Hawk led us down a steep embankment lined with trees and boulders, near the resort. In a few moments we arrived at the edge of a rushing, sun-dappled creek that ran along the bottom of the canyon.

"When you go into these waters, you're birthing yourselves into the environment of the Hopi people," she told us. "The Hopi are descendants of the star people and others who have pure medicines. They have stayed pure."

We were going into the healing waters of the stream to purge ourselves before making a pilgrimage to the sacred vortexes. Immersing myself in it turned out to be one of the highlights of my journey, a powerful rite of self-purification.

My first impression of the creek and its surroundings was of a little Garden of Eden, untamed and unspoiled. The crystal-clear waters cascaded like waterfalls over massive boulders and rocks. The air was fragrant with towering trees, lush ferns, and a thicket of foliage forming a canopy over the stream. Every boulder, stone, and pebble was perfectly placed, as if we had stepped into an oil painting. To the west, the trees sloped upward with the canyon wall. We felt captivated and seduced back into the natural rhythm and flow of life. Nothing else existed; the cold and unforgiving world felt far away. As the wind whispered through the pines, time seemed to stand still. I felt a warm sensation and a lapsing into self-forgetfulness.

Hawk explained that many Ancestors were gathered in this area. "Spirit is very strong here," she told us, describing this whole area of mountains, rocks, and forest as "a huge supply warehouse of electro-magnetic energy."

We climbed over an assortment of rocks and boulders to get closer to the water. "Wet your faces. Bond with the water," Hawk said softly. "Treat it as holy. Celebrate the spirit of water. This is how we recognize that our body is made up mostly of water. We can't live without water." She stood at the edge of the stream, with the breeze blowing through her lion's mane of hair and a faraway look on her face. She was engaged in some mysterious communication with the nature spirits.

We made an offering of cornmeal and tobacco to the stream and then dipped our feet in the icy water. Hawk positioned herself on a sturdy flat rock at the edge of the stream.

She told us that cold water breaks down energy that has crystal-lized, and it also cleanses us of the negative effects of electricity. "Pain shows us where congested energy is not flowing. Where you feel the pain is where you need to let go. Ask the water to take away the pain."

And so our healing rite began. One by one we entered the glacial stream at a point where the waters gushed with rapid force.

"Hold your breath for as long as you can, and keep your head underwater," Hawk insisted, standing within arm's length, observing carefully. The challenge was to plunge our heads in the water again and again until our aural energy was cleansed. We watched each other scream and thrash about in the water, repeatedly coming up for air, until the emotions gushed out. After this experience we felt freed of the tension and pain that had lodged in our bodies, and ecstatic from newfound energy.

When it was my turn, I entered the stream, struggling to stand upright on the pebbles and stones. A Thunderbeing stood on either side for me to hold on to as I crouched down. Taking a deep breath, I submerged myself, the impact of the rushing water pounding against the top of my head—oh, what agony! It felt like a stampede riding across my head. My reality was reduced to a deafening blur, and I emerged, gasping, exploding from the shooting pain in my head. I had never felt anything so piercingly cold; this was an elemental force!

Drenched from head to toe and shivering, I looked up at Hawk, waiting for direction.

"Again. You're not clear yet," she said sternly.

I plunged a second time, then a third. The force of the water struck me until I began to lose physical contact with my surroundings. The only thing that existed was myself and the water. Finally I surrendered to the spirit of the water. It entered and flowed through me, down my body, out through my toes until my instincts took over, spilling and gushing out of me. I burst into tears; whatever tensions I had been holding on to were released. I was reduced to a vulnerable child, dazed; I had merged with the consciousness of the stream.

As I stood there, two dragonflies with beautiful jewellike colors hovered above me—was it a dragonfly and a damselfly? Hawk explained why they suddenly showed up: "Are you looking for a relationship?"

"Yes, I guess so."

"Well, you're gonna get one." She smiled, sounding pleased for me.

Her prediction proved to be accurate some time after that.

Hawk held out her arms like a loving, compassionate mother, and I fell into her embrace.

When we had completed the water ritual, we walked back to our cabins. I felt clear and calm, emptied of all rambling thoughts. I was inside the stillness at the center of my being, charged with the healing energies of Oak Creek, reconnected to my life force. When I reached my bedroom, I lay back on a chair and observed a beautiful white light dance around in my head. The center of my consciousness had shifted to my heart; I felt tranquil and at peace.

Later that evening Hawk spoke about Sedona–Oak Creek Canyon as a primary focal point of the electromagnetic energy grid that connects many vortexes around the planet. When we're at a vortex we experience a huge change in energy. The sensation that we feel, for example, when we're near a shimmering body of water or a stunning vista is magnified a thousand times. It is as though we enter inside a whirlwind of energy and spin deeper into ourselves until we are freed of the categorizing habits of the mind; the larger picture of life is revealed to us. As she put it, "The vortex assists you to connect to the massive huge potential of what you are. It is the ultimate passageway."

We learned about three types of vortex energy: electric, which tends to be masculine in nature and stimulates our emotional and physical aspects; magnetic, which tends to be feminine and stimulates our sensitivity and subconscious self; and electromagnetic, a combination of both that enhances creativity and self-balance. And we learned that each vortex in this region has a name: Bell Rock, Boynton Canyon, Cathedral Rock, Schnebly Hill, and Airport Mesa. She also noted that vortexes exist at Apache Leap, near Bell Rock; Indian Gardens, just down the road from our resort; and, ironically, at the post office in Sedona!

We were excited and curious about these vortexes.

"Tomorrow we will head out to Bell Rock," Hawk announced, advising us to wear good hiking shoes and carry backpacks.

The next morning David came around to our creek houses and asked us to get ready. We drove back along the same route that had led us here, past sheer canyon walls and extravagant foliage. We stopped at a bridge to enjoy a spectacular panorama of red and sandstone walls merging with mountains; below was a sheer dizzying drop covered with greenery. As we continued into Sedona, the crimson monoliths appeared in the distance silhouetted by the sun.

At a junction of two highways, we turned and drove another few miles past giant fire-red buttes, spires, and pinnacles. We could see Bell Rock, which is shaped like a bell, long before we arrived there, and nearing it, we pulled off the road to a little parking area.

"Look at that!" exclaimed Daniel.

"It's—it's awesome," I stammered, absorbed with the view of this massive monolith.

We made an offering of cornmeal, requesting the spirits here to be in harmony with us. We used cornmeal because it embodies qualities of nurturing and compassion. The ancestral teachings are that corn, the source of the meal, was an original gift from Creator for man's sustenance. Man ground it in prayer and a labor of caring and love. We offer it back to acknowledge the worthiness of the gift, to say that we remember and we remain as one.

When Hawk led us into a sandy red trail marked with stones, I felt excited and happy, as though I had embarked on an adventure. As I looked up at the fiery red structure known as Bell Rock, it seemed to draw me; I felt compelled to come closer. We climbed up a rocky slope, surrounded by juniper, manzanita, and scrub. Lizards darted by. Was this some fabled mountain hiding ancient mysteries? I wondered. Or was some marvelous temple concealed beneath the surface? Bell Rock was so alive that it seemed to breathe. As we stepped onto the brilliant red rocks, I felt agitated; a nervous energy erupted inside me. The hike became challenging as we climbed up and over the massive rocks. With each step I felt more exhilarated until, about one-third of the way up, we stopped. When I looked down, the highway seemed very far away, yet less than fifteen minutes had passed.

"There is a great energy here," Hawk said quietly as we gathered around her. "If you stayed here for an entire day you would get a tremendous electric charge. But," she added, "it would be disrespectful to climb to the top of Bell Rock. It is considered an altar by the natives. People have gotten sick and vomited because they did not heed the warnings about climbing this sacred rock." Noticing its precipitous sides, I wondered how anyone managed to climb it.

Hawk explained that when natives made a pilgrimage to the top of a mountain, they would fast and purge themselves before undertaking what to them was a spiritual voyage. "The mountain is a sacred place. It is vulgar and blasphemous to think of conquering it. That's an ego thing."

As we followed Hawk across the rocks, I felt a buzzing sensation like a low-voltage electric current in my head. I peered down into the valley, covered with greenery that stretched far and wide into the surrounding canyon walls. I felt as though I was looking at a jewel of creation. For some strange reason, some of us started to weep, and Hawk explained why: "It is so real and honest here. Bell Rock is a tremendous electric vortex; it constantly disperses electrical movement. Many of us were here at the birth of this rock 500 million years ago. We paid a high physical price for this land and it hurts. That is why you feel like crying when you're here.

"Drink in what you're feeling," she said softly. "The vortex has survived in spite of everything."

We each found a private spot to absorb the energies. I sat on a rocky slope between a small pine and a clump of prickly pear cactus. I was engulfed by the endless horizon of the panoramic view. I didn't see a beginning or an end; I could no longer see any limits. I became agitated; I rocked back and forth. I had an impulse to get up and jump around. I turned around to study the summit of Bell, which consists of huge columns that looked to me like totem poles clustered together. I saw interesting shapes, faces, figures; one face reminded me of an Indian woman who had to be a thousand years old.

As I meditated, certain unresolved issues came to the surface. Does the energy here move them forward? And just as quickly I let them go. I had to restrain myself from jumping up and laughing. Why had I allowed these bothersome issues to keep me from peace of mind? It was not difficult to let them go. An unresolved emotion about someone close to me surfaced, and I also released that with great ease. Does the force of energy here move emotions that quickly? I lay down on the crimson rock, and to the right of my inner vision a presence appeared that had a head and a long, flowing body. When I asked the others, they said that they too felt the presence of something.

Later I picked up a book that described Bell Rock as a dynamo of cosmic energy that is being used by extraterrestrials as an interdimensional portal to Earth.

Too soon it was time to leave. Hawk signaled for us to come down.

As we got back on the highway, I was feeling extremely energized. Within a few moments we turned onto another road and drove a short distance. On our left we looked up to an amazing sight: a chapel nestled into the steep cliffs! It was a narrow structure built around a huge cross, jutting out of a towering rock wall. We continued up around a steep, winding paved road, higher and higher to a parking area at the top. Then we walked up a serpentine concrete ramp built into the rock, which took us to the front door of the chapel. From there we had a breathtaking 360-degree panoramic view of dramatic rock formations ranging in color from sandstone and pale pink to orange and crimson.

"Look over there—there's Bell Rock and, next to it, see that massive butte? That's Courthouse Butte," David pointed to the distance. "And if you look over there, see those four citadels? That's Cathedral Rock."

"What's that over there?" I asked, pointing to two towering rock monoliths east of the chapel.

"I think those are called Twin Buttes or Twin Nuns," David replied.

They resembled two figures merging into each other, and they had distinctive facial features. They were so eerily alive that they could have been souls incarnated in stone. Immediately next to them was a rock pinnacle that looked like a mother holding her child.

We entered into the chapel where a Gregorian chant was playing. Many people were standing around or sitting on the wooden benches. I found the environment extremely tranquil; I could easily have spent a whole day there just dreaming about life. The front and back of the chapel, which is all glass from floor to ceiling, offered spectacular views of the red rocks. We spent some time there and then returned to our vehicles.

At this point Hawk asked if we wanted to visit another vortex. We all said in chorus, "Yes!" She spoke about the energies we could expect at Cathedral Rock, which she described as a time corridor.

We returned to the highway, and within moments we were on a winding dirt road. A magnificent structure appeared on the horizon. A group of red rocks formed several sculptured columns, creating the appearance of a temple having an aura of graceful splendor. As we drew closer and closer, at each turn along the road I felt an immensity of tranquillity. When we reached the parking area, Hawk asked us to make an offering of cornmeal before starting on the trail.

We followed the trail into a primitive jungle of juniper, pine, manzanita, cactus, and all manner of shrub and scrub shooting up from the red earth, flowing into each other and merging. The slope became very rocky, and I climbed and leaped over massive red rocks, higher and higher. I stopped now and then to study the crimson columns that dominated this entire structure. I marveled at their beauty and simplicity, yet I had an incredible feeling of complexity. How could something be so beautiful and complex and still look so easy to assemble? There seemed to have been no effort in the work, and yet it gave pleasure while delivering a message. Was this Creator's abstract art? It touched something deep inside me; it felt familiar. I was struggling to retrieve a lost memory. While I couldn't understand my reaction, I was happy just at the presence of these feelings.

As I continued my climb, I felt overwhelmed by the stillness. Except for a slight breeze, I saw no other movement. Surrounded by this perfection and harmonious balance, I was getting giddy, as if I'd seen something that I shouldn't have seen, and wanted to keep it all for myself. I stopped to catch my breath. Looking out at the panorama, I saw the chapel we had visited earlier.

After a while I felt entranced, as though I'd fallen into a void. I became very aware of my body. It didn't seem to end with its form; in fact, my form seemed to have become intertwined with the rocks. I had become part of them; I had expanded into them. I felt nurtured, as if I were being cradled in someone's arms, as though the Earth were saying, "You can be who you are; nothing will harm you here; you are loved."

I realized how ludicrous any attempt to dominate nature is. There was a power here that demanded our respect. For too many years of my life, I had believed I was somehow superior to and separate from nature. Little did I think to look beneath my feet for guidance! The Earth Mother provides majestic places that are natural altars. They exist in order to stretch us beyond our five physical senses.

On the way back to our cabins, we stopped for groceries. That evening we talked about our experiences at the two vortexes and agreed that the energy at Bell Rock was different from the energy at Cathedral. Bell was much more active; it seemed to intensify whatever we were feeling. If we were anxious we felt more anxious; if we were elated we felt more elated.

Nora told us that when she looked up at Bell Rock she had a flashback that she had been there before: "I saw an entranceway, and I saw myself walking through it. I could point out exactly where the entrance was that led to a chamber deep inside the mountain. I *knew* I'd been inside!"

And Hawk confirmed her perception: "Yes, you have."

* * *

Over the next few days we also visited Airport Mesa, an electric vortex situated upon a hill. This site offered breathtaking panoramic views in every direction: on one side we could see Bell, Cathedral, and Courthouse rocks; and on the other, a sweeping view of West Sedona and the many towering giants that form the background of the town. We didn't have time to go to all of the vortexes, for we had to squeeze in jaunts to the Grand Canyon and to Hopi villages. We carried sketch pads with us, drawing the landscape and the many faces and animal shapes that appeared to us in the canyon walls. Halfway through our journey, we started to create shields, converting our inner experience into symbols and pictures on deerskin stretched over a round frame.

"You are avatars," Hawk told us as we sat on the grass behind the creek houses. "You are to humanity as the heart is to the body. You must love every part of yourself. Avatars are here on Earth now to fulfill a prophecy."

We talked about our hopes, desires, and dreams, for the vortexes had reawakened so much in us. I mentioned that I'd dreamed about being pregnant. When I asked Hawk what this meant, she said I was giving birth to my spiritual self. "I've watched you open up on this trip," she said, her hazel eyes twinkling with delight at the progress I'd made. "You're striking to look at. Stop hiding in the dark shadows. Don't let the past rule you. You are a light."

I will never forget that first journey. Sedona will always remain in my heart. Two years later I would return.

CHAPTER 6

CONVERSATIONS, DEEDS, AND DREAMS

Soft peace she brings, wherever she arrives
She builds our quiet as she forms our lives,
Lays the rough paths of peevish Nature even,
And opens in each heart a little heaven.

—MATTHEW PRIOR

ONE EVENING IN MAY of 1991, some time after six o'clock, we stopped for dinner. We were somewhere in Pennsylvania. Daniel and I had been driving for about five hours.

"Look, there's a truck stop. Let's pull in there," he said with excitement.

I turned off the highway, drove around the gas pumps at the front of the restaurant, and parked my car.

We walked past the truck drivers sitting at tables in the smoke-filled restaurant.

"I think I'll just have some coffee and soup," I said, perusing the menu.

"I'm going to have the bean soup and chicken," Daniel responded.

When the waitress came over and took our order, we were already deep into a discussion about change and consciousness.

"Have you noticed how everything seems to be moving faster? It feels as if time is moving faster and faster," I said.

"Yes, the last part of the great change has begun. Earth is getting ready to do her transformation. We are experiencing time differently; things are speeding up and they'll continue to speed up even more. The mind has to go through a rapid acceleration as it becomes enlightened."

"How do you think those truck drivers will handle the change?" I said with a mischievous expression on my face.

"They will go through it too. But they may not understand what's going on. If they're not comfortable with change, they might fight it tooth and nail."

"So people who continue to follow the accepted doctrines of the mind will feel very frustrated?" I continued.

"Yes. For the next twenty-five to fifty years we must learn to feel again. If we let the mind dominate, it will make us crazy."

"All the Thunderbeings will offer their help," I suggested.

"Yes, I think we as a group need to show people what they've forgotten. The potential we have is present in everyone, it's just that ours has evolved."

"Yes, that's true," I agreed.

"You know, I truly feel in my heart that I now have a purpose. It might sound silly, but I feel I have a duty to this planet. I feel like a soldier."

"I don't," I said. "I feel more like a parent or a mother."

"I believe we have done this on other planets, you know, acting as catalysts for change."

"You mean that we are system busters who go around to different planets?" I laughed.

We chuckled as the waitress approached and poured more coffee.

"How many Thunderbeings do you think are on Earth now?" I asked, pushing the coffee aside.

"Possibly 144,000? That's the number mentioned in Chapter Seven of Revelations. José Argüelles said this was the number set aside by God for us to be free of the curse of ego and false time. He said that the gate to the new world can be opened only by the 144,000 chosen souls."

The waitress had come over with our bill and we continued our discussion in the car.

• • •

It was midnight when we arrived at Hawk's place. Some of the Thunderbeings were chatting, catching up on each other's lives. I briefly said hello, climbed upstairs, and fell asleep the minute my head hit the pillow.

The next morning most of us were up at dawn to greet the sun. Hawk arrived after breakfast. As her car turned into the driveway, we rushed outside to greet her.

"Hello, my little Thunderbeings. Come over here and give me a hug," she cried with delight, affectionately reaching for us.

She hugged every single one of us under the big oak tree in front of the house.

"Why don't we sit outside? It's such a beautiful day," she suggested.

We formed a huge circle on the grass. Hawk sat right up near the trunk of the oak tree. The day was perfect, about eighty degrees; shafts of sunlight streamed through the trees. And I sighed because we were all together again.

Hawk looked radiant; she had the presence of a living church. Being with her was like stepping into a church and feeling clean and pure again. It made our minds go in a particular direction; we started to visualize what we needed to work on in our lives. And we found that our hearts opened up; the defensive walls we had built around ourselves started to come down.

While all of the Thunderbeings had their own dilemmas, one thing they didn't lack was feeling. In fact they had an excessive depth of feeling, and that in itself could sometimes be a problem in a world where feelings were considered a weakness. In many ways we were like everyone else; in other ways, we were very different, for we were being transformed at an astonishingly fast pace. We were making quantum leaps from month to month.

"How is everybody doing?" Hawk asked, looking around at each of us, gathering data with a few glances. "Let's start with Phillip. I want to hear what is happening in your life."

Phillip, an engineer, was recently divorced.

"Well, everything is going pretty good right now. I've been putting all my energy into my business. I don't think I'll be ready for another relationship for some time. Lately, though, I've been having some very unusual dreams about masks. I dreamed about a parade of six or eight masks. What does that mean?"

Hawk explained that the masks symbolized the many selves and dimensions of our being: "When a mask comes to you in a dream, allow a face to emerge and take shape, and then talk to it. You are not a single anything. You are a multifaceted being. You change with each person you're with. You are multiple people. You don't need to make an issue out of it. There is nothing schizophrenic about it."

She turned to Joan.

Joan, a nurse in her late thirties, talked about her difficulty in letting go of the past. Many of us could identify with her because of how quickly we were changing; we had developed an old self and a new self.

"I am actually dreaming in gray," she said, her voice cracking with emotion. "There are no colors in my dreams."

In a tender voice, Hawk said, "Joan, life itself is the teacher. If you focus on any part of your life or your past as unimportant, it goes to a gray area. Your old experiences are comfortable shoes. You cannot separate yourself from them. When you start acknowledging them, they will take on color. You would not be in the position you are today to even ask this question if you did not have those experiences. Even if it's fear or pain, we have created these things. They have taught us choices. Old experiences are your elders. Respect them."

She then turned her attention to Lynn, a very attractive blonde who worked for a large corporation: "Lynn, you have come from a real physical place. I have watched you go from being a manipulative female to someone with sensitivity. You are not a body. If you glorify your body as a tool for getting what you want, you will lose your self very fast."

Lynn nodded, and a grateful tear rolled down her face. She *had* changed a lot, and she knew it.

Liz, a college teacher about thirty years old, complained about not being in a relationship. Hawk advised her to get busy with her own life: "Relationships are not easy to maintain or nurture. A period when you're trying to fill a void in your life is not the right time to seek a relationship. The best time is when you don't *need* one, when your life is full and active."

At this point I had known most of the others for at least three years. I started to think about what they did for a living and how this had clouded my perception of them. Society in general has all kinds of notions about what we are because of our job or profession. But a janitor or a truck driver may be more fulfilled or knowledgeable about his life than a lawyer or a president of a corporation. The job or profession becomes like an outer garment or cloak that obscures the true person beneath it. And it works: most of the time we don't even question their authority and they themselves become convinced by the cloak.

Similarly, the IQ tests that our schools administer do not measure true ability. For example, if you brought a Bushman from Africa and gave him an IQ test alongside a learned scholar, obviously the learned scholar would get a higher score. But would that make him better? Let's take the same situation and turn it around. You're in the middle of an African jungle, you have no food or water, and you find yourself in absolute desolation wandering through the wilderness. Who would you rather be with, the learned scholar or the Bushman?

I was deep in thought when Hawk turned to me and asked what was happening in my life. I told her about a recent dream.

"I am cleaning an old desk. As I open the drawers I find dust five inches deep. There's stuff in the desk that's been there for twenty years, like blankets and pillows. I want to remove it and throw it out, but it's too heavy. I find Phillip and Nora, who are supposed to help me remove this old rotting desk. They take me to their friend, a six-foot-three-inch, two-hundred-pound Swede, who will help me."

Hawk explained: "The desk represents your mental and value processes. The pillows and blankets are your unconscious tapes. You are getting rid of your parents' program. You are getting rid of what has impaired you; and you're persistent in looking for someone to help you. The Swedish man represents aspects of yourself: healthy, beautiful, clear-minded, honest, robust and happy."

Eventually Hawk taught us how to interpret dreams on our own. Of course, other people can be very informative and helpful, especially if they have a knowledge of dream symbology, but once we learn to analyze our own dreams, nobody can do it better.

She emphasized how very healing it was to bring problems out into the open like this. "Have the courage to be open with each other," she told us. "My people didn't have secrets. There was no such thing. It wasn't healing if it was secret. If you do something you don't like, I want you to be able to say to each other, 'I know what I did. I don't feel good about it. I don't intend to do this anymore.'"

We had truly started to feel comfortable about sharing our thoughts. Hawk had the ability to put us at ease. She demanded no more from us than honesty and openness, just as we expected this of her. She told us that mistakes were necessary for our growth, that within our own being we would find all the answers we would ever need. She said that problems were opportunities. *What* and *who* was upsetting and challenging us was really our best teacher. The emphasis was always on the beauty in being human and our potential to obtain whatever our heart desired; total prosperity was not an idyllic goal.

"Do you want to take a break now? Let's get up and stretch." She puckered up her face like a little girl to break the mood of seriousness. "You've got five minutes to pee," she said in that delightfully playful way of hers.

I lay back on the grass and enjoyed the warmth of the early afternoon sun. I loved these weekends with Hawk. It always felt as though we were in a big cozy cocoon far away from the busy technological world where people were constantly traveling on the information superhighway. We were traveling too, only on a different highway. Even when we were in the midst of some intense discussion, Hawk was taking us through all the dimensions with her; we traveled *interdimensionally.* Feelings and emotions deep within us started to stir, and again we felt the promise of love and hope.

When we gathered after our break, Hawk told a story I had first heard four weeks earlier when she and her son, David, had driven to Toronto. As usual, they had stopped at one or two restaurants along the way.

"We stopped at this one place, and there was a couple in front of David and me. Suddenly I was drawn into paying attention to them. Here was this little old man in his late seventies, wearing a coat and suit that definitely were from the 1940s, dust-ridden, but very well pressed and very dignified. I told David to go over to the man and give him some money. The old man came over to me and said, 'I thank you for this, but I cannot take it.'

"And I said to him, 'Why can't you take it?'

" 'Because I would feel guilty.'

" 'Would you feel guilty if I told you that if you *do not* take this, it will ruin my whole day? That if I thought that I let you walk away without sharing what I have been blessed with, I would not be able to go to the end of my day feeling good about myself." [She said this to him with a certain tenderness and humor.]

"And he looked down, and said, 'That's a great deal of money.'

" 'And I have a great deal of money today.'

" 'I can take care of my wife. I don't need the money.'

" 'I have no doubt that you're a very good provider.'

" 'Yes, I am."

" 'But it would make me very happy to know that you would take this. For whatever the reason, God made me notice you, and what I noticed is that you have a need and I have more than I need. Take this. Enjoy it. Make us happy.'

"Big tears ran from the corners of his eyes. 'Do you understand what you're doing?'

" 'Yes I do.'

" 'What do you understand?' "

Hawk paused a moment. " 'I understand that, whatever the reason, I feel very warmed by you. I know that you're on a final pilgrimage with your wife. She's dying and you know that. You've left your home state of Virginia and gathered every possession that you had to give her one final journey and that you've been very good company all these years. And in this, with all your heart, you want to give her a very eloquent meal. You want her to have a very wonderful time. You want it to be an experience that will connect the two of you forever.' "

" 'How did you know all these things?' he asked me."

Hawk just smiled.

" 'In these days of watching her illness, I have come to believe that there is no God. But now that I have met you, I have come to realize that there are other good people.'

" 'If you can embrace that fully with all its worth, would you bless me one step further?' "

Hawk reached into her wallet and pulled out two more bills.

" 'Would you buy her a dress? Before you take her to dinner, let her pick the prettiest dress she's ever had. And let that also be the dress you let her meet her new life in.'

"He looked at me and said, 'Do you know that has been a concern of mine?' "

Hawk went on to deliver the point of the story: "Shortly after arriving in Toronto I received fifty times what I gave. So I had even more to give to the next lesson that God passed through my life. Do you understand what I am telling you? You can give someone a gift of a lifetime because you have more than you need. That is what wealth is. Money is but a piece of paper. You designate what gift it will be. That is what I give back to Creator."

It's just like the old saying, "What goes around, comes around." As Hawk expressed it, "I understand somewhere much deeper in my mind that this principle works. I don't know the science of it. But I know the goodness of it, and I know it works."

I was fascinated with how she nurtured everything around her, always touching and trusting and giving; it seemed effortless for her.

We asked her how she could love us if she didn't see us for long periods of time.

And she replied: "Loving you is not measured by the amount of time I've know you or how often I see you."

And we would feel an intimacy and a sacred trust with her unlike anything we had felt before.

At this point she launched into a lesson about the importance of appreciation. The key to getting more of what we want in our lives is absolute appreciation for everything that we already have—even when we feel it's meager, even when we're in pain. Appreciation of that which we take for granted will free us. Appreciation abolishes all of our complaints and our doubts. If we were ever going to be completely awakened we had to realize there were no limitations, only our own limited vision and lack of appreciation for what we had been given.

All of us had everything we needed to fulfill our life's purpose; we were born perfect for our life's purpose.

"When life is too much to handle I say, 'I appreciate, I am thankful,' and I find power in that," she told us. "It always brings me back on top. Appreciation acts like a magnet that brings more of the good things into our lives. So it's important not to complain to God or Creator or whatever higher power you're addressing."

And she would always take us closer to glimpsing our God self.

Wisdom is already perfect in our bodily form. We are the cellular memories and patterns of all that has ever been created. Our organic bodies as well as the planets and the solar system are held together by the same substance: love. This love is a magnet that lives in the center of everything.

"You are the mystery. A cord connects you directly into the black hole behind the Milky Way, which the Mayan people call Hunab Ku. Hunab Ku is the mystery that lives inside the black hole that scientists have found behind the Milky Way. Black holes are windows that go outside our universe. Everything that exists outside or inside our universe, you and I have created: the planets, the stars, the debris. We are cocreators of God. That which has birthed us is inside the black hole, Hunab Ku, source of all things. You are the most loved of Creator's creations."

When she spoke like this, I started thinking about how we all came from one cell. This cell then divided into two and split again into four, and so on, but each time it divided, it automatically took on a role: it became the cell that forms a nose or a nerve or the nails on our fingers. Otherwise we'd look like one huge nose. This in turn made me think that we all come from that one source of energy and that our bodies are like tiny working models of the universe. Therefore we can look into the farthest reaches of the universe simply by looking into ourselves; the time scale is irrelevant.

I realized that I do not have to seek to transcend my body; I do not have to spend so much time seeking what I already am. The reality of what I am *is* transcendence. My search ends the moment I begin to understand that I am in the experience of life and there is no greater place that I need to go to find myself. What I am seeking is not "out there"—it is within. I am like the turtle: I carry my home on my back.

As Hawk says: "We are here to perfect our mind and our body. We're here to manifest our potential. Why would we want to transcend into oblivion? The notion of transcending the body is a mind game."

Hawk personifies the belief that existence on this planet is a blessing, not a curse. She explained that feelings of being cursed or damned are not experienced by people who live close to nature.

"There is beauty in everything that is in this dimension," she said. "This is a place of beauty and paradise. Our true purpose is to create beauty wherever we happen to be. In order to come into the experience with Mother Earth we had to make an agreement that we would create beauty. All it takes to change the world is to embrace the knowledge that all we are ever expected to do is create beauty."

She said that beauty is found in harmony. It is the balance of opposite force fields—female and male, negative and positive. When we have equal forces of each duality, the result is harmony.

"You can behold beauty in whatever you see," she said. "It can be the most hideous creature you have ever seen. Yet if you will take the time to use the divine covenant of why you exist, you will be able to find one focus of beauty in that creature. Until you move past your point of judgment of what is beautiful and what is not beautiful, you will limit your possibilities in life. When you have done away with judging from your own scale of beauty, you will also be able to see the trolls and the rock people and the many presences that live among you that you would consider hideous, grotesque, or ugly."

If we are to remap our thoughts in this direction, we have to break the chains that have been imposed on us. These chains are made from many links constantly being added and strengthened. They are society's rules and expectations and the fear of punishment and guilt. Although invisible and inside us, they are as strong as steel, for they have created limitations and imprisoned us to the extent that our instincts and feelings have become deadened. We have become people of destruction because these chains have enabled a small number of people to control the masses. When we disconnect from our feelings, there is no compassion and no understanding. We become too heavily weighted in abstract thinking. Distinctions, comparisons, and judgments arise that exist only in our minds, and the truth of who we are and why we're here is lost.

When we free ourselves from these chains, our mind and our spirit will take flight into a boundless experience of life. We will think and feel differently; we will be more understanding and accepting, more inclined to discard our criticisms and judgments.

Humans are always *dictating* to each other. We are always trying to control one another. We should be more like nature, which is *all-allowing*—in nature each part allows the other part to live as it has to live. In a more spiritual society, we will stop this tyranny of control and have a more accepting attitude. That does not mean that we have to love every person; we cannot love everyone. The most we can do is to let them live and to care.

"Today," Hawk said, "relationships are trashed; there are no fruitful relationships because people are playing games of control with each other. Many people don't really know what they want out of a relationship. The chemistry becomes a prison, whether it's mothers-daughters, fathers-sons, lovers, it doesn't matter. Relationships are at their very worst in the history of this planet. Why? Because you've extracted every right relationship of yourself out of your mind. You don't know if there's really a God. You're trying to find out. You wonder what your role in it is. And on days when nothing is going the way you hoped, you even question the existence of a God."

And since we're on the topic of relationships, what we're seeing today is a polarization of the sexes. There is much conflict and confrontation, each side pointing fingers and blaming the other for our ills. Even with mere word association, when "male" and "female" are spoken, the words evoke a response of opposition. Instead, the response should be one of perfect balance of yin and yang, as in Taoist teachings. The healthy interplay between male and female causes new growth; the harmony between them causes great peace.

"We're afraid of being spiritual in our relationships," Hawk continued. "But as we become more spiritual beings that doesn't mean solemn and serious. In fact, spirit *is* carefree and lighthearted. Pure spiritual persons laugh, have fun, have sex, and so forth, and at the same time honor themselves. Life is an adventure for them because they know that being human is sacred and powerful: we were not conceived in sin but were made manifest in joy."

These are some of the qualities that will help us navigate through the gateway into the new world. All the old ways and belief structures will no longer work. If we choose to hang on to them we will engage in a futile struggle, for we will be working against the universal forces.

The winds of change are upon us—the very center of our existence is changing. We must quickly expand our ability to love and trust. Now we have countless books, songs, and movies inspiring us to the expression of love, but still we do not embrace love as a practical way of life. As Hawk noted, love is the true principle of evolution. Our true nature is to move toward harmony. We are meant to be happy, not to suffer. We must give up the need to suffer, or we will not be able to tolerate the more refined atmosphere of the new world. We don't have to suffer to achieve our enlightenment, contrary to what many programs and schools of thought would have us believe.

But the transformation can't happen without a cleanup. The cleansing must happen before the new world begins. As Hawk said, "Just as the seasons weed out malfunctioning growth each year, the larger cycles of the universal calendars change civilizations. The weaknesses in our civilization have to be weeded out."

Hawk always encouraged us to live our dream and our vision. "The mysticism *can* materialize," she would say. "Do it now, not tomorrow or next week. Become the best self you can be. Write about what you want out of your life. Be drunk with the dream of your own adventure." And she would remind us that there is no retirement from life. "This is an action planet. Stay busy and purposeful. Find a new adventure."

Although it was well after midnight, we were still going strong, feeling alive with the magic of being together. In this tiny, little-known corner of the Milky Way, the Thunderbeings were plotting and planning the new image of humanity that would someday have far-reaching implications for the entire universe. We stayed up until the small hours of the night because there was far too much work to be done! We dreamed about eradicating all the nightmares of the world and about a new world of peace and harmony. We dreamed about life on Earth returning to its original state of paradise.

We were drawing up the blueprint of the new humans. So far we had decided that they would be spiritual yet earthy creatures capable of tolerance and compassion. The new humans would have expanded their ability to love and trust. The new humans would no longer doubt themselves as spiritual beings. They would never think they were deficient or flawed in any way. Oh, sure, they would get angry and obnoxious, but they would never try to control or deceive for the purpose of dominating their fellow humans. The new human would still be ambitious but not ruthless. They would have obsessions, but without the destructive component. They would make mistakes freely without judgment and they would be able to forgive themselves. The new humans would enjoy laughter and communication, but not gossip. The new humans would never take themselves too seriously. They would be more cosmic in their outlook and would experience a oneness with Great Spirit.

Considering the condition that humankind is in today, I didn't think a mere makeover would suffice. We needed radical surgery.

CHAPTER 7

THE BEAR SWEAT

Have you descended to the springs of the sea
or walked in the unfathomable deep?
Have the gates of death been revealed to you?
Have you ever seen the doorkeepers
of the place of darkness?
Have you comprehended the vast expanse of the world?
Come, tell me all of this, if you know.

   —*The Book of Job*

TWO MONTHS LATER, IN July, we set off again for another long drive. This time Nora had joined Daniel, Katherine, and me. Nora, a tall, lanky brunette in her late thirties, was a copywriter for an advertising agency. We found ourselves stopping at virtually every mall we passed so that Nora could indulge her love for shopping.

   When we encountered dead animals on the road we would move them onto the grassy shoulder. If it was unsafe to stop, we would still make an offering for the animal and pray for it to be released to the all-knowing realm. It was something that Hawk had taught us; the animal in its innocence has no comprehension of being struck by the vehicle, and it keeps reliving the experience until the ravens come to free its spirit.

   By late evening, after pausing one last time for dinner, we had tacked three hours onto our trip. We were having so much fun that it was well past midnight when we finally arrived at our destination.

The next morning during breakfast, I looked around and noticed a couple of new faces in Hawk's kitchen. Jim, a business executive from Detroit, and Brian, a carpenter, who lived in southern Ontario. All together, twenty-five of us had assembled for another weekend of learning and adventure.

By midafternoon, we had gathered wood and brought it to the back of the house. We chanted as we carried the logs to Hawk, who placed them in an orderly arrangement. She then lit a match, and we watched in silence as the wood burst into flames.

The fire swirled and spiraled above our heads, changing color from yellow to orange. Our ceremony had helped to release the spirit of the wood. It allowed the trees to speak to us and share their knowledge. Dancing before us was the very soul of the trees we had used. We were witnessing the energy of the sun and the nurturing of the Earth and all of the elements, for nothing is more interconnected with these things than the tree. Within the flames is revealed all that the tree has ever experienced.

"The fire is bringing you a bright orange," Hawk said. "Normally you can see violets, yellows, and blues. Orange symbolizes total transformation. The fire in itself is a living being. So nothing determines the color of the fire other than its spirit. This is a fire of transformation. It's time to surrender all your confusion and the parts of your self that don't serve you. You want to go beyond the realm of your mind because you know its potential to defeat you. I want you to function at your maximum, at one hundred percent of your ability."

She proceeded to tell us a story about how fire came to Earth. She told it in poetic language, using what seemed to me ancient words and although I didn't fully understand it at first, it still made an impact on me.

> *When man was in his darkest state and lived instinctually, he was like all the other creatures—he made no choices. From the mother universe, the Pleiades, there was a thought. Man was ready to explore his intention to be. So there was a very powerful movement sent from the Mother Sun and it was sent through fire. It was the first light to pierce the pattern of forms.*

And humans gathered around the great flame and gave celebration for its light.

After watching it for days, they made their first choice: to keep the flame alive. They began to explore themselves by making more choices. They began to stand upright and walk in the sun and experience themselves with the ability of their consciousness. They had full consciousness. They thought with their whole brain. And the top of their head stayed soft, bringing much energy and fire. But they began to use this powerful intelligence to manipulate and trick each other. As the Above Beings in the realm of light watched, they heard them say, "Maybe we are smarter than God." And the grandmothers cried. They realized there would have to be a great suffering. Only then would we be cured of the illusion that we are superior to those who gave us the fire. The Above Beings warned that in the days ahead we would think only from the part of our minds that made the choice to separate. We would think we were alone and our cries would be heard all over the universe.

Humans began to compete with each other, and this has gone on for a duration of four worlds. As we come into the cycle of a new world, we will arrive again at the opportunity to reconnect with our original and pure intelligence.

If we are ever to experience the acknowledgment of the Above Beings again, we must turn away from all destruction. In the next world we will realize that we are not separate from God. Many will still choose to compete with God, but they will have to come back through the trials of fire.

Like teenagers who think they're smarter than their parents, as our civilization matures, so will we come to realize that we are not superior to that which gave us life, and we will start to show respect. Those who continue to be self-centered and refuse to acknowledge the Above Beings will not be spared. They too will have to come face-to-face with themselves, however painful their trials of fire might be.

Later in the day Hawk announced that we would have another ceremony: a sweat lodge. She preferred more formal terms such as "rock lodge" and "stone elders' lodge," because she said it is a sacred place where we renew our connection with Creator.

In preparing our rock lodge, we placed several large rocks in the fire. The lodge is made of willow saplings bent into the shape of a turtle shell; these form the ribs of the lodge, which are covered with cedar and canvas. Natives say that the covering is like the night sky or like the skin of a great animal in whose body you are being held. It can also be the skin and body of your own mother when you were in the womb.

Just outside the entrance to our lodge is an altar, where offerings, including feathers, stones, and gems, are placed. The altar is made from the earth plug pulled out of the center of the lodge, which provides the pit for the heated stones. The pathway that leads to the altar is the neck of the turtle.

The rock lodge represents the womb of the Earth Mother: to be inside the lodge is to be inside the womb of the Earth. It is an altar between the material world and the spirit world, where shamans do most of their healing work.

The sun was setting over the valley as we started to gather outside the lodge. We women wore cloth wraps made of cotton fabric cut wide enough to wrap around our bodies and tied at the front. And the men had fashioned wraplike shorts for themselves, tied at the waist. Hawk arrived wearing a yellow and white wrap, with her hair tied back. She checked us over: were we wearing cotton? Synthetic fabrics are not comfortable in a sweat lodge. She instructed us to place our jewelry on the altar outside the lodge. We must approach the lodge with the deepest respect, as a place of prayer and purification; we must walk around it from east to south to west, the way the sun moves. And we must always walk around the head and neck of the turtle.

"I want you to enter the lodge with the awareness that it is the environment of Great Spirit," she said quietly. "You close yourself off from the outer world when you are in the lodge. You look inside yourself. You are going back into the void. The mystery lives in the void."

I wasn't sure what Hawk meant by "the void." Did she mean an emptiness where nothing exists? Or is there no such thing as nothingness? But then, what existed before humans, before the planet itself—one huge void?

She continued: "Our stone relations bring us many gifts that we may be purified in our sweats. They send messages through their cells to aid us. They bring us many revelations of our true nature. They are true and loyal friends."

Hawk entered the lodge first and chanted as she crawled around. Then she sat down and said, "Come on in." We proceeded to file in, one by one and on all fours, chanting softly.

Although this was my second sweat lodge, I was still nervous. My first one had been a fiasco. I'd felt confused, not knowing what to do or how to do it. Shortly after commencing, I had wanted to escape, and halfway through, I did. I was afraid of being in a dark space, closed off from the outer world of light and sound. I had felt claustrophobic at having to sit so close with so many other people; twenty-five bodies had made for a crowded lodge.

While I waited my turn to enter the lodge, I watched the sparks from the fire as they danced upward. My attention turned to Hawk who was sitting at the doorway. She was telling people to circle to the left of the lodge. When it was time to enter, I crouched down on my hands and knees. The entrance was very low and narrow. In the semidarkness I crawled slowly, making sure I did not go near the stone pit. As I sat down, the straw on the floor of the lodge rubbed against my legs. Finally, when all of us had entered, Hawk asked us to stop talking.

Alison and Don remained outside the lodge as stone keepers. They were responsible for tending the fire and bringing in the heated stones between rounds. The lodge would become hotter and hotter over the course of four rounds, one round for each cardinal direction.

The stones, which were heated in the fire we'd built and then brought into the lodge, were referred to as "our elders" because they were older than humans and therefore had great wisdom. Water was poured over the heated rocks, causing immense amounts of steam to emanate from the stones, which released their heat into the lodge.

"Bring me ten stones," Hawk said. The stone keepers carried them on pitchforks.

"Hello, stone elder," she greeted each stone and splashed water on it as it entered the lodge.

Doreen and Brian, who were seated near the opening, assisted in placing the stones in the pit.

We bowed our heads reverently in acknowledgment of the stones.

"Stone keeper, close the tarp!" Hawk pronounced.

The door flap was closed; all was dark except for the glow of the stones. Hawk poured more water onto the stones, causing them to make a hissing sound; the lodge filled with a light mist.

She proceeded to speak with such force and power that her voice reverberated through the lodge. She spoke of the Earth Mother: "She is the mother of our bodies and we are in her womb." She called out to the heavens and to Creator. She invited the spirit keepers of the four directions into our lodge. In an intimate and heartfelt tone, she prayed that there would be no more war, that all peoples would be healed of their bitterness and anger; and that we would again be one family of two-leggeds.

"We need to heal and restore the value of life and the joy of being on this beautiful planet. She is also alive and intelligent. Man creates pain and fear and uses it to control people by giving power to negative and destructive energies. This is not intelligent thinking. We cannot continue to separate ourselves with religion and racism. We now need to heal and regroup. Our elders have kept their sacred ways, ensuring that all humankind would have the opportunity to awaken to full realization."

She splashed more water on the rocks, and the mist permeated the lodge. Together we entered into the void, eyes closed. Suddenly I had nowhere to go but inward. I was afraid. What would I find there, inside myself?

"The rock," she continued, "represents our skeletal system. You came into the Earth as a message. The message is in the pattern of your bones. The rock elders are ready to give all of their wisdom to help us. They teach us the strength of the winds and fire. They teach us to penetrate density and be invisible. The stone elder has come through all these things with wisdom. It is fire and water in the same moment, resolving the contradiction of duality."

I understood her, yet I had never really looked at a stone in this way. I realized that I could no longer treat nature merely as an object, for she provided me with everything I needed. I couldn't live without her—we were one and the same.

"You come into the stone elders' lodge with a desire and a willingness to give up all your denials," she said. "Are you ready to give up any part of your self that denies the totality of what you are? Are you ready to do that now?"

The ceremony began. Hawk called upon the spirit of the east: "Grandfather, Great Eagle, come, give us your gifts of vision and inspiration. Help us to rise above our limitations and dance in the clouds. Teach us to see through your eyes."

Together we shouted, and the lodge swayed with a crescendo of voices. Hawk banged on the water bucket, signaling us to stop. The spirit keeper of the east had come into the lodge!

"Welcome, Grandfather. We thank you for coming to our lodge. Let the prayers begin."

One after another we Thunderbeings said our prayers. We were by now accustomed to a certain formality; we would say our names and when we finished our prayer, we would signal to the next person to start.

Katherine prayed first: "Gatekeeper of the east, this one known as Katherine asks for your vision to rise above the confusion in my life at this time."

When the first round was completed, Hawk asked the stone keeper to bring in more stones: "Stone keeper, open the gate!"

Ten stones were added to the pit. As each stone entered the lodge we put our forehead to the ground in a posture of respect.

"Welcome, stone elder."

The door flap was closed. As Hawk sprinkled water on the stones, they hissed and sang, and the steam rose. The reality of the outer world was fading as we descended into a realm where our conscious thinking minds could no longer have power over us.

"Embrace the mist. Wash yourselves with it. You're inviting the elders into your being."

The entire lodge shook with the force of Hawk's call as she called upon the spirit of the south, represented by the wolf. In a tender, loving voice, she asked the spirit keeper to teach us how to laugh and play and to understand the meaning of family.

Together, in unison, we screamed and wailed like wolves. We began another round of prayers. As the moist heat clung to my body, I felt a wall of desperation closing in on me. I couldn't let go of my control! What would happen if I let go? I dared not let go of the self-control I had cultivated. But I really did want to release myself from the dreary mechanisms of my mind.

On this third round we called upon the spirit keeper of the west, symbolized by the bear. Hawk prayed: "Give us the understanding of the bear. Give us the strength to transform our weakness into courage." She continued to pour water over the rocks. The steam rose like a serpent, coiling itself around my body. I turned around and pressed my face to the cool floor of the lodge.

"Embrace the heat. Don't tell your mind that you're in arctic weather. Become one with the heat."

We had already learned to accept the true reality of heat in the fire walk, and it was the same now. Indeed, this is a powerful technique that can be applied in our daily lives: Don't deny what is. Denial will never get us anywhere. It is easier to go with the flow. It is an easier, more harmonious path, and it feels better.

When we completed our prayers, the door flap was lifted and twelve more stones were brought in for the final round. Hawk called upon the spirit of the north: "Source of the creative force, place of wisdom and freezing winds, from your frozen waters comes the promise of the future."

As the water cascaded over the stones, we were engulfed by steam. I couldn't breathe. . . . I turned around to bury my face in the Earth. The heat drove us deeper into ourselves, and some of the Thunderbeings were panting their prayers.

The sweat lodge wasn't merely a ceremony; it was a challenge in the physical sense. I always had a fear of dark enclosed spaces, and now I found myself in absolute darkness. The air was heavy and choking. I didn't know what represented the front, the back, what was up or down. Direction had no meaning. East, west, north, and south no longer existed. I truly found myself existing in a void, but to my surprise, instead of the space contracting around me, I was experiencing an expansion. The darkness was unfolding into a size that I felt was larger than the universe and I was *floating* in its very center. No matter how much I reached out I couldn't touch the edges. And now the sweat lodge had accomplished its goal: it forced me to depend on myself. It forced me to grasp for my own resources. I was thrust back onto myself—my inner self became my whole universe.

In one final prayer Hawk offered her appreciation to our stone brothers, to the wood and the water, and reminded us of our divinity.

"Stone keeper, open the gate!" she shouted.

"That was a good sweat. You got the toxins out!" she said, pleased with the results. She asked us to put our forehead to the Earth and thank all our relations as we left the lodge

When I came out, I flung myself to the ground. I felt as though I had fallen into someone's arms. The Earth was blowing softly over my body; I could feel her coolness nurturing me back into oneness with her. The experience of being in a dark enclosed space filled with heat seemed so simple, yet I was mesmerized by its power. It caused me to reevaluate my long-held beliefs. It made me realize that the way I was living my life was misguided. Up to this point I'd had no idea of the healing and transformative powers of the Earth. It was the Earth that had purified my body and lifted my spirit. It was the Earth that was waiting to soothe me and hold me in her arms. I truly felt loved and embraced, as if she had reached out to me.

Eventually I got up and walked over to Hawk. Lynn and Kevin were helping her wash the mud off her feet

"How do you feel? Did I cook you enough?" Hawk joked.

"Oh, yes, it was the hottest thing I'd ever experienced," I sighed.

"I thought one of those rocks was going to blow up," Kevin said jokingly.

Eventually we all headed back to the house for a feast.

"You all look so beautiful," Hawk told us. "The rocks have given you their soul and wisdom. When you are in the lodge, you start burning where you are the weakest. After you sit in that intense heat you're willing to forget all of your long-winded miseries. When you look into your life you realize there is a lot for you to feel good about."

In August of 1991 I arrived at Hawk's place for the bear sweat. Nothing in my life could have prepared me for this experience. It is difficult to describe. It is truly beyond words.

The bear sweat is the hottest sweat lodge we will ever experience. "You're gonna cook," Hawk warned the thirty Thunderbeings who had gathered. We knew the lodge was going to be between 600 and 800 degrees Fahrenheit, and we had all freely made a choice to be a part of it. We also derived comfort from the fact that some of the Thunderbeings were here for their second bear sweat; that gave the rest of us hope. But now, as the moment approached, I was wondering if I could go through with it.

What? Impossible. No way, my mind screamed its protest.

The bear sweat was our initiation into bear medicine. It was our initiation into the shamanic otherworld. The bear would teach us to draw upon our inner resources. Bear medicine would teach us to act from a position of power. Completing the sweat called for great perseverance and strength. We would enter the lodge to conquer our fears or the bear would devour us. Its claws could cut deep into the flesh.

We had been fasting for several days, eating only salad, fruit, and juice in preparation for the sweat.

At three o'clock we gathered, wearing our cotton wraps; the mood among us was very solemn. The afternoon sunlight streamed through the windows.

"Make sure you understand what it means to have bear medicine," Hawk said quietly.

"This is not a power trip. Having bear medicine is applying gentleness without the need for recognition. It is using power with gentleness. Bear gives us many medicines. Many fear the bear, but fear, like the bear, can be our strongest ally. Treat it with respect and move through it. Fear is never real, but its gifts are valid.

"The bear we will encounter is within ourselves. It is all of the judgments and critical opinions we have about other people. Every time we judge someone we are seeing ourselves in that person. Every judgement we make reveals what we hate or cannot accept about ourselves. Our dislikes, resentments, and fears live within us. Observer and observed are one and the same. We are that which we see in everything and everybody.

"Each time, for instance, you think some other person is clumsy and ugly, you are looking at an undeveloped part of yourself."

"The bear forces us to confront ourselves. In the subconscious environment of the rock lodge we come face-to-face with all the dark and ugly aspects of ourselves, all the things we choose to see in others but not in ourselves.

"I want the bear to rid you of your self-importance. Bear medicine kills form very fast. Bear can devour you. Bear has no predator except for the intelligence and cunning of humans. Humans have the ability to outthink the bear."

Since we were going into the rock lodge to defeat the bear, we could not show weakness. Once we entered, we had to stay until the end. No one would be allowed to leave between rounds. No one would be permitted to break the lodge, as some had done during the first bear sweat, the previous year, when some Thunderbeings left halfway through. As well, no pail of water would be passed around. Neither could we put our faces to the ground when the steam got too intense; we had to sit up at all times.

My heart was pounding. There was no way I could do this! How could I get out of this? And my fear turned into a panic that clawed at my soul. Perhaps I could approach Hawk and tell her I wasn't ready for this rock lodge!

Hawk went on: "In the bear sweat you leave your physicalness behind. You stop being human and start being godlike. The soul is the master."

Gulp.

My hope was that Hawk could look into the future and see if things would go smoothly or not. Perhaps she had already caught a glimpse of our bear sweat? Perhaps she had seen us defeating the bear? But at this point she did express concern for one of the Thunderbeings.

"One of you has a death wish."

There was a tense silence as we all looked around to see who that might be. At whom was the warning being directed? Hawk said she would keep a watch on this person—and that was all she said. The tension in the room shot up. Hawk started us chanting. There was a quiet intensity in our voices. Our chant sounded like a lament, as though we were reaching deep inside our souls to find the courage to take that leap into the unknown.

We chanted as she led us outside to the veranda. Because of our week-long fast we were starting to show signs of fatigue.

"You will be allowed one glass of water prior to going into the lodge."

As we walked to the lodge, I tried very hard to keep my fear under control—but I couldn't. Hawk gave strict instructions not to walk across what represented the head and the neck of the lodge.

Like a fool I walked over this area. Why did I do that after she told us not to?

Her words pierced through me: "Just know that you will feel truly alone when you are in the lodge."

Did my walking across this sacred area symbolize the kind of experience I would have? I was frantic. I did not know what to do. I wanted to run away.

Meanwhile, she had gone back to the house. My emotions were boiling inside me. How could she say that? I wanted to run over and tell her that I couldn't go into this rock lodge. I just could not! I walked over to the house and tiptoed into the kitchen. She was cooking bear meat.

"Hawk . . ."

"Get out of here!"

Her anger came at me like a bolt of lightning. I flew out of there with the speed of a frightened deer. Nobody was supposed to be in the kitchen while she was preparing the bear meat. She was putting her medicine into it and needed complete privacy.

Later when she came out and I told her I didn't want to go in the rock lodge, she admonished me: "You are always setting yourself up for a letdown."

And I knew she was right. I knew I could not admit defeat even before I encountered the bear. Deep within me, I knew I must not quit.

Just before we entered the lodge, we watched a sunset that was pure gold. The land looked absolutely luminous. Perhaps it was a sign that we would come out of the lodge spiritually renewed?

We resumed our chanting. Aletia, a beautiful Thunderbeing with piercing brown eyes, was in front of me, and as she bent down to enter the lodge, I heard Hawk whisper mysteriously, "See you on the other side."

Later when I asked what that meant, Aletia confided that she had left halfway through the first bear sweat. "Hawk was saying, 'Don't worry. You're going to complete it this time.' "

Hawk arranged the seating order in the lodge. Experienced bear sweaters would sit next to novices. I watched as the others entered the lodge, stepping over the border into this underworld of death and rebirth. We sat trembling, for we knew there was no turning back now. We were only moments away from encountering the bear. Hawk asked the stone keepers to bring in the rocks.

"We will do 108 stones."

Forty glowing rocks, some the size of watermelons, were piled onto the pit. That was as many as I had done in an entire four rounds! The stone keepers handed the water bucket to Hawk and sealed the door flap. Darkness descended. Hawk ordered Don, who was sitting in front of the other door flap in the back of the lodge, not to open it at any time: "On no account are you to open that door."

Hawk poured water on the rocks, and they hissed. The lodge filled up with steam. She told us to keep our eyes closed. As the lodge grew very hot, I felt that I was falling down a deep black hole. The steam was coming down and there was no place for it to escape. I was drenched in perspiration from head to toe. She told us not to fight the heat: "I don't embrace the pain of the heat. I *become* the heat."

My back and shoulders were rigid with fear. Hawk splashed more water on the rocks, and they spit out their steam. She told us that we *could* get through this because we were not limited by our physical form. We were born pure and whole; and all we needed to do was connect back to that internal knowledge that was within us.

"You are spirit," she said. "Your body is sacred and holy. There is nothing new to learn. You need only awaken and remember what is already inside you. It is time to awaken all the gifts of your mind and body. And to know they are the expression of the Creator. If you were attuned to this, you would transform the planet on a conscious level."

The steam rose from the rocks. The lodge grew hotter and hotter. I tried to push my head farther into my chest, but there was no escape from the steam.

The first round of prayers was now under way. There was much moaning and groaning, emotions spilling out, secret desires revealed, tearful requests, promises to be good . . . and when it was over, Hawk called out, "Stone keeper, open the gate!"

As it opened, I gulped the air. I felt as if I were drowning. I had to swallow as much air as possible to see if I could survive the next round. I tried to shake off the heat while the stones were being carried in. The second round began. Hawk splashed water on the stones, and the lodge filled with scalding hot steam. It was hotter than an oven! Let me out of here! I rocked to and fro in a frenzy. Had I descended into hell? An aching aloneness came over me, just as Hawk had predicted. Even though I was surrounded by my fellow Thunderbeings, I felt isolated and cut off from everyone and everything. The others no longer existed. I wanted so badly to grab Aletia's hand, but no, I couldn't. . . . Finally I took her hand. She whispered, "It's okay."

The lodge swayed with our whimpering and wailing. I gasped for air, couldn't breathe . . . Oh, no! I just wanted to get out of there. Let me out of this subterranean oven! Some of our prayers sounded like tortured requests. Deeper and deeper we sank into the sweaty inferno. My head was spinning.

"Stone keeper, open the gate!" Aaah . . . More red-hot rocks were piled into the pit. The door flap was sealed. I felt a panic in my heart. Hawk called upon the spirit of the west. She prayed for us to find the courage to defeat the bear. She asked us to growl like bears.

"Growl! Louder! That doesn't sound like a bear. I want to hear ferocious growls."

We growled and growled, our bodies swaying in a frenzy. The lodge was now an impenetrable cloud of steam. We were cooking in a huge pot of boiling water, cut off from the knowable world, swirling in darkness, deeper and deeper into a strange underworld. My eyes rolled around in their sockets. My growl was more like a desperate cry. Was some monstrous ugly thing coming at me? I could feel something looking at me with vengeful inhuman eyes. Let me out of this inferno! Can't breathe . . . suffocating. Primitive moans, groans, and grunts were being forced out of us by the heat.

I heard some commotion to my right. Some Thunderbeings were attempting to get up.

"Sit down! You are not going to break this lodge!"

We started to chant. My chanting sounded like a tortured cry to me. The heat was burning my back and my arms. I was drenched in sweat, semiconscious. Was I going to die? I could not stand it any longer. Let me out of here! Panic gripped my heart with a clenched fist. My breath felt like hot steam. The chanting sounded like whimpers. The heat drove our foreheads down. We were spiraling down through time to the beginning of the Earth when steam rose from the molten surface before the creation of the waters.

"Stone keeper!"

I heard Hawk asking for more rocks and another bucket of water. My sweat-drenched eyelids slid open to catch a glimpse of half-slumped feverish bodies. This was the last round—we were almost there, she told us.

"We can't!" we moaned. "We can't take any more! We have had enough. We feel as if we might pass out!"

She said, "If you feel as if you're going to pass out, pass out!"

The entrance to the lodge closed ominously.

She tossed all of the water from the bucket onto the rocks.

"This is going to be intense!" she warned. "In this round, we will all say our prayers at the same time."

A scalding hot wave rolled over us. It was a blast of heat. Hawk called upon the spirit of the north. In my semiconscious stupor a prayer came to my lips. My skin hurt. It felt as though it were being seared. Oh, my God, I'm on fire! My body is on fire! I sank into numbness. I was a reptilian brain with no eyes, a primitive brain bound by nothing . . . no past, no future, no thought. I finally surrendered to the heat.

Then I heard a strange sound—*WHOOSH*. Suddenly I was moving through space, spinning and spinning . . . out of my body, hurtling through space into the blackness between the stars . . . through galaxies into some nameless dimension . . . on wings of light, weightless, feeling no pain, surrendering. I entered a vast space of white light. How long had I been gone? I didn't know. Time didn't exist.

Then I heard Hawk's voice: "Stone keeper, open the gate!"

The steam billowed out of the lodge, like a lid coming off a pot of boiling water. Steam was coming off our bodies. Hawk had a big smile on her face. "You all flamed! It was beautiful. Your bodies took on the presence of a flame. All I could see was one sphere of brilliant fire. Your bodies were emitting fire. And then I saw a blue flame shooting through the roof of the lodge."

And it dawned on me what that *whooshing* sound was: it was all of us bursting into flames!

At this point Hawk splashed cool water on us, and sighs of relief reverberated through the lodge.

As we started to leave the lodge, the stone keepers helped us over to the grass. As I buried my face in the ground I could feel the Earth Mother soothing me with her cool breath; she was rocking me in her arms. It was the sweetest embrace I had ever experienced. I felt loved; I felt like her equal. I felt wonderful; I had been freed of all the psychic baggage I had been carrying around for years.

When we finally got up from the ground, Hawk gave each of us two pieces of bear meat. We ate one piece, which tasted quite sweet; the other was for us to carry with us in a pouch. She said that she obtained it through a Native American hunter she knew had hunted the bear in a sacred manner. Tribes who hunt in a sacred manner do not kill out of greed or a desire for gain. They do so with prayers and chants; their objective is to kill the animal quickly *without suffering*, and some will not consume the meat if the animal suffered. They consider the animal pure, meaning it does not hold to life in a selfish way and does not fear death, but it fears the pain of death, so the hunter must ensure that it does not suffer.

We hugged each other and reflected in silence, communicating more clearly than we had ever done with our voices.

I had experienced the strength of the bear. I was now able to recognize the bear inside me and instead of feeling fear, I took comfort from his presence at my side. He walked alongside me. I remembered the saying, "What doesn't kill you makes you stronger." Now I really understood its meaning.

We ran down the hill in a burst of energy, laughing with delight, for we had come to the realization that very few things were really impossible.

We showered and dressed and then gathered for a feast. I glanced around, marveling at how radiant everyone looked. Their faces were beaming! I felt a deep sense of peace. I felt lighter, as though emptied of all troublesome thoughts and misplaced responsibilities. It was the closest I had ever come to a feeling of bliss.

Hawk told us that just before we burst into flames we had gone beyond our minds into another realm. "It gets so hot that your mind finally gives up its struggle and allows itself to be totally ignited into consciousness." The heat weakens your struggle until you just don't struggle any more. It breaks you down and stops your thinking or conscious mind from dominating. Finally it releases you from the realm of time and boundary so that you can take flight.

"I think I passed into another world," Tonya said, smiling. "I heard the sound of drumming!"

"My hand went right through my shoulder," Lynn said, her eyes wide with bewilderment.

A lot of us just left our bodies. An experience of that magnitude had taken us out of our limiting, common reality.

In spite of the tremendous heat that we had endured, not one of us was burned, although one of the stone keepers had burned his hand. We were not engulfed in flames because of Hawk's great medicine. Rock lodge leaders must be strong and capable and unconditionally loving; they cannot be judgmental, for the dross that we burn off in the lodge escapes through them, and it is the dross that burns.

Hawk told us that very few people have bear medicine. "Physically," she said, "no one can live through that, at least according to conventional science."

We did it. We overcame our limitations.

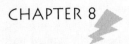

CHAPTER 8

TIDE OF CHANGE

There is a pleasure in the pathless woods;
There is a rapture on the lonely shore;
There is society, where none intrudes,
By the deep sea, and music in its roar:
I love not man the less, but Nature more.
    —LORD BYRON

I NOW FELT READY for any challenge. While I knew I still had a distance to go in my development, at least I was on my journey; I was headed in the right direction. When Hawk called upon us to assist her in redirecting a destructive force that endangered the East Coast, I didn't hesitate. I knew I had to be there.

In the spring of 1992 I arrived, along with fourteen other Thunderbeings, at an island off the southeastern coast of the United States. We met in a charming little town where we had rented three cottages, built on stilts, overlooking the ocean. After locating our cottages, we went to meet with Hawk. When we had all gathered in the living room of her cottage, she explained the urgency of the situation: the Atlantic ocean might come inland, and much of the East Coast could be covered by water.

"The land is shifting, and the ocean will come in five hundred miles unless we change the consciousness," she told us. "If we don't want the East Coast to become an island, we have to talk to Mother Earth. We have to ask her, 'What can I do for you?' We have to tell her, 'You are an experience that touches my heart.' We have to love her with all our heart, touch her with love, stroke her. Touching water is like touching the tears on her face. Touching the wind is touching her breath."

The problem, she said, is that most people only *take* from the Earth. We must replenish what we take, for if we forget the law of give-and-take, we will starve. This is one of the fundamental rules of nature that must be followed.

At this time we were witnessing extreme and erratic weather patterns around the globe. This could possibly be symptomatic of the maelstrom of emotional energy being released by humanity. Instability was becoming a fact of existence; rules and regulations at all levels were being questioned, and demands were being made for change. There was disillusionment in the workplace. Work that involved repetitive tasks made people feel like cogs in a wheel, which is not natural or nurturing. They felt as though they had lost the ability to control their own lives. Families were in disarray and at a loss as to how to regain the sense of continuity they once had. Organized religion was dying, but the world was on the verge of a massive return to spirituality. Meanwhile, newspapers had become catalogs of disasters happening every day somewhere in the world. Many humans, especially those who had not opened themselves up to expanding their consciousness, were feeling the intensity of changes playing havoc with their peace of mind.

Hawk warned the Thunderbeings: "Things are going to get very intense. Everything you think will be made manifest. As fast as you can embrace a thought, it will happen. Be responsible for what you say and think. Start trusting in your own abilities. Keep your heart open to the power of love. Stay in close contact with Creator."

She told us that we would probably see new dimensions of destruction as the 1990s continued to unfold. She said there was not one major land mass that was not going to shake. We would have to contend with earthquakes, floods, hurricanes, landslides, extremes in the weather, and other natural disasters. Many large bodies of water would come inland; the great Mississippi would take a new direction. We would see hurricane-force winds that we have not seen in this century. Earthquakes would occur with increasing frequency and in places not traditionally considered earthquake zones. We would see vast changes in the geography around the world; islands would disappear, and new coastlines would form.

The Earth would have to go through these changes if the natural order was ever to be restored. The great purification was necessary. We had stored so much chemical waste that there was no way we could backtrack and solve this problem. Mother Earth was undergoing a cellular change and eventually—according to the scrolls and drawings of indigenous peoples—her physical appearance would change: she would become long, lean masses of land.

We would also have to contend with massive virulent epidemics.

But, dismal as all this might seem, a possibility had arisen that we might avert one of the greatest of the prophesied catastrophes, which would cause the globe to shift on its axis. This possibility is a result of the work of the Thunderbeings and other peacekeepers around the world who have been focusing on peace and harmony. We have succeeded in tipping the scale away from total destruction!

Is it possible that the consciousness of the few filled with heartfelt intent can move the many?

We had one week to accomplish our work here. If we were not effective, the Earth would shift, and the ocean would come inland.

Sitting in the back porch of Hawk's cottage, I had a clear view of the ocean. I could feel the presence of nature spirits. I could see them out of the corner of my eye.

The roar of the ocean called to me like some distant forgotten song in my deepest and most primitive memory.

"It's beautiful here," we agreed, chatting about the different things that appealed to us, such as the unspoiled sandy beach and serene atmosphere. I found it soothing and relaxing. I felt like a child being held in my mother's arms. It was a perfect place to go on an inner journey.

"The waters are our emotions," Hawk said as we gazed out at the ocean. "We have put huge bodies of water between us. But they will subside as we return to being a human family. The only species that creates disorder on this planet is man. Our DNA carries the genetic pattern of warlords. We need to break that pattern. We still live in fear, and that fear feeds the prophecy of destruction. Peacekeeping is the only principle that works. Peacekeeping will bring Earth and all of her inhabitants into harmony."

Hawk was gearing us up for our assignment here. We had only three or four days to unify ourselves into One Thought. We had to empty ourselves of any doubts about our ability. Self-acceptance would help us enter into a state of surrender and trust in order to attune ourselves to the universal source of energy. Two things could stop us from reaching that ultimate state: one is fear, and the other is a belief that there might be something out there that is more intelligent than we are.

"There is nothing on the other side that will help us," Hawk said sternly. "There are no guides. *Something* is not more intelligent than you. You *are* the guides. The place you are looking for is inside you, not somewhere else. Do not be afraid of the power of your self. You can move in and out of your body to anywhere in the universe. You can fly and disappear on the wind. Why have you lost this ability? Because you started listening to others who said that it couldn't be done. The only resource you have is inside of you. Ask Great Spirit to guide you. Invite your mind into the stillness of your spirit. Stillness is not inactive; it's concentrated activity."

In terms of numbers, we were right on target. We needed at least ten Thunderbeings to turn the forces around so that the Earth would not shift. Where two of our minds could create a tremendous resonating force, ten could change the galaxy.

I looked around at everybody and realized that although we sometimes locked heads with each other—we were all strong leaders, and that made for all chiefs with no Indians—we had also developed a comfortable closeness.

Many of us still carried a certain amount of fear or embarrassment as to how we were perceived by others. Did we seem like fanatics? Did we appear to be unstable, radical people? Were we merely a new breed of sixties hippies? Was our belief a passing fad? This made us hesitate to expose ourselves to criticism.

Meanwhile we had work to do!

Because the force of our thoughts and our love could prevent the East Coast from becoming an island, we had to enter into the deepest part of our being—we had to trust ourselves completely. If we wanted to maximize our abilities, we had to first step outside the constraints of linear time. To that end, we removed our watches and covered any timepieces in our vehicles and cottages. It was important to get beyond linear thinking and into the vast ocean of consciousness. Second, we thoroughly cleaned our cottages because we wanted them to sparkle with our energy; we wanted everything in our environment to be in harmony. Pillows, for example, contain the thought forms of those who have slept on them, so we whacked them against a wall or pounded them with our hands. Last, we entered into a period of silence. This was the only way we could tune in to the master computer, the God within us. This was the only way to focus ourselves into a sense of oneness. Through silence, through shared ritual and prayer, through probing our dreams, we would start to resonate as One Thought.

The next morning I awoke with the first gray of dawn. I walked across a wooden plank, down several steps to the beach, and threw my towel on the sand. The ocean was calm. I let the waves play at my feet like harpists tuning their harps, allowing myself to tune in to the spirit of the ocean. Plunging into the water, I acknowledged the spirit keeper of the east and then returned to the cottage. I crawled back into bed and forced my mind to stay in a lucid dream state. If an unpleasant dream came to me, I would reenact it and give it a beautiful ending.

The phone rang; that was our cue to get dressed. We prepared and ate breakfast in silence; we had decided ahead of time who would prepare the food. Then we tidied up the cottage and waited until Hawk called again. When the phone rang, we grabbed towels along with a change of clothes and drove over to her cottage, a short distance away.

"Okay, first I want you to spend some time in the ocean," she announced just after we arrived. This, I thought, must be a warm-up for our major assignment.

"Get in touch with the vastness of the ocean and of yourself. Feel the volume of love and patience in these waters. The whales and dolphins are our ancestral beings. They wait patiently for us to communicate with them. As you go into the water, allow yourselves to open up to the feelings that the ocean is communicating to you. Notice how eagerly the ocean comes to you. This is a reality, not just your imagination. You *are* important."

I strolled across the white sandy beach and stood at the water's edge. There was nothing to be heard but the constant rhythmic pulsation of the waves and the cries of the gulls patrolling the shoreline. As my gaze sank into the ocean, I realized I was looking into another world where creatures floated effortlessly among others like themselves. It made me think of the whale and the dolphin and why they are such magnificent creatures; they are travelers of two different worlds—and I found myself in the same position at the edge of the water.

We made our cornmeal offerings to the ocean and then submerged ourselves in the water. After about fifteen minutes Hawk came out and joined us.

"We're going to speak to the whales and the dolphins," she said. Following her example, we stood in a row within the foam of the waves. We watched as she became very still. After a moment of deep concentration, she opened her mouth wide and out came a loud, piercing, vibratory two-syllable word that resonated into the horizon. We watched as she proceeded to show us how to create this sound, which took a considerable amount of practice.

"This is how the Australians speak to the whales and the dolphins," she explained. "They imitate the sound of the deep." She called it "toning."

This involved creating a hollow sound and combining it with body movements that approximated martial arts maneuvers. After synchronizing the first syllable with a sharp twist of the body and one leg raised, on the second syllable we brought the leg down and thrust one hand forward as if we were punching the air. Doing this in the water with the waves crashing down was a challenge, to say the least!

We must have presented quite a scene: fifteen people fighting the breakers with judolike movements!

Thirty minutes later, our voices began to sound strained. But we noticed that something unusual was happening: the crests of the waves had started to rise.

"See, she responds to your toning!" Hawk exclaimed, pleased.

The waters were responding to us; they were greeting us! Exhilarated by this accomplishment, we threw ourselves into the effort with all of our energy.

"Look!" shouted one of the Thunderbeings.

We looked up and saw several dolphins bobbing around in the water. They were coming closer and had obviously heard our communication!

We were ecstatic, overcome with emotion. We could feel them touching our minds. We could sense their purity and gentleness. These intelligent creatures just wait for us to respond to them. Their unconditional love for humans has never diminished. Dolphins used to walk among us as earth dwellers. There is a very close kinship between humans and dolphins—they communicate telepathically.

"Dolphins are pure intelligence," Hawk told us. "When they saw that humans were separating, they went to the waters to wait. They wait for us with absolute trust that one day we will return to the great gathering when all the creations will communicate with one another again and there will be no more separation. They have never judged us or abandoned us."

At this point the ocean had become very calm and was changing color. Before we started our work it was a metallic blue; now it was a much lighter blue. Not only had we calmed the ocean, but we had brought healing to her waters!

Heady with this accomplishment, we expressed a loud yelp of joy before returning to the cottage. Hawk told us: "You changed the color of the ocean. See what you can do? See how powerful you are?"

And we could feel our hearts opening up. She reminded us that we had the ability to call upon and therefore manifest the power of the Thunderbeings simply by concentrating our thoughts. These powers consisted of our ability to communicate with the forces that control the thunder and the wind.

She said that this ability was natural to us, but we had forgotten it, and that the only thing that prevented us from consciously realizing this was a thin veil of forgetfulness.

"There are many on this Earth that are not *of* this Earth," she said, mentioning Stephen Hawking, the theoretical physicist and author of

A Brief History of Time. From his wheelchair, Hawking, who has Lou Gehrig's disease but whose mental travels are more extensive than most, writes with authority on distant galaxies and alternate dimensions because he *journeys* to them.

"Hawking is a Thunderbeing," she said. "He is a soul that has totally rejected his body. His eyes are alive because he's living out in the universe. He says, 'I journey.' Although his tongue won't cooperate, he has perfected a computer, a synthesizer, that responds to his thoughts and sounds."

That afternoon we went out to one of the restaurants in town. Despite the magnitude of our purpose, Hawk encouraged us not to get too serious or take ourselves too seriously. We joked and played throughout our time together, cultivating the child within, protecting the delicate innocence of that child. Plus it was just plain fun to go out together. We found a little Italian restaurant about two miles away, tucked into a row of tourist shops.

"I want the spaghetti with lots of mushrooms, green peppers, and onions," Hawk said in that playful, childlike tone that always made us smile. She turned to her son, David, who was sitting next to her.

"You look handsome today. It's too bad your personality doesn't match," she teased him. "There are days when he just shines. But when he's gloomy you don't want to be near him."

We laughed. The conversation zigzagged from topic to topic; we talked about marriage, movies, and movie stars.

"Paul Newman is a tremendous humanitarian."

"Robert Redford is a dreamboat."

"To watch Redford, the way he sticks his hand in his back pocket, you can almost feel the temperature rise in the room."

"I think Patrick Swayze is a doll."

"Yeah, he has a set of buns on him that's absolute bliss. And he's such a good dancer." That was Hawk's opinion.

Anyone who overheard our conversation, would not have had the slightest clue that we were Thunderbeings attempting to save the East Coast from being submerged!

•   •   •

When we returned to Hawk's cottage, we gathered on the back porch with a full view of the pounding waves and the shrieking gulls. The ocean shimmered, kissed by beams of sunlight; big billowy clouds hung low in the sky. We savored the sights, scents, and sounds; we were becoming attuned to our new surroundings.

But our anxiety deepened as Hawk prodded us to explore the depth of our inner space and confront our fears.

As we sat around her in a circle, I noticed that she was wearing a simple white sundress and her mass of tumbleweed hair was tied back. She seemed very buoyant today. Her eyes revealed a dreaminess and serenity; I could tell that she loved it here—she loved the ocean.

"Death is your biggest fear," she started softly. "Listen to yourself. You are your own psychologist. When you tell your problems to a shaman, they ask you questions but they do not give you answers. Why should you fear death? If you don't know what death is, why should you fear it? What you fear is being unable to control the experience. Really ask yourself what it is that you're afraid of. And consider the possibility that you alone determine when and how you will die.

"The only parent we have is the Mystery," she went on. "Your biological parents are just the womb and the seed; that's it. Love your parents, but don't make them responsible for your feelings."

She wanted us to reach deep inside ourselves. She wanted us to remember the full capacity of ourselves as spiritual warriors who had come to Earth to deliver a message of the heart.

"You have the ability to achieve whatever you want," she continued. "Let go of the need for pain and suffering and self-importance. Pain is congested energy; it's a denial of life. You don't have to suffer to grow. The best thing for you to do is to embrace total awareness."

Now, just as we were entering the deepest part of our being, we were also having to fight off the sand fleas that were leaping up at us. They were inside our clothes, and we were trying to shake them off. Here we were trying to get spiritual and an army of sand fleas had launched an attack on our bodies. We laughed uproariously as we imagined that the sand fleas were Thunderbeings of the sand flea society and we were the great spirit people. They had come to communicate with us. The Thunderbeings of the sand flea people had come to speak to *us*, the great spirit people! We laughed until our sides nearly split.

After about an hour of battling the fleas and giggling, we agreed to move back inside the cottage, where we continued our discussion.

Hawk said that the key to our success was to love ourselves: "The one thing that takes is trust. Don't judge yourselves, even if you're having negative thoughts, because the totality of the mind consists of a good balance of negative and positive thoughts. We have both of these within us; we can't have one without the other." For so long we had believed that we were failing in some way if we were not being positive all the time.

"If you're not having negative thoughts, you're not experiencing yourself as a full being," she told us. "You have made negativity something that is *bad*, but that is not a reality; that is not a principle. You can't be positive all the time. You can't be blissed out. We are not here to kill negativity but to have a balance of positive and negative. The best you can achieve is a delicate balance of give-and-take. Being more positive is not a truth. The cycles of the moon are constantly dancing through our negative and positive cycles. There are times when you are more sensitive. Harmony is fifty percent negative and fifty percent positive."

Hawk was fine-tuning us for our assignment. She wanted us to understand that we were more positive than we thought we were and, in so doing, to reclaim the power that was inside us. She wanted us to believe and trust completely in ourselves.

All she needed was ten Thunderbeings sending out the right frequency and we could turn the forces around!

"Your hearts show the purest intent, but you have to find that unique feeling that will make you just soar," she continued. "Fifty years ago we were still using our sixth sense. Now we're down to three physical senses; we don't believe what we see and we don't accept what we hear; even our sense of touch has become impaired. In the original consciousness that we began with, we had fourteen senses. Think about it. Every cell of your body has its own central core of intelligence; it receives, puts out, and records. There are at least sixty billion cells in your body. Where is all that data going if you're only using three senses?"

She assured us that we could extend the electromagnetic force that surrounded our bodies. We could project our minds as far as we want them to go.

And as we discussed *how* we would save the East Coast, we started to appreciate the value of ceremony and the various tools we had acquired. When we rattled, drummed, chanted, and danced, we activated more of our senses; we evoked the energy that lay within our organic vessels. We started to plug in to the universal forces. Ceremony helped us enter into a trance, which was extremely powerful.

"All of you are psychics and trance mediums," she told us.

When some of us raised the subject of channeling, she said that she didn't believe in channeling: "I think it's just a profit-oriented scam." Channeling, she said, comes from the God within us. The so-called channelers are not expressing the thoughts of some highly evolved spiritual being that has temporarily entered their body. No, they have simply entered into a trance and plugged in to a source of universal information.

In order for us to discover ourselves further, Hawk sent us out on the beach for what she called a medicine walk. Using all of our senses, we recorded the first three things we saw, heard, smelled, touched, and felt. Then we wove a story out of this. I spent what seemed like two hours simply absorbing everything about me and then with a passionate fury I put my thoughts on paper, and the following poem emanated from me:

When I feel alone and love is war
I raise my head to the heavens
To meet your eyes in every star

When I feel alone and life brings pain
I raise my arms to the clouds
To feel your tears that come down upon the rain

When I feel alone and happiness is merely a tease
I raise my ears to the sea
To hear your soothing whispers spoken by the breeze

When I feel alone and survival is a fight
I raise my face to the sun
To receive the warmth of your love that comes in the light.

Later that day we did more exercises with words, dreamcatcher symbols, and colors, to help us get into the flow of right brain creativity.

We also spent some time discussing healing techniques. Hawk told us that as Thunderbeings we were natural healers. We would never use the power of our thoughts to harm somebody. Wishing somebody ill or planning revenge was not the way of our medicine. We did not have to do that—the natural law of the universe would take care of wrongdoers and balances everything.

"You don't want to focus on a bad thought to someone," she said. "Instead, you want to take the principles to their highest ideal and focus on the good in that person, even if the person hates you. Focus on saying, 'I reflect back all that is sent to me; I am blessed; I am loved by the source.' "

She said that love was a powerful source of healing: "Ask for harmony and balance for the person who has come to you for healing. Hold the image of the entire spectrum of the rainbow. The rainbow represents peace, harmony, and hope. The rainbow does magical things for people."

She chastised us for acting as though we had solutions for others: "Stop giving spiritual advice. Get off the ego trip of thinking you have the solution for other people. They have God within them too."

We spent every moment of our day working toward a deeper awareness. It was important to enter into a mind-set of oneness in order to be successful here.

That evening Hawk asked us to bring our drums and rattles to her place after dinner. When we arrived, the aroma of sage and cedar permeated the cottage, drawing us into sacred space.

Hawk brought out her kettledrum, a huge drum nearly three feet in diameter. We all sat on the floor, with the lights dimmed, and started to drum and rattle, softly at first, and then more intensely until the entire two-story cottage was vibrating.

"Pound those drums! We want it to resonate out into the universe."

The kettledrum had to be struck hard so that it would express our primal force in its raw and pure state.

We became immersed in the sounds. We felt the intensity of fire and thunder within our being. Between the pounding of the waves and the pounding of our drums, all of our separate individual beings were harmonizing and surging together as one.

Our drums brought forth the strength of the Earth's vibration while our rattles were stirring up the atmosphere.

"Okay, stop for a minute," Hawk said in a low tone. "Allow yourself to stay in this meditative state. I want you to imitate an animal or a bird."

We became bears, wolves, monkeys, crows, owls, seagulls, frogs, dolphins, panthers. The cottage shook.

"You're afraid of losing control," she said. "Just as you move into an in-depth meditation you snap back. Really let yourself go."

The growling, howling, and hooting grew louder and more insistent. And we felt a wild delight as if we were surfing the waves together, shrieking our war cry for the return of harmony and peace on this planet, for the return of the chants and dances that once created the greatness of humanity.

I delighted in the power of feeling connected with the others, as though nothing could stop us. Emotions flooded my being—I felt ecstasy and pain, understanding and confusion, all at the same time. Every emotion I'd ever experienced I re-experienced in one moment: joy and sadness, panic and tranquillity, anticipation and disillusionment. Every part of my being was reacting, and I felt incredibly invigorated.

And that evening, out of our deepest and most profound feeling of oneness, we gave birth to a new chant: "Peace and harmony surround me and dwell in me." We sang it over and over and over again; we couldn't get enough of it. "Peace and harmony surround me and dwell in me."

"This song will be remembered throughout the ages," Hawk said passionately. "This chant will be carried on, and you will be remembered one day as the Ancients."

Chanting could move us to the spirit realm; and this particular chant seemed to be especially effective in calming doubts and destructive thoughts.

The next morning we awoke as usual at dawn and performed our morning ritual; we each took a turn walking out to the beach. I stopped at the shoreline, dug my feet into the wet sand, and gazed out at the first reddening of the sky. For several moments I had a vivid, intense feeling that I was in a dream. I felt as though I could go anywhere and fly high and be above it all. Taking several steps into the ocean, I felt the waves surge at me with an eagerness and love I had not noticed before. I plunged into the water and offered thanks for the new day. Back in my room, while taking a shower, I recalled the dream I'd had the night before.

The phone rang while we were in the middle of breakfast; we put everything down and rushed over to Hawk's cottage.

After we arrived, I noticed a beautiful vibrancy in all of us; we were starting to relax into one consciousness. We were feeling fused with each other, with the ocean and with the sky. It had taken us three days to achieve this feeling of oneness.

"I want you to use the totality of your mind's capacity," Hawk said in a serious tone. "I want you to commit to this with your entire being."

She said that we would go out on the beach and appeal to the elements. "Only an imbecile thinks that he can command the elements," she said firmly. "They come because they're our companions. They are in relationship with us. All it takes to work with them is complete trust that we're interconnected. We cooperate with them; we cooperate with the cloud people and the water people."

At this point she also told us that we would be working in connection with a group of elders on the West Coast. They had a telephone contact who would keep the communication moving with us.

The big moment we had been waiting for had arrived. Silent and anxious, we carried our drums and rattles out to the beach and arranged ourselves in a straight line—all fifteen Thunderbeings, with Hawk in the center—positioning ourselves a few feet from the shoreline. We waited, practically holding our breath, while Hawk began the ceremony. From her mouth came a high-pitched chant that resonated with so much passion and love it was as if she had called in the entire line of her ancestors to help her.

She signaled to us to begin. We pounded our drums and shook our rattles with every fiber of our being, exploding with the intensity of our purpose. We squeezed out every drop of love that was in us. We broadcast our message to the water beings and the cloud people; we sent our prayers to the Earth and to the galactic spirit.

Within moments a great body of motionless and opaque clouds filled the sky. The land and the water were smothered in dark gloom. The waves rose and pounced like a wildcat at our feet.

We chanted and chanted until we were One Thought resonating out with the force of our collective love. We continued for some time until it seemed that we'd entered into a trancelike state and coalesced with the sky and the earth and the clouds, as though we'd walked straight into another dimension. The body of clouds hung low with an impenetrable darkness. The waves whipped our feet. We stood in a row, facing the ocean, intensifying the heavy rhythmic pounding of our drums and swinging our rattles until our consciousness converged into a deep mystic oneness. We were soaring together, beyond words.

Suddenly I had a glimpse of my childhood and remembered the swing set in the backyard of my house. A friend used to push me until I was screaming and pleading to be pushed higher. I stared into the sky and felt as though I were disappearing into the clouds, and as I gained momentum, it seemed that nothing could hold me down. It was the same now in my feeling of connection to the elements.

Hawk raised her hands and motioned in symbolic sign language. We did the same, our outstretched hands sending the message from our hearts to the elemental beings.

And then, almost immediately, a thunderhead rolled and crashed over the ocean like a pirate ship emerging out of the vastness of space. We watched in amazement. Lightning danced across the sky. The four winds started to blow. We screamed with joy as the rain came down and kissed our faces!

It had all happened so fast! We were stunned.

The rain continued to come down until we were drenched. We huddled together on the beach and chanted.

I don't know how much time passed, but after we had gone indoors the cloud veil started to lift and the sky turned blue.

Hawk confirmed that our ceremony was a success.

The thunder and the lightning had danced around us as if we were in the center of our very own vortex. We had made a connection! We were loved! We experienced a tremendous feeling of belonging. I knew what it felt like to be lightning and thunder and rain and wind; it was such a strong feeling that I couldn't separate myself from them. I truly realized that I was the rain and the thunder and the lightning and the wind. I was made from the same ingredients. I was no longer just this form that I now carried and that would continue to exist even after I left it. One day I would become the winds and the seas. All of a sudden I felt no beginning and no end. I had a sense of infinity. I now had a vastness that I could draw upon. I felt this without anyone explaining it to me. I was the wind that blew across the ocean; I was the rain that danced upon my cheeks. I was the thunder that shook my body; I was the lightning that illuminated my eyes. I would never feel alone again because I would always have the elements to turn to for friendship and guidance. Now I felt a yearning to spend time with my new-found friends so that I could get to know them even better. They could teach me; they could soothe me and bring excitement; they could take me on a journey.

"We've accomplished what the elders asked us to," Hawk said, beaming. "They asked us to be there before the crescent moon showed its face. We've resolved the congestion that hung over the continent. We lifted it, and the cloud people dispersed it."

"You saw the effects of your medicine," she continued. "You drummed, and the elements responded. All the prophecies say that the Thunderbeings will save spirituality. You are a spiritual vessel. What else could you be?"

That evening we received a phone call from the spokesperson for the elders on the West Coast. Hawk answered the phone and passed on the message to us: "The elders say we are loved. The plates have shifted!"

• • •

The next day I awoke with a headache. As I walked out to the beach, I saw that a thick gray mist had blanketed the ocean and the land. This environment would enhance our ability to receive visions. Was that why I had a headache?

"The vision gate is here," Hawk announced as we gathered later that morning on the back porch. "The mist is a gateway for souls that work in the dimensional drapes. This is the reward for our work."

We received a second phone call and learned that a beautiful rainbow had formed on the West Coast. "There is a massive, shimmering wall of rainbows along the mesas," Hawk told us after she got off the phone, smiling.

We spent most of the morning inside Hawk's cottage. The mist and the fog would continue for the entire day. I found myself in a deeply introspective mood, just longing to lie back and do nothing but daydream.

We talked about the power of our thoughts and that we did affect everything around us, contrary to what we were raised to believe. Someone in the group made the comparison that we'd been taught to move things with sticks: we'd come to rationalize that if something went wrong, it was the stick's fault. We had set it up so that we could blame the stick. We could say that the stick did it, but we were the ones who manipulated the stick.

"You have seen the results of your thoughts," Hawk told us. "You do not create every thought, but you are responsible for the thoughts that you convey. Stop thinking the unwanted thought and replace it with a chant or an affirmation. When you've seen the results, you just can't be casual about anything anymore. You are that powerful all the time."

She said everything we think and do affects the next seven generations. Therefore we must consider the effects of our actions on future generations. "This is called purposeful thinking," she told us.

The discussion turned to dreams, and Hawk answered several questions. One of the Thunderbeings, a graceful and slender woman with long blond hair whom I didn't know very well, started to weep as she talked about how fragile she was feeling.

"Your gracefulness is your strength," Hawk told her. She said it was a good idea for the rest of us not to feed the woman's weakness.

"She needs tough love," Hawk said gently. "Go up to her and startle her. Break those energies. Toss her. Make her jump up and down."

I felt sad, for in the blond woman's eyes I could see a frightened animal, huddled and cornered. (A year later when I saw her again, she had blossomed; she was into a new relationship and was planning to get married.)

Hawk reminded us that there were no victims and that all of us were magnificent beings who emanated from the Mystery. To describe ourselves was to limit ourselves to that particular description. We were multidimensional beings who were constantly changing. We were different with every person in our lives. Who could determine where we began and where we ended? Our full potential was a never-ending story.

She said that we were sprouting the new generation: "We are in the most intense fire of transformation. We are finding God in our self, and if our self is fifty percent negative, that's okay. We can't be positive one hundred percent of the time or we'd go insane. If everything has to be right all the time we will never learn."

At this point, we broke for lunch. David made a huge pot of spaghetti and we gathered in the L-shaped kitchen with a view of the beach. The fog was a thick haze, a massive cloudscape. You couldn't see where the horizon ended and the clouds began.

We talked with the close and intimate rapport that came from having been part of a momentous occasion.

Soon it was time to say good night. We walked out to the driveway and headed back to our cottage in two cars. I was with Jackie, Vanessa, and Ellen while Julian, Matthew, and Marian were in the car ahead of us.

As we got on the road, it started to rain and thunder with such ferocity that we had to slow down. Jackie, who was driving, doubled the speed of her windshield wipers, and in about five minutes, just after we turned onto our street, the rain began whipping our car. The road had become almost invisible, and we drove past our cottage twice.

During the few moments that it took to emerge from our vehicles and walk up the dozen or so steps to the door of our cottage, we were drenched. Once inside, I opened the sliding glass door in my room. The waves crashed and clawed at the very edge of the wooden stilts supporting our cottage. Gale-force winds unleashed their fury and lashed our cottage. I felt a fear, but a stronger emotion—excitement—also arose in me as I fathomed how all the elements had come together in this perfect union like a giant symphony. I could feel that we were being danced by the universe.

As a result of our work here, a new balance had been achieved—and perhaps we had succeeded in postponing the disastrous earth changes that had been foreseen for this area.

I left the window slightly open before I went to sleep. The next morning all was peaceful and calm. I awoke with the most exquisite sensation, which I can only describe as a beam of love radiating throughout my body. One of Hawk's chants, a beautiful song that always touches my heart, surfaced in my thoughts. I had a strong urge to weep with joy and didn't understand why.

We spent several more days on that beach. On the last day we shopped and had an uproariously good time at a local eatery playing some memorable tunes from the fifties and sixties on an old jukebox.

CHAPTER 9

JOURNEYS AT NIGHT

Miracles are not contrary to nature, but only contrary to what we know about nature.

—SAINT AUGUSTINE OF HIPPO

A FEW MONTHS LATER, Hawk called for several Thunderbeings to accompany her to Arizona. There was important work to be done there, and she needed our assistance. Timing would be of the utmost importance. The West Coast was in danger of breaking off from the continent, and something had to be done immediately. There had been many predictions that California would disappear into the ocean, but perhaps we could delay the event.

In the fall of 1992 I arrived at the Phoenix airport. As I walked past the car rental counters, I noticed David waving at me. We greeted each other, and he told me to tell the others to wait in the baggage claim area.

Several Thunderbeings were here who had not traveled with Hawk before. While waiting for our baggage to arrive, I studied everyone carefully. Henry, a dentist, had arrived from Florida. George and Victor, a biologist and a waiter, both from Quebec, had flown in with their friends, Lois and Jacqueline, who were both artists. Leslie, a designer of jewelry, and Ann, a graphic designer, were from Ontario while Caitlin, a musician, lived in Ohio. Ellen, a nurse, had driven in from Texas with her friend, Laura; they both looked in need of spiritual repair. There was also Dale, Maura, and two couples, Jennifer and Bob, Carolyn and Irving.

David came in and said hello to everyone. "When you've got your bags, meet me outside," he said, stepping briskly through the automatic glass doors. When we had retrieved our baggage from the carousel, we stepped out into the sweltering heat; all of our rental cars were lined up at the curb. I hopped into the lead vehicle with David; the others would follow us.

"Mom arrived a few days ago to spend some time with the Hopis," he told me.

"How long a drive are we in for?" I asked, feeling excited to be back among the palm trees, cacti, and mountains.

"We probably won't get there until midnight," he said, checking the rearview mirror to see that the others were following.

This time we would follow the route into Sedona, then continue on into the northeast corner of Arizona, close to the Hopi and Navajo reservations. During the drive, David and I talked about the landscape and various topics, including the time he had lived in Arizona and how much he loved it there. As we approached Sedona, my heart leaped up at the sight of those red rock monoliths. We drove through Oak Creek Canyon, and then the terrain changed again into miles and miles of ponderosa pine. It was sunset when we approached Flagstaff, a small city surrounded by pine forest. Up ahead in the distance appeared some enormous snow-capped mountains.

"Those are the San Francisco Peaks. They're supposed to be the highest mountains in Arizona," David said. "That's where the kachinas live." Some of the native tribes believe that these kachinas, powerful spirits, inhabit the area of these peaks; this is a sacred region to these tribes.

We stopped at a fast-food eatery in Flagstaff. As we continued on, we passed the massive cinder cone of an extinct volcano and then miles of blue-green sagebrush growing in profusion along the highway, followed by a vast stretch of plains dotted with low-lying shrubs, yellow grasses, and wildflowers. Then we turned onto another highway; it would be another hour before we reached the dry remote mesas and scrubland of northeastern Arizona.

"We should be there in about thirty minutes," David said a little wearily, peering into the darkness. The trip ended up taking longer than that after we made a couple of wrong turns.

The narrow two-lane road was so deserted we had only to contend with an old pickup truck for most of the way.

"Isn't this where Canyon de Chelly is?" I asked.

"It's northeast of where we'll be."

According to my guidebook, the first inhabitants of Canyon de Chelly, where "sheer sandstone walls rise up to 1,000 feet," were the Anasazi who flourished between the first and thirteenth centuries. The Anasazi, or Ancient Ones, inhabited the Four Corners region where Colorado, New Mexico, Arizona, and Utah meet; here they carved their homes deep inside the cliffs. Their disappearance is a still a mystery to archaeologists; it is considered one of the great puzzles of pre-Columbian North America. Hawk would later offer her theory of how and why they disappeared.

We finally turned off that long dark road and arrived at Second Mesa, one of three major mesas that make up the Hopi Indian Reservation.

In about ten minutes we arrived at the Hopi Cultural Center, a pueblo-style motel. As we entered the parking lot, the glow of the moon was all that illuminated the sheer blackness of the surrounding area, creating an almost eerie setting.

I peered through the car window. Hawk was waiting at the other end of the parking lot. She was wearing a dazzling purple and white ceremonial dress, with a bird feather dangling from her ear. The air around her had a presence, a force that was in turn affecting me; I was mesmerized.

Fluttering about her were several bats moving in unusually slow motion. I stared with fascination. There was something strange about these bats, but at the time I couldn't figure out what it was. Later, when I asked Hawk about them, she said the bats were shape-shifters, medicine people who traveled with her in one form or another.

"Hello, hello!" Hawk called out exuberantly, holding out her arms. At this point the bats suddenly vanished!

She embraced each of us the way she always did, with loving, nurturing, heartfelt hugs that penetrated to the core of our being. I secretly marveled at her ability to move with total ease among us while simultaneously moving through the dimensions. Her mystical eyes reflected back to us whatever face we showed; looking at her was like looking into a mirror. Like a creature of the night, she could see through darkness and perceive things that were hidden from others.

She then asked us to make an offering of cornmeal and tobacco at a small stone shrine in the courtyard of this stark stucco structure.

"When you give a love offering to the land, say, 'I come in peace.' Learn to be in harmony with the land."

After we had found our rooms, we gathered in a tight circle in the center of the courtyard. Hawk told us that the Hopi in this region lived a ceremonial life. "We're in their sandbox," she said metaphorically. "This is their land and we have to honor that. The Hopi way is what we study if we want to learn the happier course of life. The Hopi are remnants of the people of faith and hope. They consider it their duty to take care of the land and the Earth. Early every morning, they run several miles to their cornfields, and every cornfield has a ceremonial altar."

She described the Hopi as "unsophisticated, naive, and extremely trusting." When we visited them, we women must wear skirts and shawls, and we must all practice silence, for "silence is where we meet spirit." She asked us to go there with respect and without making judgments.

I looked up at the moon; enormous black clouds swirled all around, creating mysterious faces and shapes. When I closed my eyes, the moon reappeared in my mind. Subtle unseen forces were at work.

In a hushed voice, Hawk announced: "Three Hopi chieftains are practicing their medicine here, and our souls are aware of them." Suddenly the clouds covered the moon, and we found ourselves in complete darkness—our souls were being taken to a place between the physical and spirit worlds. Whatever we were feeling, whether fear or anticipation, was intensified.

Hawk sat cross-legged, opposite me. I stared into her amber eyes, which burned right through me, and I squirmed. The shamans' gaze could be quite uncomfortable because they look into your past and future and into your innermost secrets. Their intense awareness can even read your blood pressure. "When you are in movement with the soul, you find yourself totally aware of what each individual is thinking and doing," Hawk had said on another occasion.

Some of the others looked anxious and full of hope for an answer to what they were searching for. She acknowledged their unspoken questions and assured them, "You are shaman souls. You are sages. There's not one of you who doesn't have roots somewhere in a medicine society."

My heart started to pound with excitement, for I knew that we were now in movement with the greater forces. The experience was incredibly intoxicating. We traveled as one consciousness, focused and silent. It was such a freeing experience to merge with the Earth and the sky and each other. Our days began with ceremony and ended with ceremony in accordance with the movement of the sun. We were slowly regaining a sense of connection with "all our relations."

Hawk asked us to be up at five-thirty, to get in sync again with the movement of the sun, our natural clock. "At dawn we will pick up the sun's song."

Before we went to our rooms, she spoke to us of dreamtime medicine—she called it dreamspeaker—and said we would start to explore and work with it. When we're in dreamspeaker, we're in a very deep, deep sleep. We enter a larger dimension of the brain beyond our five senses—we expand into the sixth, seventh, and eighth senses. We become global beings and connect to the wisdom of our ancestors.

In dreamspeaker we're healing our shadow self, made up of parts we've rejected because we think they're flawed or weak. We have relegated them to the subconscious realm, a vast reservoir of creativity. Indigenous people who live closely connected to nature function in a fully conscious state; for them there *is* no subconscious.

"You must learn that your brain is one hundred percent available to you," Hawk emphasized. "Your brain cooperates with *whatever* you tell it."

She said that when we're in dreamspeaker we're inviting the ancestors to help us fully remember when we were children, "before anything or anyone ever told us that our dreams weren't valid."

I understood that in dreamspeaker I could reclaim the forgotten part of myself. If I brought the conscious and subconscious to life I could experience both of them fully. I could live twice the life and experience twice as much. It would be as though I had two children: I would nurture and play with one of them but call the other one my dark child and distance myself from it. Even if I couldn't understand my dark child, I could at least *try* to understand. The child would still need to be embraced and nurtured or it would pull further away from me.

Hawk responded to several questions and then bade us good night. I walked to my room, burned some sage and cedar in a small earthen bowl, and started to prepare for sleep. As I lay in bed, I made a point of inviting Hawk into my dreams.

I immediately found myself plunged into a deep dream state. I was in a place where I saw no boundaries; I experienced a sensation of infinity. At first it frightened me and I felt alone among huge spheres made of marble, crystals, rubies, and emeralds; the spheres seemed to be floating around me. Then I realized I was among the planets! I saw no beginning and no end, yet I felt embraced. As I looked over my shoulder I found myself face-to-face with three beautiful creatures. I could feel their radiance and love; I understood they had come to comfort me and invite me into their world. Then I realized they were dolphins! Two of them were larger, obviously adults, and the smaller one had a certain juvenile playfulness to its movement. With their perpetual smiles, they beckoned me to travel with them; they would show me the beauty of their home. I felt truly blessed by their genuine friendship and their desire to share with me. As I looked into their eyes, love emanated from them as though windows to the entire universe. It almost hurt to look into their eyes—they seemed to expose and reveal everything that ever was and ever would be. I couldn't fathom it all. I felt a warmth; emotions that I had never felt before flooded my being. I could feel my body vibrate as the sound of the dolphins entered me; we were like two minds coming together.

As I looked down, I found myself transformed into one of these gorgeous creatures. I had no legs, no arms; I was a perfect form that was now able to swim through the energies emanating from the planets. The movement was effortless. I was a form of silky skin that glided and cut gracefully through my environment.

Upon awakening, I felt that I had returned from a faraway place. For a moment I was dazed and confused. The experience had felt so real, as though I had been offered an alternative. I was in a panic because I had to choose where I wanted to be. But later on I came to realize, to my delight, that I now had the power to go there any time I desired; my dream world was always there.

We rose at dawn and met outside. Positioned at the edge of the parking lot, facing a field of juniper and shrub, we watched a blaze of orange and gold fill the horizon. Breakfast followed; everybody nodded with approval—the fried Hopi bread, dipped in honey, was delicious. The Miami people were deep into a discussion of Hurricane Andrew: the medicine work that Hawk had done with the Thunderbeings who lived in that state saved Florida from total destruction. The hurricane, Hawk told us, "had danced out of the Atlantic Ocean" to do some important balancing for the contaminated nesting areas around the East Coast. "The waters were dangerously polluted," she explained. "How are you going to live without water? Nothing will survive if the air and water are not purified. The weather beings made a unanimous decision to bring in the big guns."

After breakfast we gathered once again in the parking lot and set off on the day's adventure. We drove through rocky, barren land which changed to a savanna-like plain filled with shrub and cactus. As we approached Navajo country, multi-hued sand dunes and red rocky escarpments dominated the landscape.

We continued in a southwesterly direction until the San Francisco Peaks appeared in the distance. Soon we were turning onto a long paved road lined with pines. We had arrived at Sunset Crater, where a black cinder cone rose a thousand feet above jagged lava flows. The final eruption, some nine hundred years ago, had given the rim of the crater a distinctive red glow.

As soon as our vehicles came to a stop, we bolted out of them, like children reaching an amusement park. We wanted to experience everything about this place, its sounds, its fragrance, its sensations. In retrospect, considering how tranquil the place was, I am fascinated by how alive it made me feel and how it stirred me.

As we walked to the base of the cinder cone, I felt as though I were looking up at an enormous presence that possessed awareness and sensation; the peak seemed protective and caring toward its human friends. Surely it was one of the Ancients, an intelligence that could be tapped, for it seemed to breathe its essence over this entire area.

Hawk led us over to an enormous white pine tree. "This is our teaching tree," she said, pointing out that it had a blue and gold aura. We sat under the tree, with an unobstructed view of the volcano.

As we sprawled out on the grass, I could feel my eyelids begin to droop as Hawk took us through a meditation. Her tone of voice was irresistibly warm and passionate: "Many spirits stay in this particular region. . . . Allow your umbilical cord to re-form itself, envision it entering the Earth and moving through the fire and the lava, down to the crystal core of the Earth Mother. Just breathe and quietly listen. . . . Learn to respect what gives you life. Be in awe of yourself. What could threaten you? Don't be afraid of really living. What you're denying is what you pray for. . . . All of your sciences can't explain you. They can't even *touch* the vastness of what you are. The more time you spend in quiet places like this, the more you become aware of what you are."

She went on to say that we had been conditioned to think of ourselves in terms of what we did for a living. We had been taught to define ourselves through an artificial structure, and our interaction was colored by that definition. If we had been raised to experience ourselves primarily as beings of nature, our interaction would instead be colored by our common love for the Earth.

As I listened to Hawk, I felt an intimacy with her, and I felt the power of the volcano as though it were communicating something. Indeed I could feel the ground beneath me vibrate ever so gently.

By now it was getting late, and we returned to our motel. That night, I invited Hawk into my dreams, and again I awoke with a sensation of having been in boundless space, although this time I knew I had been a more active participant in a very intense experience. I felt strange and disoriented.

When we gathered in the motel courtyard, my feelings were confirmed. Hawk told us that we had all journeyed in the night to Sunset Crater, the volcano that we had visited the day before.

"Every one of you went to Sunset Crater with me last night." We had journeyed with Hawk and worked medicine at the volcano! Trekkers might say that we beamed ourselves to that volcano. The Mayans might say that we were part of a matrix of energy lines that encompassed the entire universe, a crystal grid network or a vast information web that connected all places, times, and events.

Hawk explained it this way: "Your body has the ability and circuitry of a huge electromagnetic switchboard to connect you to everything."

I didn't doubt it for one second. I *knew* I had been journeying in the night. I *knew* I had been part of a significant event. It was clearly evident how I had allowed myself to be conditioned over the years to be bound by the limitations imposed on me. I was always told that I couldn't do this or that because it was impossible or unrealistic or because I was just dreaming.

With the help of dreamspeaker I hoped that I could break through the learned preconceived notions of my conscious mind.

As Hawk continued to speak about the benefits of dreamspeaker, she asked, "Why can't you be happy? What is happiness to you? Wouldn't happiness be to know that you are truly divine and that there really is a God and that you have nothing to fear. Wouldn't that be happiness?" Her voice became very gentle. "Wouldn't peace exist everywhere? That's where you're returning to. You're returning back to pure energy."

I realized how often I'd look at people and thought they looked as if they were battling everything around them. Their movements seemed awkward; they didn't seem to be in flow with the energies around them. Even athletes had to work very hard, using their mental abilities to get into a frame of mind that would allow them to move in a fluid and graceful manner. On the other hand, a deer, a dolphin, and an eagle were always in flow. For them, there was no wasted energy; every movement had a purpose; they were in unison with everything in their environment.

Our energy had become askew, however. We had fallen off the tree of life and drifted away to become lost souls. That was why we had this yearning to come to something, to find out where we belonged. The pure energy that made us was going to have to return to a purer form or we would self-destruct. It would become so haphazard that it would collide with itself until it blew up. In order for us to be happy again, we were going to have to return to a pure state.

With Hawk we were learning that there were no limits and that we must use all of our abilities. In communicating with the volcano at

Sunset Crater, I believe we succeeded in saving the West Coast from major geological damage.

Several months later I asked Hawk about our interaction with the intelligence at Sunset Crater, and she explained that when we approached the volcano we asked, "How can we help?" and it answered, "Take some of the pressure off."

She went on to explain exactly how we did that: "Remember, I told you we had to be there at that time to make sure there was no separation of the continent on the West Coast."

We were able to take the pressure off the volcano through what she called a transference of energy. "There's no limit to how much energy we can run through our body," she explained, "as long as we don't try to control it with just our five senses. Our body can handle a lot because it lives and breathes and experiences the totality of the universe."

We were able to reroute the force of that volcano because in dreamspeaker we entered into a state of consciousness where there were no limitations.

"It takes megatons of energy, more than the atom bomb, to stop a volcano," Hawk continued. "Energy is intelligence and has its own language; you have to be able to talk to it. So we interacted with what is really a fire god, a soul that's in charge of particular lava activity at certain levels of Earth energy. Some people call them devas. There's a deva, for example, that takes care of the ocean. You're talking about a soul—they simply choose not to walk on two legs.

"Each vortex has a different frequency, a different sound. So does your soul. Every soul has a soul tone or soul ray. If my soul ray is gold, I will be more skillful at certain things than you, because that tone or quality is very natural to me. It's the same thing with different places on the Earth Mother. She has all these different vortexes, just as your liver tissue is different from your kidney tissue and your heart tissue. All of the various things that make up your body are different cellular groupings. Every one of your organs has a different tone. In the Earth, each mass has a tone that becomes a soul, a deva, a consciousness, an intelligence that works in total coherent interaction with it, just as your soul is in conscious interaction with your body."

She described Sunset Crater as "an individual in the volcano clan."

It became the eyes of its community and said to the community: "I've come and touched with souls that live in two-legged form, and this is the assistance they gave."

It was obvious to me that when we become connected with the Earth, we will feel a strong, passionate yearning when those around us reach out for assistance, whether they are four-legged creatures or something as big as a volcano. This must be what dedicated environmentalists and animal protectionists feel in order to continue in their endeavors. It's the same feeling we get when we see a baby bird that has fallen from its nest: we want to help it and hold it and return it to its nest.

Everything needs assistance because we're all part of the same community called Earth. Separation from nature doesn't work; we have become too destructive. If we are always enclosed by the four walls of our homes and offices, that's what we identify with. Therefore it's hard to think of ourselves as beings who can journey among the planets, let alone communicate with a volcano.

Yes, I thought, we can live in the mediocre environment of our four walls; we can swim in that pond, but that doesn't mean we have to drown in it. That pond is an infinitesimal fraction of what there is to experience; there is a whole ocean out there. If the pond is all that we ever experience, we've lost it—we're not even alive anymore.

Hawk went on: "We tend to take the vastness that we are and keep narrowing it down, thinking this makes us more secure. We think that we'll be safe if we can restrict the vastness and make it into a little thing we can put in our hands. But then we begin to die because that's not what we are."

Once I reflected on her comment I realized what it meant. As human beings we've gotten into a habit of categorizing everything; we don't even realize that we're doing it. It's what we've been taught in our schools. Our sciences teach us to categorize: is this substance a solid, a liquid, or a gas? Is this creature a fish, a mammal, or an amphibian? Everything has to fit into one of our categories or it doesn't exist. That makes it smaller and allows us to feel as though we are in control. When we meet someone, we immediately categorize him or her: friend or enemy, male or female, rich or poor. That, too, limits our understanding; we've lost the ability to understand people. Everything has to fit somewhere, and if it doesn't, we'll *make* it fit. Then we feel secure because we've explained it, and now we know it and control it. Our whole society is geared like this.

When we were at Sunset Crater we were able to communicate with an intelligence as big as the sun—even bigger. It's the cosmic storm of fire that creates planets. We were talking to a volcano clan. This intelligence doesn't just exist on this planet. It's out there in the universe, blowing up and exploding, spewing and creating new planets.

We made friends with that volcano, and it was impressed with us as a people who were willing to assist it. That volcano used our frequency and our tone to help disperse some of the tension and the stress it was experiencing.

The proof of what we did at Sunset Crater appeared several months later when an earthquake rumbled through the region. Arizona is known to have the smallest earthquake potential of eleven western states, but on April 29, 1993, an earthquake registering about 5.4 on the Richter scale occurred in the vicinity where we had been. The natives knew that someone had worked medicine at the volcano.

CHAPTER 10

THE DANCE

Lo, the poor Indian! whose untutored mind
Sees God in clouds, or hears him in the wind;
His soul proud Science never taught to stray
Far as the solar walk or milky way.

—ALEXANDER POPE

WORKING IN THE "MIDDLE world" is a profound experience. It brings me closer to realizing my interconnection, that the sun and the moon and the wind and the whirling forces are all within me and that my soul is a part of the Great Spirit.

Like the hero in *Indiana Jones and the Last Crusade*, we need only to believe with all our heart that we can leap across the great chasm that separates us from the Holy Grail. This is an old spiritual lesson that is difficult to learn because we have separated ourselves from the Creator, which has no limitations.

Our experience at Sunset Crater brought us closer to knowing what is possible. It helped us to understand that it is the emotion of the soul that takes us through time and space. When we utilize the frequencies of the soul, there are no restrictions.

Afterward Hawk told the Thunderbeings: "You are the power. Feel good about it, but don't brag about it."

Like the others, I won't quit until I have dislodged myself from the chains of a civilization that has kept us estranged from the Earth. We have all been taught that the environment around us is "just physical"—but nothing could be further from the truth. Our environment is alive; it has feelings, and it communicates. We have been taught not to trust our own feelings. But the time has come to trust and have faith again, to go through the doorway into deeper spiritual realities.

Early the next day, Hawk took us to one of the Hopi villages that are spread over three mesas that rise up to about seven thousand feet. We drove a short distance from our motel through barren terrain dotted with colorful rock formations, cacti, and shrub. Our vehicles lurched up a narrow rocky escarpment to a mesa top. We turned onto a dusty dirt road bordered with dry thistle and sagebrush. Up ahead stood a small village consisting of a cluster of sandstone huts. As we drove onto this crumbling yellow sandstone shaped like a flat-topped ship, we felt as though we had traveled back thousands of years in a time machine. There were no modern conveniences, no electricity, and no running water, no indication of the tentacles of mass communications that clench and clasp every corner of the globe. Traditional values still prevailed here, since the ancestors of the Hopi were guided to this region by their prophecies. Families belonged to clans, and each clan had a name, usually that of a bird, beast, or other living deity.

After we parked, Hawk reminded us to keep a respectful silence. "This village," she said, "is as old as the mesas."

From that mesa top the desert stretches emptily away to the buttes and mountains. This barren plateau is probably one of the least welcoming landscapes in the country. The Hopi must rely on the power of their prayers and ceremonies to evoke rain; indeed, they say that it is only by their faith that their fields are watered. They say that those who live along running water will be the first to lose their faith because they do not have to depend on prayer. The men run several miles every day across the desert to their fields of corn. They have disciplined themselves to awaken early in the day to work in the fields and then come back to the village before breakfast.

Hawk told us that the Hopi begin their day with offerings of cornmeal, asking for happiness and food for their people: "They say, 'I begin to care again this day.' Caring is like a big stone dropped in a still pond whose impact resonates outward into all relationships."

She said that when the Hopi perform a ceremony they send

prayers to all parts of the Earth: "Their medicines are vital in knitting the Earth together."

Hopi ceremonies, rituals, dances, and songs have been documented as being as complex and esoteric as any modern sophisticated system of today. A *National Geographic* article noted that kachina dances are among the most important art forms in North American history.

I think of the Hopi as global beings whose ceremonialism helps maintain a balance with the Earth. Nothing is excluded from the blessings they invoke: the earth, the seas, the plants, the animals, and humans. They are keepers of ancient knowledge. It is their destiny to preserve a fragment of the ancient culture so that we who live in modern times will understand that the human race is much older than what our learned ones tell us.

We walked over to a cluster of thick-walled stone dwellings. A woman with dark wrinkled skin and black hair emerged from one of the huts. I felt instantly comfortable and at ease with her; I felt warmth and gentleness. Hawk embraced her and then introduced her to us. She greeted us with a hello that was more than simply a repetitive behavioral response; it was heartfelt.

A year-long schedule of ceremonies and dances is a way of life for the Hopi. From what I understand, almost all of the dances in the village plazas and kivas (underground ceremonial rooms) are prayers for rain and fertile crops. In the kachina dance, the participants drum and chant from sunrise to sunset, inviting the kachinas, who reside atop the San Francisco Peaks, to manifest themselves as clouds. When the men are dancing, they call the kachinas to come into their bodies; and the kachinas *dance* the dancers, who move in a trance. Some of the Thunderbeings who witnessed the kachina dance told me that they observed a clear blue sky become dark with clouds directly above the village after hours of dancing. They saw the rain come down. The rain means that the Hopi have performed their ceremonies properly and have lived a virtuous life.

I'll never forget our first trip to this area in 1990 when we visited another Hopi settlement on the First Mesa. Our cars labored up a steep, narrow path to a village built on solid rock with ominous cliffs all around. This isolated skytop village seemed to be sprouting out of the rock. What a strange sensation to be surrounded by nothing but endless sky and bleak terrain, as if the village were hanging in midair. On that day, the Navaho and the Hopi were performing a mixed kachina dance. Spectators filled the square and crowded the rooftops. Some thirty dancers, in elaborate masks and colorful costumes, paced around in a circle, chanting. They turned rhythmically from right to left; and then from left to right, shaking their rattles and stamping their feet.

As I watched, I found myself wanting to come closer. I wove my way through the crowd. I was fascinated by the dancers' movements; they moved as one body. Their movements were astonishingly in sync and in harmony. That huge circle of dancers was perfectly choreographed. The movement of their feet pounding the ground resonated out through the Earth, and I was able to sense the pounding beneath the soles of my own feet. I was not merely watching and hearing; I was actually *feeling* the dance, like the vibration of the kettledrum that captivates your whole being with its spellbinding rhythm.

As I watched, I felt as though I were looking into golden fields of wheat and flowing back and forth in unison with them. It is the same feeling I've experienced while watching the rhythmic movement of the ocean's waves. As the waves are moved by the ocean, so are the dancers moved by the history of their clans, their families, and their ancestors. And as the ocean is moved by the planets, so have these families and clans been moved by the forces of the universe. Suddenly the dancers, their families, the ocean, the planets, all seemed to be one body. I felt a sense of interconnection. I felt tied with the ones who had danced this dance one thousand years before. I *felt* their energy; it was in the air, in the cactus, and in the sage. Even today when I look at the ocean and its waves, I am taken back to the dancers upon the First Mesa in Arizona.

My mind was filled with the image of the dancers as we visited another Hopi village and met with Black Eagle.

Black Eagle will act as our guide through the land of the Hopis and accompany us for the remainder of our journey. His six-foot frame was attired in simple shirt and blue jeans, belying the importance of his role in the village. He was a humble and naturally warm soul, who often looked down rather than directly at you. His black eyes, intense and unfathomable, seemed to conceal a depth of knowledge.

Our first stop was a little village of huts built around a central plaza. Off to one side of the village stood the ruins of an old church built in 1901 by a Mennonite minister in an attempt to convert the Hopi to Christianity. The villagers did not like the church, and neither did the spirits. It was consequently destroyed by lightning, rebuilt, and then destroyed by lightning again. As we continued through the village, one Hopi woman gave us piki, a thin, waferlike bread, along with bags of blue cornmeal. In another home we were invited to study the kachina dolls and other handmade crafts. I was touched and humbled by the Hopi's appreciation of their few possessions. It seemed that they wanted only to live simply and in harmony with nature.

We came to the opening that led into the kiva, an underground chamber where the Hopi pray and make preparations for kachina dances and other ceremonies. Hawk asked Black Eagle if he could take us inside, a privilege that is usually forbidden to outsiders.

Cautiously, he agreed. Keeping a respectful silence, we climbed down a ladder about twenty feet below the surface. It was cold and damp; there was a fire pit in the center and seating ledges along the sides. I shuddered at the thought of how dark it must be when the opening is covered.

Hawk had once told us that the kivas are corridors to the other worlds. For that reason they must always be approached in pure silence and with respect. Before going into the kiva, the Hopi will fast completely, and they will stay inside the kiva for fourteen days. On other occasions, such as before the ceremonial dances, they will go into the kiva every night for a month.

When they are in the kiva, the dancers become merged with the Earth Mother. They become one with the trees, the rocks, the sun, and the wind. This environment deep inside the Earth plunges them into a state of ultimate awareness to a point where, even in utter darkness, they know where the sun is. I've personally never witnessed the dancers, but others have told me that when the dancers emerged from the kiva they seemed to be hovering above the ground—they seemed to be riding the wind.

We climbed out of the kiva and made one more stop at the Hopi craft shop to purchase silver jewelery, books, kachina dolls, and weavings. On the way back to our motel, I started to read a book about Hopi prophecy. In it found this passage, which I feel captures the Hopi spirit:

> *In the beginning, we are told, Taiowa, the Creator,*
> *gave us his life plan, which we call the Prophecy.*
> *If we hold fast to the sacred way as he devised it for us,*
> *what we have gained, we will never lose . . .*
> *Beware of the other way,*
> *the way of life of those who do not pray . . .*
> *This time of confusion, in which many will choose either path,*
> *   is called a time of purification.*
> *So it seems we now are all at this point in our lives,*
> *where indeed purification is for the world, the order of the day . . .*
> *Give love to all things, people, animals, plants,*
> *and mountains; for the spirit is one . . .*
> *The Prophecy says the Earth will shake three times:*
> *first the Great War, then the Second One,*
> *when the Swastika rose above the battlefields of Europe,*
> *to end in the rising Sun sinking in a sea of blood . . .*
> *Now, what would the third one be?*
> *This, the Prophecy does not say*
> *For it depends on which path humankind will walk:*
> *the greed, the comfort and the profit,*
> *   or the path of love, strength, and balance.*[1]

The next day we returned to the Hopi village to get Black Eagle. He guided us through hilly terrain dotted with flowering yellow and white sagebrush to a hidden sacred mesa near his village. We stopped at this deep gouge in the Earth framed by immense white cliffs, austere and dreamlike, strong with an otherworldly mystique. While we stood at the edge, I felt myself being magnetically pulled in.

"Put an offering of cornmeal into the mesa to the spiritual entity who walks this place," Hawk instructed us.

We all put out cornmeal offerings. Two days later when we returned to the mesa, she said, "The woman who walks this place has gathered your gifts."

Hawk told us that some time ago she had gone into the mesa with her Hopi elder, and they had encountered the female spirit. "When we were there, we heard singing," she said. "Then we felt a presence coming toward our campsite; it was singing softly. As the presence came closer, the song got louder and I realized I could feel the form. My elder welcomed her to our fire and in just a split second there was a woman sitting with us, with her legs crossed, near the fire.

"The presence appeared to be maybe twenty-two or twenty-three years old, very serious, not quite beautiful, but handsome in a way. There was a stateliness about her, very much like when I see a good balance between male and female energies in a woman. Anyway, she sat and talked. When the presence got up and moved away, we thought we were seeing it walk away. Then we realized it wasn't here. The next thing we saw was a little white rabbit or a desert rabbit running away. We followed the footprints, and where the human prints ended, the rabbit prints started.

"It was either the second or third night we were there, what actually came to our campfire was a rabbit. It just sat there and listened. My Hopi elder said, she's a shape-shifter. She simply has the ability to be a hawk, a rabbit, or a human. So she sat there with us in her rabbit form."

Hawk told us that the spirit lives inside the mesa and she will live there forever. It is her home. She protects the mesa, which contains the sacred minerals and stones the Hopi use to make their masks and kachina paints.

On this second visit, we descended in our vehicles to the bottom of the mesa down a steep, treacherous path. In the hot sun amid sand and sheer, angular cliffs we entered a vast haunting silence. Hawk said, "It is so quiet down here that you can hear the wind sing and the movement of the coyotes and wolves."

The mood of primordial isolation was perfect for what would unfold. Hawk instructed us to find a private spot and just meditate.

I noticed the many layers of time written into these pallid cliffs. Some of them were shaped like huge sculptured fingers etching their forms into the sky. Two distinctive lines indicated where the water's surface must have been when this place was an ancient ocean. I lay back and bathed in the sun's light. It was so tranquil. I could feel the presence of spirit, as though it were the very warmth that was breaking through my skin.

After a few hours Hawk called us together and asked us to build a fire with the wood she had gathered.

As the fire grew intense, she became agitated and started to speak in a tongue that was unfamiliar to me. A surprisingly vivid red fire leaped out at us. I had never seen a fire that red!

Hawk entered into a deep communion with the fire, and we sat completely still with our attention focused on her. She became more agitated and charged with energy. Her face was flushed, her eyes wide and piercing. She was obviously hearing and seeing something that the rest of us couldn't. As I watched her, she seemed to expand in stature and tower over us.

In a commanding voice she said, "The fire spirit shows a lot of red. It shows that many of your issues are about anger and that you're not dealing with it in a balanced way. This is a warrior fire and it can spread your anger."

Her eyes became dark and intense, riveted to something in the distance. She spoke slowly, passionately: "There's a face of a great chief on the wind, Chief Joseph. And Crazy Horse is very strong here. The people of Siberia have come on the winds, and the powerful warriors of Australia are here and an old Anasazi chief. Many have come to counsel with you. The ancestors on the wind say, 'Grow up, grow strong, and be in awe of who you are.'"

We looked around at each other, confounded and dazed.

"The winds," Hawk went on, "are our oldest communication frequency. They're our global telephone line."

She went on about the importance of dealing with our anger and the need for wisdom and self-love. "Wisdom replaces hardship. Love yourself. What you don't like about yourself is where you need to focus your strength. You have to heal yourself before you can heal the world."

It was midafternoon and at least 100 degrees. The sky, which had been clear, suddenly clouded over, and the winds started to blow.

"The clouds and the wind have come in response to your presence," she said softly. "Seldom do they come here."

I looked around and saw glimmers of appreciation. Irving nodded, apparently enjoying the fact that the natural forces respond so lovingly. George was deep in thought, seeming to appreciate this as well, while Henry smiled with obvious delight.

"The trees will move, the ground will become very busy, and the winds will bring elders to try to be a part of you—that's how important you are."

She said she couldn't understand how we could deny our connection to the elements: "I watch your minds, and I respect every bit of how intelligent you are. And I wonder how you can be so intelligent and deny your relation to a tree? How can you look at the sky and not know you're there? How can you be mesmerized by the twinkling of Venus and not know she's talking to you? The twinkling is a communication. But you don't see it that way because someone you trusted and loved—called family, teachers, scientists, clergy—told you that none of these things are valid. But if there is no validity to these things, what are you? If you are not all these entities, what are you?"

At this point, I became painfully aware of how much we'd lost in our intimacy with nature. Primitive tribes were part of the local ecosystem. With the industrial revolution and urbanization, however, we drew away from the land, believing that we had conquered nature and entered into a new form of existence. In the process, we shut ourselves off from the many communications around us, including the plants and animals on which we depend for our daily existence. Even though they respond and speak to us, we are unable to understand them. The plant and tree people continue to give of themselves and nurture us even though we have become indifferent or unresponsive. We don't hear the tree invite us to sit under its branches. Yet when walking across a plateau under a hot sun and finding a tree, who doesn't feel a yearning to sit in its shade? The tree beckons us—it says, "Come rest under my limbs"—and we instinctively give thanks to the tree for being there.

The plant and tree people prepare us for the change of seasons. When the leaves turn color, we know that winter is coming. When bushes and plants are laden with fruit, we are being informed that winter will be long and hard; the animals will be well supplied. Our tree and plant relations speak to us, but we've forgotten and don't give credibility to *how* they speak. Instead, we turn on the television or radio for a weather report.

Our other relations, the animals, are not so unconditionally giving. They no longer trust us: they run away when we approach them.

"The plants give endlessly to their last root for man," Hawk said, her voice filled with passionate caring. "Many of our other relations have abandoned humans because man has violated the fundamental laws of nature. But the trees say, 'No, I align myself with man.' The plants will sacrifice in magnitude for us. They will bring us what we need. They are totally allowing of us."

I realized that despite our arrogance and indifference and abuse, the Earth continues to love us unconditionally.

When it was time to leave, we made a final offering to the mesa and got back on the winding road that led to the highway.

Early the next day we left Hopi country and drove along the same route that had taken us to Sunset Crater. This time though we headed toward the south rim of the Grand Canyon. Late that afternoon we arrived at the edge of this stupendous chasm: 277 miles long, one mile deep, and ten miles wide, it takes in part of the mighty Colorado River. Many writers have been pushed to their limits trying to describe the wonders of the Grand Canyon. It *is* difficult to describe hundreds of cliffs and slopes stretching far into the horizon while the sunlight dances on the rock walls, creating brilliant hues of all the earthly colors made only more sensational by massive looming shadows. A gentle wind blew through the canyon as though the sacred breath of Creator had emanated from the great Mystery. The fragrance of juniper and cedar permeated the air. I felt as if I had arrived at a great temple that has been created for the sole purpose of my spiritual or philosophical awakening.

As we perched precariously on a rocky ledge, I had an overwhelming and powerful feeling that I might be swept into the gorge. I grabbed a clump of sagebrush and held tight.

When I learned that every year some people fall into the depths, I wondered if they had experienced this same irresistible impulse to throw themselves over the edge as I did, but were unable to hold back. They were mesmerized and beckoned into the canyon!

"Don't you feel as if you can fly?" Hawk exclaimed. "This is the heart of the Earth Mother. When you stand here before this magnificent creation, how can you doubt that there is a Creator? See how much you are loved," she said, gesturing with her hand along the vast, colorful horizon.

Black Eagle guided us through a prayer acknowledging the spirits that reside here. "We are in the land of the Hopi. Guide us through our journey," he said softly. According to the Hopi, this is where the story of the world began. Black Eagle told us that the Grand Canyon is the doorway through which life emerged. This is the *sipapuni*, or place of emergence, for the Hopi people.

Within moments, clouds, mists of light, and lightning voices gathered around us in response to our prayers. Three crows emerged seemingly out of nowhere, and I wondered if they, like the bats around Hawk when we arrived at the Hopi Cultural Center, were shapeshifters. Just as we got up to leave, a light rain started, and within moments of getting into our vehicles, a torrential rain came crashing down on us, making the dark road a challenge to drive. We drove for a long time through enormous mountains that looked like looming giants of the night.

NOTES

1. Robert Boissiere, *Meditations with the Hopi* (Bear & Company, Santa Fe, NM: 1986).

CHAPTER 11

UNFOLDING OF THE UNIVERSE

Sooner or later every one of us breathes an atom
that has been breathed before by anyone you can
think of who has lived before us—Michelangelo or
George Washington or Moses.

  —JACOB BRONOWSKI

GOING IN A SOUTHEASTERLY direction, we approached Oak Creek
Canyon. My heart jumped with excitement as the road snaked through
the steep-walled canyon I had first seen two years earlier. As we drove
downward along a precipitous road, the pine-covered canyon wall rose
to a dizzying height. Returning here was like returning to my sacred
home.

We arrived again at Junipine Resort, nestled on the banks of Oak
Creek. This was to be our home base for the next seven days.

At 10:00 P.M. we congregated in the living room of one of the
cabins. There were two couches and we grabbed chairs from the dining
room or sat on the carpeted floor in front of a huge stone fireplace.
We could hear the rushing creek outside the sliding doors, which
opened onto a wooden deck and a view of the craggy canyon wall.
What a perfect place to dream or to learn how to dream and understand the language of our dreams. Once we were all comfortably
seated, Hawk told us why she had brought us here: Sedona, she ex-

plained, is an important energy center. It is one of the planet's most sacred sites, a power point on the planetary energy grid.

After my first trip here I had read a fascinating article by Martin Gray, who had visited more than three hundred sacred sites in over forty countries. Gray wrote about receiving visionary information dozens of times while experiencing the energies of various sacred mountains. In one of his revelations, the Earth spoke to him "of her sadness concerning human alienation from the land." In another, he "received" information that led him to conclude that the power points on Earth are similar to the acupuncture points on the human body. At the power points, "a unique energetic dynamic exists which allows for a mutually beneficial relationship between the planet and humans." Humans, he felt, may assist in the energy-balancing and thereby the healing of Earth by visiting the power centers of the world.

And that was exactly why Hawk had brought us to Sedona. We were here to assist in the healing of this area, which is part of the Grand Canyon. From the larger perspective of the Earth as a conscious being, this place is comparable to her spinal cord. The spinal cord is such an important region of our body that we can be paralyzed if it is injured. If other parts of the Earth were destroyed, she could still carry on. Similarly, if we lost a limb we too could carry on, but to have one *vital* organ destroyed means the destruction of us as a whole.

Like acupuncturists, we would thrust ourselves into the point where the flow of energy has been blocked or interrupted, so that the Earth could be liberated of her pain.

Hawk talked about the desecration that was happening in Sedona, which is the location of numerous vortexes. She said that the proliferation of tourist shops and buildings was hurting the energies of these vortexes. "Even the residents have tried to stop the expansion," she said, noting that the building of major hotels and high-rises had been halted. "The expansion is like a tight collar around the Earth Mother's neck," she said.

Hawk told us that the Old Ones had warned about building on this sacred red rock country. When we are at the vortexes, the spirit of the Earth is felt very strongly, and nothing should interfere with that. Erecting buildings changes the vibration of the land.

"Man is not meant to build among these great rocks and canyons," she said with a mixture of sadness and anger.

She needed at least ten Thunderbeings to help her alleviate this condition. We would prepare ourselves by entering into a state of silence and cultivating pure thoughts.

"It is easy to fall in love with this place," she went on. "Everybody who has come here has some reaction. We're in the wind canyon. Hundreds of ancestral spirits can become manifest here because of the vortex."

Much has been written about the power and magic of the Sedona vortexes and how the energies help people make dramatic shifts in their lives. We change when we come to a vortex because we become synchronized with the energies, and the dormant circuits of our central nervous system are activated.

"A vortex is a gateway in which the cosmos creates an altar where time and space meet," she said, noting that recent scientific discoveries support the existence of vortexes. Scientists refer to them as "wormholes."

She said that some vortexes, like the ones here in Sedona, are earth temples: serene, majestic places where man has found God and where time stops. Here we are able to touch the deeper dimensional energy flows of the universe. Here we can experience seven dimensions at the same time!

The Earth Mother provides these temples for the sake of changing us. They are heart medicines because our hearts are touched and changed when we are in their presence. And we, in turn, empower them by spending time loving them. The Earth waits for us to respond to her, even if we question her. She is lonely and eager for us to speak to her. Consider, for example, a famous tourist attraction: Niagara Falls at the Canadian-U.S. border. There is a huge presence there. The Falls is an intelligence. We need to speak to the presence there. We need to communicate with the spirit world that is there. Every time we pray, we make a difference.

It had been a long day, and Hawk decided to send us back to our creek houses. She reminded us of the importance of maintaining silence.

At this point we also removed our watches so as to disengage ourselves from mechanized time. The sun would be our timekeeper; we would move according to the way of Spirit. As before, Hawk would call or send David to wake us up as well as reassemble us.

"In the morning, after you have gone to the stream, I want you to start writing about your dreams. Okay? Sleep well."

When we dream, with Hawk nearby, we go into a very deep realm; we enter the larger community of galactic intelligence. And what an exquisite place to dream—Oak Creek Canyon! It was situated in a column of energy that increased our dream activity manyfold.

I had no idea how long I had been sleeping when I awoke to a knock on the bedroom door. It was time to get up. The morning light peaked through the vertical blinds. I scrambled out of bed, put my cloth wrap on, and grabbed a big towel. It was a good five-minute walk to the creek along a beautiful lush trail, with hummingbirds greeting us along the way. We walked in quiet serenity, like monks, with our heads bowed, not looking at each other. We then gathered at the edge of the creek and took turns immersing ourselves and giving thanks for the new day. Nothing shocks you into full awareness like a plunge into icy crystal-clear waters!

Returning to the cabin, I jumped into the shower and crawled back into bed with my journal. I wrote and slept until the phone rang. It was our cue to get dressed and have breakfast. We attempted to prepare breakfast in silence, but we started hand-signaling to each other. It would take us a couple more days to get used to cooking and eating in total silence. We spent the rest of the morning in solitude.

I stepped outside and sat on the deck. It was so peaceful, with the songbirds and the gentle gurgling of the creek. The sunlight streamed through trees, which sloped upward with the canyon wall. I could feel myself slipping into an introspective state and becoming aware of all the issues in my life. Gazing at the canyon wall, I noticed that it was tinged with white, gray, and rust; I could see faces and shapes looking back at me. I imagined that real beings were infused within the rock formations.

There was another knock on the door.

"Everyone's meeting outside in ten minutes. All you need to bring is your notebooks," I heard David shout as he entered the hallway. I threw on a skirt and a light cotton shirt and grabbed my sunglasses and hat. Not a word was uttered while we got ready; all you could hear was the opening and shutting of drawers and doors along with running water and footsteps.

We gathered in front of the cabins and sat on a grassy area. Hawk was wearing a flowing white skirt and a mauve-pink flowered tunic. We chatted for a while, and she taught us a chant, which we would sing on our visits to the sacred vortexes over the next few days. Singing puts our minds and our hearts in perfect unity, which will help us accomplish our work here.

Some of the Thunderbeings here were new to our organization; they had not been with Hawk as long as I had. For that reason she spent the next stretch of time trying to jar some awareness into them about their everyday belief systems. This is true for all of us—our lives are either enhanced or limited by what we believe to be true about ourselves and the world around us.

"I want you to start activating your brain so you can work with it on a conscious level all the time. Terms like 'higher self' and 'subconscious' are not valid. Your brain cooperates with whatever you tell it. Get rid of anything that makes you think you are less evolved in the spectrum of intelligence. Inside the mystery schools as far back as Lemuria the priests started that concept in order to control people."

As I listened to Hawk, I realized what a great motivator she is. I have often found myself revved up and feeling empowered after listening to her.

"Start saying to yourself, 'I can do it. What is there that says I can't!' You have to break that belief. There is no hierarchy of God. It is a privilege to be in the Earth and to show your creativity in form. You are not cursed. There is nothing more beautifully balanced than this body. You are the maximum."

She was especially concerned that some of the Thunderbeings believed in the existence of nonphysical guides.

"Don't take on guides you think are smarter than you. You have the ability, like a multiple switchboard, to plug in to any universal information. There is nothing out there more intelligent than you. You're it! Do not deal with anything that degrades you. Intelligence has been enslaved because someone found out how easy it was to do so.

"I want you to stop using phrases like 'I can't' and 'I don't know.' These only impair your full consciousness. It doesn't matter what your parents' plight was—you have a gift to deliver. We're not trying to build massive egos out here. Change those tapes in your head if for no other reason than to know the joy of self-realization. When you begin to know the God within, you are the humblest of all meek people. Because you sit in quiet, in a state of awe. And there's a love that I can't even begin to tell you about until you learn to feel it," Hawk said, her voice becoming as gentle as a caress.

She then handed us a folder with several papers in it; one was titled "Five Steps to Dream Interpretation." She noted that there were three types of dreams: anxiety-release dreams, in which we rehash the day's events; prophetic dreams, in which we gain insight into some future event; and direct-communication dreams, in which we receive a message from someone or something. And she added mysteriously: "Many worlds will be sending communications to us while we're here." I figured that this was somehow related to our upcoming work with respect to visiting and healing the sacred vortexes, and that our work with dreams was leading up to that.

"Dreamtime medicines are extremely powerful to medicine societies like the Australian Aboriginals, the Siberian people, and the Dogon of Africa. The natives of Australia are actually called the dreamers; they spend most of their life working in what is called the dream lodge.

"And we're not talking about astral projection, where your light body gets up and goes someplace. We're talking about you physically being able to clone yourself. Many Eastern teachers, people you call yogis, have recorded that. As your body lies in its intermittent position, you clone your pattern just a short distance away. A short distance for you here would be any part of North America."

I found myself wondering about this, and after giving it some thought, I concluded that this was not impossible. I had found that I could close my eyes and picture myself anywhere in the world. Maybe the yogis had developed this skill to a higher level.

And she went on with softly urgent passion to convince us that we are born perfect for our life's purpose. And that what has been demonstrated by shamans and wizards, yogis and spiritual masters, is something we are all capable of.

"You have many thoughts in your head that you aren't particularly capable of manifesting these powers. But if someone else is, why aren't you? There is no God that selected the chosen. Do you understand that? No God sat up there and said, 'Well, you've been a good child, so I'll make you this very special person and I'll call you the chosen, and the rest of these children will just have to follow you.' There is no God that does that. You do that. You are here and you chose to be here. Now you have to decide to participate as a chosen. You're full of doubts and denials because they were fed to you."

She told us that she had asked Black Eagle his thoughts about us: "I said to him, 'If only one thread could be cut that would set them free so that they could fly, what would you say that is?' And he looked at me and said, 'If they would but truly submerge themselves in appreciation.'"

As before, she talked about the need for us to appreciate everything about ourselves: "Appreciation abolishes all doubts that you're not blessed with everything you need. And when you begin to appreciate the things you take for granted, you start realizing how much you *do* have. Appreciation births tolerance and acceptance."

Then she talked about the dream work we would be doing, explaining that "the practical step-by-step stuff" was only a start. At first we would draw our dreams in words and pictures: "When you go into the dream state you want to say with absolute strength and conviction to your mind that you're no longer the captain of this ship. You're teaching the mind that your soul is in control.

"The soul's not caught in here," Hawk said, touching her chest to indicate her body. "The soul isn't in here. How much importance can you give the soul and think it's lost in this? It is not the mind that controls this vessel. The soul does. That's why you have problems with people you think are taking your power. You don't *have* any power. There is only one power and that's *love*. We all have that. There is really nothing anyone can steal from you. They can get you to play their game, that's all. There are a lot of sorcerers who do that—to what advantage I don't know; it doesn't make too much sense to me. I think it makes a lot more sense to see a bunch of people get together and make dinner to feed some people who are hungry. I am more impressed with that than I am with sorcerers who make you afraid of them because of this and that."

That night we would go to sleep singing a chant about the virtues of tolerance and compassion. Now, that seemed like such a simple thing, but when Thunderbeings chant, their thunder is heard in the distance. Our chanting would help set the framework for our work at the vortexes. It would allow the energies of the greater forces to come through us.

Over the next two days we acquired a massive amount of information about dreams. Every morning, upon awakening, we wrote about the feelings evoked by our dreams; then we extracted the theme or summarized the dream's plot and analyzed the symbolism. Some nights there was a great deal of activity in my dreams. In particular I dreamed about the future course of my life (which did materialize within two to three years). I also dreamed of being out in the desert at the vortexes with Hawk. Overall I had a sense of dreaming so deeply and so profoundly that I couldn't even begin to comprehend where I had gone. It was only later, after our journey, that I understood how much we had accomplished in our waking life through this deep level of dreaming.

That evening Hawk announced that tomorrow we would begin our pilgrimage to the sacred vortexes.

She talked about the different forces that characterized each vortex. She explained more about their tremendous energy fields and said that some of them contained passageways or corridors—what scientists called wormholes. She handed us a magazine article about Harvard physicist Sidney Coleman who described wormholes as "Invisible, submicroscopic rips in the fabric of space-time that tunnel out of the universe, linking it to an infinite web of other universes."

"What did you think of the article?" Hawk asked. "Coleman is trying to show how solid the universe is. We think it's empty, but there are tunnellike passageways throughout that interjoin the past and the future."

She added that the passageway looks like a beautiful spiderweb. "And that is how we travel and how we move through everything in what you consider the invisible ray. We *can* move molecular structure; we *can* break it down. Our physical form can break down and disperse and come back without misplacing an organ or missing a breath. And that is not impossible. Everybody is born with the possibility of it." And we discussed the theory that faster-than-light travel is possible because of the existence of wormholes.

"Aren't the passageways too small to travel through?" Irving said.

"Yes, Coleman says they are too small to move through," I added.

If scientists believe that wormholes are microscopically small, like a strung-out thread, Hawk said they're measuring that through their current understanding of time and space. "Once you move past that," she went on, "wormholes are big enough to drive a bus through. If you moved at the frequency of the passageway, within less than a split second you could materialize on Mars, Venus, the Pleiades, or any system outside this galaxy." She emphasized that this is not magic—it is pure, clear intelligence—and scientists will catch up with it as soon as they stop denying that mysticism is the mother of science. Mysticism is not something that has been dreamed up—it is not "woo-woo." Mysticism represents the principles that are the formula of a life-giving force.

Interestingly, physicists are now beginning to think it's possible that we could travel, as though in a time machine, through a wormhole and emerge in another part of this universe or a different universe.

"All ancient histories talk about people who walked between the worlds. It's no different than getting on a highway and knowing we're going to end up in Arizona in fourteen hours. These people knew how to get into a frequency and travel upon it, like the pilot of an airplane who knows it has to follow a certain course. That's how the natives could make their star mappings so accurate."

Astronomers are realizing that native peoples' maps are true to the detail of where the star systems are, as in the case of the Dogon people of North Africa who possess information about the rotation and relative position of the star Sirius, which they have claimed consists of two stars, one of which is a white dwarf invisible to the naked eye. The Dogon have known about this invisible star for thousands of years—and their understanding of the two stars' orbits coincides exactly with modern astronomical findings.

For Hawk it is *practical* to get inside one of those wormholes and travel to any planet. Most people consider feats such as teleportation, levitation, disappearing and coming back phenomenal, but she does not. "It is not new in our history for people to report how natives come and go on the wind and how they are there and then disappear," she said. "There are documents of tremendous historical importance which confirm that chieftains and medicine people have actually been viewed disappearing by spinning off the ground into midair." What they do, she explained, is put themselves into synchronization with the vibration of a particular passageway, and then they can travel upon its form.

It occurred to me that perhaps that's how mystics and sages received divine revelations. When Christ was in the cave at Quarantana, when Moses was on Mount Sinai, and when Buddha was beneath the bodhi tree, maybe they had wandered into a vortex of energy that zapped them through a corridor in space.

Black Eagle told us that some of the elders in his community said Moses stepped inside a passageway into a parallel world and came back through tremendous frequencies—and that was why his hair turned white!

Hawk said that galactic passageways can be found at the Grand Canyon. There is also a passageway at the site of the post office at the corner of Highways 89A and 179. Because the building is situated in a time-warp doorway, the movement of mail is disrupted.

She said that the Anasazi disappeared through a passageway like the one at the post office and went on to other planetary realms. This would possibly explain the great puzzle of why this sophisticated prehistoric tribe suddenly abandoned the Four Corners region. For it is said that in the late 1300s these intelligent, highly civilized people vanished almost overnight. The Anasazi had developed excellent methods of farming and irrigation, created multistory cliff dwellings, and apparently lived without war for hundreds of years.

"Why did they leave?" I asked.

"They moved away from this dimension because they didn't want to experience or learn the destructiveness and separation of our present world."

Basically she explained that the Anasazi foresaw the coming time of spiritual darkness on Earth and didn't want to be a part of it. Having highly evolved psychic as well as intellectual and spiritual abilities, they understood that their being transcended bodily form. And so they vanished through a wormhole.

She said that all the gentle-natured spirits—such as Pegasus and the unicorn and others that we now consider mythical creatures—used to exist on Earth as real physical beings, like you and me. But they could not survive in what had become a coarse and negative atmosphere. These pure spirits took reclusive positions in this dimension because they can live only where the tonal vibration is in absolute harmony. They cannot survive amid prejudice, hatred, and separation. But they continue to exist just beyond the veils of our atmosphere and can still be seen by those with a pure heart—babies and little children, for example. They will return to Earth when humankind becomes pure again.

It was getting late when we returned to the subject of vortex energy, but everyone was wide awake; emotions were riding high. I was on Hawk's right; she sat there like some middle-world goddess. Her aura seemed to expand and enfold us into the volume of her being. I was fascinated by the degree of her intensity; she never seemed to tire—she could go on for hours and hours. Her hands constantly moved to amplify what she was saying; she rhythmically rubbed her thumb against her fingertips. I knew that she was traveling between worlds even as she spoke to us. Many times I have been in a conversation with her and I have suddenly lost the thread of what she was saying. I would be spinning with her on some dimensional beam and found it increasingly difficult to focus on what she was saying. Now my mind was spinning again.

"When you're in a vortex, it creates an electrical exchange in the dormant corridors of your mind, which in turn connects you with those tunneled passageways."

What? I did not completely grasp what was being said, not from *not* believing but merely from not being able to fathom it.

At this point Hawk announced that tomorrow we would visit the sacred vortexes. Of course we would receive the vortex energies, but more importantly we would *give* our offerings. When we're offering we're really giving love. Because we are in a relationship with the Earth, she wants our love as much as we want hers; she is sad when we're indifferent to her. By visiting the vortex points we could help heal her. Our loving hearts would act as acupuncture needles and stimulate her.

The next morning Hawk awoke us early so that we would have time to bathe in the creek and prepare backpacks. She was going to send us to Bell Rock, the incredible red monolith we had visited two years earlier.

"When you're at Bell Rock you will be in a tremendous electrical energy field," she told us. "You will be doing ceremony with Black Eagle when you're there. You are going to talk to the stones, sit on them, hug them, kiss them. You are going to rattle, drum, and sing. You will be offering your love to the vortex."

She instructed us to clear ourselves: clear our mind of conflicts, opinions, judgments, future worries, and past regrets. "Allow yourself no form, no color, no light," she told us. "Just be an opening on the face of the Earth. Entertain no thoughts. Be very focused." This silent, meditative state will allow the vortex to take from us what it needs.

"Remember, you are Creator's intention in motion," she said, reminding us that we would act as channels for greater forces. When I asked her about meditation exercises I'd read in a book on vortexes, she replied, "Do whatever helps you get in touch with the stone and the earth. The problem with those written exercises is that you're so concerned with doing them right that you can't do them. Be the director of your meditation. All you need to do is keep your spine straight and grounded; and if you are sitting, sit cross-legged. Use your breath and your heartbeat to put yourself in a centered place."

Mysteriously, Hawk stayed behind at the cabins, but she instructed us to watch for her while we were at Bell Rock!

She stood in the parking lot and waved to us as we drove off. In about ten minutes we reached highway 179 in Sedona. In the distance loomed the massive Courthouse Rock and, right next to it, Bell Rock.

As soon as we arrived, Black Eagle guided us along a trail to the bottom of the rock. He sprinkled the ground with sacred cornmeal, requesting the spirits to be in harmony with us. When we had climbed partway up the rock, we made another offering of cornmeal. Then we wandered off on our own.

I climbed up to a slope shaded by a juniper tree. Taking several deep breaths, I concentrated on what I was feeling. I sang softly the chant that Hawk had taught us. And I started to feel the charge of the rock, the same intense energy I had experienced two years earlier. I looked around and noticed that the others were unable to sit still.

Then, after being absorbed in our meditations for some time, we heard Black Eagle call out, "Here she comes!" A rainbow suddenly shot across the sky out of nowhere! The sky was completely cloudless, there was not one drop of rain, and yet this rainbow stretched out into a full spectrum of vivid colors that was positively unreal.

Hawk was painting a rainbow for us. The natives call this a middle world rainbow: the Zunis and the Pueblos, the Southwest tribespeople, are adept at knowing how to produce such rainbows.

It was not an elemental rainbow produced by rain.

When we returned to the creek houses, Hawk was waiting for our reaction. "I painted you a pure medicine rainbow," she said, smiling. "It was as thick and dense a rainbow as we can make in this dimension."

"It was *so* vivid and *so* real!" I exclaimed.

"I was in a meditation when I heard a noise; I looked up and saw the rainbow," Henry said. "There was something a little different in the colors."

Irving, his eyes wide with amazement, added: "I'm not one to have unusual experiences but I just lay down and cleared my thoughts, and the first thing I saw was your face. I realized, Oh, my God, it's Hawk!"

The rainbow was a loving demonstration that medicine works.

That evening when we gathered after dinner Hawk handed us five pieces of paper, another part of her effort to help us reach deeper spiritual truths.

"All right, let's take a look at these papers," she said. Turning to me, she asked, "What do you call these?"

"Um, inspirational verses."

We read through one of them:

I am growing older knowing
That my disappearing youth
Hides itself in my uncertain wisdom
Growing younger all the time.

She waited for our reaction and then said, "It's very Zen. It's one of those spiral things that take you in and breathes you out and you wonder where you went. She proceeded to explain the meaning of the verse and then said, "You're afraid of death; you're afraid you stop somewhere. Your uncertainty is that you don't know what comes after death. Until you fully accept life after death you can't live fully. Live every day completely and then you won't be dying. Where does wisdom dwell? Wisdom is in the heart: that's where you live forever. What you *feel* you will never lose."

Later that evening Hawk talked about another vortex that we would visit the next day: Boynton Canyon, a magical, enchanted place of whistling winds, considered by many to be the most sacred place in red-rock country.

Boynton Canyon is a blend of magnetic and electric Earth energy. Those who have studied the mysteries of the canyon describe it as a twilight zone or an in-between place where Spirit makes itself known to us. Others have described it as "a gateway to a vast unconscious realm."

Recently, though, a world-class resort called Enchantment has been built at the mouth of the canyon. Hawk told us that nothing should be built on such sacred Indian healing and burial ground. She said that the natives had fought for a long time against the building of this resort.

There are many stories relating to events that interfered with the building of this resort. Even after it was built, people didn't want to come back after their first visit because they'd had very eerie feelings or experiences. As a result, the place went broke under its first owners. Then the next owner tried to get someone to exorcise the place and chase the spirits away. Hawk heard about this and explained to the owner that the problem was not *how* the resort existed but its very existence—how can you exorcise that?

Boynton Canyon is one of the largest power spots; it is a huge force field. The Apache and the Taos people make pilgrimages here all the way from the Four Corners area.

And Hawk informed us of the mysterious presence in the Canyon. Many people have seen an old spirit man with long white hair in a braid, having a kind but serious face. Artists who have sketched him come up with similar drawings. That's how readily he manifests himself. And he tells people who come to the Canyon, "Don't come this way," and "Don't desecrate this area." He's what we consider a guardian of particular burial places.

And so the next day we continued our work at the vortexes. Just a few miles down the road from our resort, we stopped at Indian Gardens. This is a very beautiful lush section of Oak Creek Canyon that is easily accessible from the road. Indian Gardens used to be an important ceremonial place for natives, but now, Hawk told us, the natives feel the spirits have left this area. It is situated on one side of the road, across from a gas station and trading post, which are dwarfed by a massive canyon wall. As we strolled beneath towering trees, I sensed a quiet power and imagined how pristine the area must have been a hundred years ago.

Hawk asked us to make an offering of cornmeal into the creek. While we stood together near a huge boulder at the stream's edge, she spoke this prayer: "We started off in the Great Mystery, and that is where we will return. Differences in race and belief no longer matter here. We are one consciousness. The natives are asking us to help and pray and do our ceremonies. They are asking that the principles of nature not be changed so that this river will stay clean and the land will remain healthy enough to feed us. This is our common ground."

We continued along the winding Oak Creek Canyon road until we arrived in West Sedona, the main shopping area and the site of the city hall. Along both sides of the street, spectacular red rocks soared high above the buildings. As we turned onto Dry Creek Road, on our right appeared three rock formations, including a big domed mountain—Capitol Butte, which is 6,400 feet high and looks like a huge whale. The road curved downward, dominated by a vast luxuriant forest of juniper and pine. In the distance the fortresslike rock wall of Boynton Canyon rose above the sea of greenery all around. At a turn in the road, we saw signs for Enchantment Resort. Approaching closer, I could feel the mystique of the vortex. It was *awesome!*

We turned down a dirt road and parked.

"There are various paths that go to the buttes," Hawk told us, as we gazed at the fortresslike canyon wall. "This is a powerful place. This is a place to make ceremony and to heal. Here you can connect to the essence of what you are."

We followed a meandering trail amid a fascinating variety of greenery including juniper, manzanita, prickly pear, and ten-foot-high stalks of agave cactus. The very ground, trees, and shrubs exuded stillness and serenity. As I stopped to observe a bright blue bird inside a pine tree, I could hear the sound of my breathing. Almost as a reflex I felt a sense of reverence.

We stopped where an original medicine wheel made of stones used to be. Hawk said that a group of New Age people had taken it down and rearranged it using the same stones; as a result, the shrine was destroyed.

"When you see shrines and altars on the land," she said, "you can be a part of them, but don't put one up. There were tremendous disturbances here after the original shrine was taken down. We live in a world where people are crazy with fear and prejudice."

We spent a few moments in silence acknowledging the shrine. Black Eagle sprinkled cornmeal on the ground and said this prayer: "We came here in remembrance of souls here before us. We are sorry there are no stones here. Let us have a happy journey and no hatred, just happiness."

Continuing along the trail, we each went off on our own. I paid careful attention to how the energies were affecting me: I wanted to keep walking but at the same time to be still. As I sank deeper into the silence, I felt as though I were gliding along the trail; the crimson ground felt so soft. Fixing my gaze on the canyon wall I noticed a solitary spire that looked like a human figure with a head. As I learned later, the locals have named the spire Kachina Woman. I understand that she is regarded as a symbol of the ability to rise above confusion and attain mystical wisdom.

I moved farther along the trail until I felt compelled to sit down—I just wanted to close my eyes. My attention was being diverted away from what was around me; I was not looking at anything in particular; I was not analyzing. My mind stopped rambling. I would have been happy just to sit there for hours. It was as though I had stepped through an invisible door that offered a glimpse into a cosmic realm.

The stillness was immense. I became acutely aware of the energies around me as if the outer forms were falling away and the essences were baring their very souls for me. I felt very connected to the canyon. It was now a being, a force, that existed to remind me of the benevolent energy of the universe. There was nothing here that threatened or minimized me in any way. Instead I was being invited to trust myself. I was being invited to look at my life from a larger perspective. I realized certain things about myself that I could change; in particular, I didn't have to be so impatient—one of my least desirable qualities. The energy here was allowing me to view myself in a noncritical manner, with more acceptance and understanding. I was able to easily jump back into my past and recall incidents that had happened years earlier. "Unburden yourself, free yourself, be happy," the canyon seemed to be saying.

How long had I been there? I didn't know. Time had no relevance.

When we got back on the road, we drove past Enchantment Resort but did not go inside the grounds. A few years later when I visited Sedona, I learned that mistletoe had started to eat the trees in Boynton Canyon. When I wandered into the canyon one evening, I heard music blaring from the resort; it did not feel right—that music did not belong there. When I asked Hawk about this she said that the existence of the resort is changing the vibration of the land.

"My heart almost breaks when I think of the extraordinary splendor of that canyon," she said. "The natives fought for a long time not to have this resort built. Nothing should be built there."

And she told me a story about a Hopi elder who took some children to the canyon; one was a three-year-old boy. "The boy kept spinning around. Then he sat and stared up at the canyon and started to cry. His tears hit the sand and turned blue." She explained that this was Spirit telling us we have to leave this place, for Spirit speaks through children.

She said, "All that is there will go away." Boynton Canyon would become a desert! The thought of this happening was so disturbing that I wondered if it was too late to tear down that resort. Why don't people understand that we are not meant to build in such sacred places? For in the great rocks and canyons are the voices and whispers of the elders. The beauty is there for the many to enjoy.

We left the canyon and returned to the main road, continuing along the same route for about two miles. We turned right at Airport Road and drove a short distance up a meandering road. We stopped at a small parking area in front of a bluff, the location of Airport Vortex. Climbing up the rocky slope we arrived at a flat clearing between two hills. On one side of the clearing lay a steep gorge and stunning vistas in every direction: cliffs, spires, domes, and canyons were everywhere, *vibrating* with energy. We could see the bold shapes of Bell Rock and Courthouse Rock. The four towering citadels of Cathedral Rock were on Bell's right. Then we paced about forty feet to the other side of the clearing. From there we could see the winding road we had just come up, plus a sweeping view of all of West Sedona. The vortex energy there was wonderful. I could feel the electricity in the air. In fact, I was surprised at how quickly it energized me. Although we had been there for less than thirty minutes I was bursting with determination and drive.

"This area is considered a time doorway," Hawk said. "You have a perspective of the past and the future from this one central point. When you look to your right, you see the past. When you look to your left, you see the future."

On our right was the massive panorama that included Bell, Courthouse, and Cathedral rocks; these are our ancestors. On our left we had a bird's-eye view of West Sedona and the town's background of towering rock sculptures.

"Take a deep breath and breathe it back to the Ancestors," she said softly. We all stood at the edge and did that. Then we paced to the other side of the ridge to view Sedona, which appeared tiny nestled in the valley. Hawk urged us, "Look beyond the congestion and see in the distance the mist of hope. Look to a future where there is no malice, no hatred, and no bitterness." Tears streamed down our faces. "We need more places in the world where there is laughter," she added.

We did not have that much time, so we continued on. We drove through town over a bridge, past some tourist shops. Then we turned onto Schnebly Hill Road, which soon became a bumpy dirt road. As we climbed the steep wall of a canyon, our vehicles staggered and stumbled past exciting panoramas of uptown Sedona and surprising new rock formations. Trees, shrubs, and cacti emerged out of the redrock slopes along the road, which had become precariously narrow and twisting. After about thirty minutes of sharp curves, my body started to stiffen with fear. One wrong move and our car would go over the precipice! There was hardly enough room for vehicles to pass us. After a final sharp curve we reached the summit.

"This is called paradise!" Hawk exclaimed as we gazed at the spectacular view. We could see Oak Creek Canyon, Sedona, and the outline of mountains far into the distance. We were absolutely spellbound. It was as though we had reached a higher realm where heaven and earth meet. We felt that the experience of bliss could materialize here without much effort. We could feel our potential to make a divine connection to the entire universe.

At this point we had already been in and out of so many vortexes that we were *saturated* with earth energies. We were all experiencing overwhelming and conflicting emotions.

"The Ancients left messages for us in these vortexes," Hawk said to help us understand the intensity of our feelings. "You feel excited and happy but also depressed when you're here. You're in awe of Creator, and at the same time you're distressed by the garbled tapes in your mind."

She explained why the vortexes touched us on such a deep level.

"In a vortex exist tablets of thought forms left here by people before us. Our ancestors knew through a vision of the future how far humanity would go to destroy the Earth in order to have material comfort. They left a vibration in these vortexes that touches you on a cellular level. It awakens in you the possibility that you can have the good life with its material comforts *without* destroying the Earth."

We had arrived just in time to watch the clouds pile up in a rosy flare. All was ablaze with color. The setting sun cast pink and golden hues over miles of towering red rocks and lush valleys. We gathered in a circle and shared our deepest feelings; there was not a dry eye among us.

"All of you have felt that you did not fit in or belong," she said softly. That's because you're Thunderbeings. You're here to create a world without prejudice, where people can trust one another. You want to eliminate the need to destroy."

It grew dark. Black Eagle and Hawk made a ceremonial fire and worked with the spirits and beings in this area. They prayed for all people to return to one consciousness.

Then, as we have seen on many occasions despite a cloudless sky, a few raindrops kissed our faces, and Hawk told us, "This is the elders kissing us, cleansing us, and loving us. We are loved."

Whenever she says this, there is a distant glaze in her eyes and a childlike expression of peace and joy on her face. When I asked her why this rain had come, she said it was a confirmation from her elders that she had done good work.

As our journey came to a close in the darkness, we received a powerful communication from the heart of the Great Mystery. A dazzling display of pure luminescent lightning danced across the sky. The lightning surged from the heart of the Grand Canyon. The winds swirled in from every direction; we could feel them moving in response to us. As we raised our eyes from the horizon into the heavens we were rewarded with a magnificent view of the Milky Way. It appeared ever so close in a glorious blaze, reminding us of the lost paradise that we all longed to return to. It seemed to say, "You are the promise of the new world; you will open the path of the heart."

We were being sent a message of love! We were being celebrated because we are Thunderbeings! We felt the pull of a universal force. During these moments we resonated with the pure energy of the unseen harmonies that kept everything in their orbit, for what else could hold this desperate planet together?

Most of us experienced emotional breakthroughs at the Schnebly Hill vortex. In less than two weeks, we had made a giant leap in our spiritual development. How could we have done this in such a short time? How was it possible? The vortexes are powerful transformers, but our visits were brief. One has to remain at a vortex for at least twenty-four hours to absorb the incredible amount of energy that we had absorbed. How were we able to do this?

We were able to make quantum leaps at each vortex because we visited them first in our dreams and then in our waking state. We traveled to them on two separate occasions! In the dream state there are no limitations of time or how much energy we can absorb.

While we waited for our airplane at the Phoenix Airport, the teaching continued—it never stopped! Hawk gave us another glimpse into what our extraordinary human form is capable of as we come into the full realization of our abilities. She said very matter-of-factly that we were becoming skywalkers—actual people who walk on clouds! When we achieved full consciousness we would be able to walk among the clouds. She told us she had seen a skywalker not long ago while she was aboard an airplane.

"I was very busy with paperwork when I realized the person next to me had suddenly become quite startled and uneasy. I looked out the window and recognized a Native American elder walking right into a cloud. He looked at me and waved. Well, I realized he was a physical being. The person next to me just laid her head back and started breathing very hard and acting very strange. Meanwhile other passengers had also seen the skywalker. People started asking the stewardess if there had been any cabin pressure changes. They all thought they were having hallucinations in which we saw people walking around on the clouds.

"The stewardess said, 'No, we've already checked the cabin pressure because the pilot saw it too.' Anyway, the crew explained and rationalized the sight away as a decompression problem. The oxygen masks started flying, and the pilot made up an apology for the oxygen problem.

"Everyone ended up on my side of the plane. They looked at me real strange. One man asked, 'Do you see him, too?' And I said, 'That's a skywalker.' And he said, 'You don't seem all that surprised. Have you seen them before? You're not even impressed. A skywalker? No, that's impossible! There's no one out there.' But his eight-year-old son said, 'I don't know how you can say that Dad. Look! He's right there!'

"One woman had cold compresses on her forehead. A lot of people were complaining of vertigo and saying it was an omen of death.

"And someone else asked me, 'What was he doing in the sky?'

"I replied matter-of-factly that he was going for a walk. Maybe he walked right into the next cloud and into a big kachina cloud. He was probably thinking to himself, Damn, I can't even go for a walk these days without scaring all those third-dimensional people!"

We laughed and laughed.

Skywalking, she told us, is a common practice among some of the Maya, Hopi, and Muscalara people. There are people who can rise up and walk through the clouds. And we're not talking about spirit beings; we're talking about real physical forms walking on the clouds. We're talking about the principle of levitation. Skywalkers simply reach a higher level of levitation.

I asked Hawk about the bats we had seen that first night when we arrived at the Hopi motel.

"Those were shape-shifters. Didn't you see how extraordinary the behavior of those bats was?"

And I thought, Yes, there was something odd about them. They had hovered around Hawk and then disappeared! She explained that shape-shifters had expanded their minds to 100 percent consciousness and could take on the forms of other species. They simply used that species's principle, which lived within their being. We have something of all of God's creations within our body: mineral, plant, animal, water, air, earth, and fire. Ultimately, our body can do whatever we tell it to—fly, skywalk, or shape-shift. Shape-shifters capture a particular tone and then transform themselves. The process of shape-shifting involves sounds and smells that many people would consider grotesque.

"There are people who shape-shift," Hawk said. "They can be with you as a deer. They can be the hawk or the eagle or the snake. They can even be the whispering winds. They were with us constantly on our journey in Arizona."

And I remembered that almost everywhere we had driven, we saw red-tailed hawks circling above us.

CHAPTER 12

QUESTING FOR A VISION

The goal of life is living in agreement with nature.

—ZENO OF CITIUM

I'VE FOUND THAT THE greatest hunt in life is the hunt for a vision, a destiny. The people who speak to me as I hunt are my ancestors; they are my guides on this hunt. I am hunting for my prophecy, for my destination, not what has been prophesied for me by others but what was encrypted into my soul. In order to find my vision I withdraw from the world. In my seclusion, I reach out to the intelligent spirit of nature. I turn to all the creatures great and small and to the green growing beings in the wilderness to direct me to my prize; I learn to understand their language. While I feel fear because of the danger, I also feel the excitement of attaining my prize.

Modern-day people go hunting for a visionary state too, but they do it unknowingly—they call it a vacation. They set aside time to go to the country, or they get on a plane to escape the pressures of their lives. They've become bored or bogged down by troublesome responsibilities. They yearn for new meaning and new experiences, to be rejuvenated or spiritually renewed. They just don't go far enough with their quest.

By 1993 I had completed three vision quests. In fact, the quest was becoming an annual event for the Thunderbeings. Questing was an important part of returning to a balanced relationship with nature.

Without this balance, humanity would be doomed. One didn't have to look far to see the signs of our demise. The Thunderbeings were trying to show people the importance of seeking a vision. The Bible puts it beautifully: "Where there is no vision, the people perish."

We have grown so far away from the Earth that we no longer know how to understand her. We do not follow the movement of the sun; we have made the lightbulb our sun, and yet we are beings of the sun. We hide within the four walls of our homes, and our life force dries up. We don't even understand ourselves anymore. We seek, forever asking, "Who am I? Where am I going?"

Such troubling questions are answered when we return to nature; our alienation from ourselves is healed. There are no truths as great as the ones we find in nature, for nature never lies to us. The human urge to understand ourselves, to connect with someone or something is satisfied when we embrace nature.

Vision-seeking means setting aside time to draw inward so that we may listen to the voice of Spirit. The vision happens when we put aside the needs of our mind and body to make way for Spirit. In preparation for our vision-seeking, we purify ourselves: we fast, consuming only water, for several days, and just before setting out into the wilderness, we spend time in a sweat lodge.

Hawk told us that in ancient times priority was given to vision-seeking. People of all ages would go to private places and do what was necessary to affirm themselves to the Great Spirit.

A wonderful story helped me understand how close in spirit we were with the rest of the creation in the First World of our existence.

> In the days of the Second World, the people multiplied rapidly. They started to break their relationship with the rest of creation and venture outside the great gathering of living beings, in which there was no separation. The tree people looked at their human family and said: "I would not want to live outside the forest." They were referring to the one consciousness that existed then.
>
> The Bear said: "This is different from the great sleep; this idea of wanting

to be an individual is different from the experience of dreamtime." The great sleep and dreamtime were part of a pristine state of being completely in tune with the Earth and not having a separate identity. And Man tried to tell Bear what identity was. Deer also talked to Man. Deer walked on her back legs. She looked at Man and said, "When you say 'separate,' I feel a fright because you'll never understand me. I have taught you beauty and grace. And from you I have learned how to dream." And Man said, "Oh, no, I will never wander so far away from the great knowing as not to understand you."

The Owl was listening and studying and saw the dark countenance of Man contemplating his identity alone, away from the great forest.

Then the Eagle arrived and said to Man, "Old One, I bring a message to this gathering. Think very seriously. Aloneness has never been a need. This dream to have an identity can become very complicated. Sometimes a dream is a journey that can become very long, and the trail can change. You may never find your way back home."

And Owl said to Man, "You alone will forget how to come back. You will forget to give praise, and you will not hear the song of the sun or recognize the love of the stars. You will forget to give praise for all the blessings of the day."

But Man went on his search, and drew farther and farther away from the great gathering. The trees listened and spoke, but Man did not hear. The Bear came and scolded, "You do not listen!"

Man became afraid. The Eagle flew by, and Man said, "I wish I could fly."

And the Eagle said, "You fool."

The Owl said, "Who do you think you are?"

Man watched the songbirds and saw how involved the feathered people were with the sun. He listened to all the birds chattering. "Maybe if I sit and watch the sun, I will remember," he said.

The smallest sparrow said, "Do not worry, my friend. I have got you covered."

The chattering birds are praying for Man, who does not remember.

We separated ourselves more and more as we evolved through each world. We chose to be separate from the One, to do things our own way. Now we turn to our ancestral spirits to help us out of our confusion. They are within us, they are in our blood, and they give us wisdom through visions and dreams. But we must enter into the silence to hear their silent voices.

Most of our questing took place near Hawk's home, near the Poconos, amid hills, valleys and woodlands. The first few Thunder-beings who started questing (back in 1987) were unable to accept the idea of being completely alone in the wilderness without food, exposed to the elements, even for one day and one night. One Thunderbeing hauled a queen sized mattress into her tent! Another brought a Japa-nese lantern while others erected massive three-room tents. Now when we reminisce about those days—which we refer to as our Hollywood questing days—we laugh uproariously. And no part of this story brings more laughter than Tonya's lame scheme of sleepwalking to the kitchen to get late-night snacks!

Gradually we graduated from one-night quests to two-and three-night quests and so on. Indeed, the proper way is to keep on questing until we have a vision.

Hawk told us that when she quests she does not eat or drink for as long as it takes for the vision to come: "It could be four days or more; we stay until it comes. We live as Spirit in these times. We face nature and all our relations in as natural a state as possible. We stay exposed to the elements day and night, for this makes our visions more powerful."

First we had to choose a questing site among the hills and forest. We wandered around until we found a place that felt just right, where nature spoke to us. We then said, "I have come seeking my vision. Am I welcome here?" If we received an agreeable feeling or message, we would settle in. We would smudge the area and make offerings of cornmeal and tobacco. We would call on the spirit keepers to sanctify our circle. Then we would place four stones around our tent to rep-resent the four directions. We would remain within these perimeters, which we sealed with a ring of cornmeal for spiritual protection, so no harm would come to us during the quest. Such a small space also compels us to focus on our immediate surroundings.

As I prepared for my third quest, I felt terribly apprehensive. This would be my first winter quest, scheduled for the second week of December 1993. Expecting cold weather, I purchased a sleeping bag designed for below-zero temperatures, along with insulated clothes and wool socks. I had visions of knee-deep snow and of icicles hanging from my tent. But was I ever in for a surprise! When I arrived for my quest, along with twelve other Thunderbeings, there was a complete turnaround in the weather. It was almost balmy—no snow but lots of rain.

After we put up our tents, we climbed to the top of the hill. We were nervously clutching at the candles Hawk had asked us to bring. She talked until the sun reddened the western sky.

"We have begun to extract ourselves from nature," she told us. "We are in combat with nature most of the time. It is important for you to get involved with the land. Allow yourself to become part of the terrain. Ask the Mother to embrace you. Listen and move around. Speak to everything as an intelligence. Put aside all of your body's needs and empty your mind. Place your being back to the Earth. Ask for the strength and physical courage to do the quest."

She gave each of us a piece of bread and told us to eat half of it and give the other half as an offering to the Earth at our quest site.

"When your fears come to visit you, remember this moment and all of nature will come to assist you. Stay focused. Pray with your total being. Pray that your vision comes quickly. And be willing to accept and live up to your vision."

We entered her house and placed our candles above the fireplace. After we put a match to them, Hawk said, "You have now become vision seekers. Call to the ancestors and announce that you are here to seek a vision. Send your prayers to all who are to assist you."

At our quest site we were to gather stones and make a shrine to honor the four directions, the Above Beings, the Earth, and ourselves. We were to pray continuously for a vision, stating: "I come seeking, and I ask for a vision. Help me, hear me, Ancients."

Hawk said that when the vision came, it would be unmistakable: "You will feel empowered. You and Creator will be reconnected and back in flow as one."

The sun had already set when we started to walk over to the hill to our sweat lodge. We had come prepared, wearing our cotton wraps, and holding the clothes we would wear during our quest.

"The stone elders will purify you and prepare you for your vision journey," Hawk said, as we lined up near the fire where the rocks were heating up.

In the lodge, we prayed that a vision would come to us quickly. The lodge became very hot. Once we broke a sweat we were ready to begin our quest. We changed into our clothes and headed out to our sites. We followed a narrow dirt path across a grassy slope that descended onto a wide expanse of tall grasses, framed to the north and south by forest; to the west, a deep valley extended all the way to the horizon.

When I reached my quest site, I crawled into my sleeping bag, but I couldn't fall asleep. I soon realized that a tiny pool of water had formed inside my tent and was seeping into my sleeping bag. I complained for a while and then decided the wisest course was just to accept it.

The next morning, before dawn, I emerged from my tent. There was not a single snowflake! Here we were doing a winter quest and it was warm!

I had chosen the same site I'd used for my very first quest on this land, amid tall grasses that reached up to my waist, with views of the valley and forest. This morning the mist hung over the valley—it was magical. Suddenly, out of nowhere, I was seized by an urge to dance. I danced around my tent, trampling over the grasses, swinging my body, leaping into the air, doing all the dance steps I knew. I became wild with a desire to dance. The energy erupted in my body, as if something had broken free inside me. Why was I allowing myself to surrender my self-control? This had not happened on my previous quests—I was much more controlled.

Now I wanted nothing to hold me back, and since I was completely alone, I threw off my clothes. I rolled around in the towering grasses, and I could *feel* them respond to me with their own laughter. I felt acknowledged by the trees; they were happy to have me there with them. As I spun around on the ground I felt a total acceptance by the Earth. I believe she welcomed my jubilant behavior.

Later, when I described my experience to Hawk, she said that it is instinctual for four-legged creatures to roll around in the grass. She said that I was medicine dancing and that I had let the child out.

After I had exhausted myself, I lay back and closed my eyes. In my tranquil state, my thoughts turned to questions of infinitude. Where did the wind come from? It had to originate somewhere. Was it the breath of Earth?

Then it started to rain and the sky became as gray as stone. A massive canopy of grayness stretched above me, seeming to envelop me. My mood changed, and I started to feel melancholy.

By the end of the second day, I felt as if I were floating. I wasn't focused on anything in my immediate surroundings. I had shifted my attention inward, but I was even more aware of what was going on around me. I lay on the ground and just gazed into the sky for what seemed like hours. Time disappeared as I drifted through the vastness of space. I looked at my arms: they didn't seem to be attached to my body. I envisioned flying into a mythical forest where magnificent flowers burst into light and creatures with yellow manes strolled about. When I came out of my dream-like state, I knew I had gone somewhere; I knew that I had been *journeying.*

It continued to rain; in fact it rained almost continuously for the entire three days. A big puddle of water formed in my tent, and I found myself accepting it, unlike my reaction in the past. I realized how far I had come since my first quest four years earlier.

I'll never forget that first quest.

In the spring of 1989 I had arrived at Hawk's place with a tent, a sleeping bag, and a jug of water. Aside from the clothes on my back, these were my only questing accessories.

I had been fasting for several days on fruit and water. Nine other Thunderbeings had arrived, including Kevin and Doreen, who were there to assist Hawk. They were a very friendly and warm couple in their late forties, who lived and worked in Cincinnati. They had both quested before.

Hawk had told us that all of our inner doubts and fears would be reflected in the entities that came to us during our quest.

"Try not to give in to your fears or to the horrors your mind can create," she said. "Pray harder and louder if you become weak with fear. Go out there committed to the vision. I have known people who stayed out for weeks."

When we headed out to our quest sites, our only light came from a pale moon and a starry sky. Kevin pointed a flashlight at our feet and offered some words of encouragement. I stumbled down the hill, feeling my way through the shadows. We were all very solemn as we inched our way through the darkness.

"My spot is over there," I said, staring into the darkness to see if I could find my tent. I had chosen a place at the bottom of the hill, in the midst of tall grasses, up against a barbed-wire fence, with a bird's-eye view of the entire valley. I did not want to be too far away from Hawk, who was at the top of the hill. And neither did I want to be in the forest, which felt even farther removed from my known world.

I stumbled toward my tent. The others continued on, and I waited until their voices faded. I looked around at the darkness, full of anxiety. What lurked there? I remained still, listening to the night sounds: crickets, a gentle breeze playing with the leaves, a dog howling in the distance. I had been dropped outside the confines of my orderly structured world. What now?

Over the course of the next three days, I danced around my tent, prayed to the spirit keepers, chanted, examined caterpillars, snails, spiders, a bee, and other tiny creatures that came to visit me. A graceful, long-legged spider made her home in my tent, and once I overcame my apprehension, she became my quest companion. What had at one time seemed insignificant now became an important part of my survival. I realized that we think these little critters are unimportant only because we're not paying attention to them. During my quest I came to realize their significance.

I lay on the tall grasses and enjoyed the feeling of sunlight bathing my face. I played with the foliage of the trees near my tent. I experienced the pangs of hunger, and during my second night I dreamed about—of all things—lemon meringue pie! I listened to the voices in my head until all the issues of my life shouted at me. My mind became a tyrant; it wouldn't stop. I remembered what Hawk had said: "When you listen to your mind, you realize what a lunatic it is, with all of the doubts, the fears, and the devaluing of your experience." *How true.* I felt trapped; like a mountain cat, I paced around my tent dozens of times, wanting to pounce out of my lair.

I found that my greatest challenge was having to exist minute after minute and hour after hour in absolute silence with myself. This forced me to just sit and breathe and observe, which is not easy when you're used to racing through life. I propped myself up against my tent and studied every detail of the landscape. Sometimes I retreated into my tent to stare at the spider; she stared back at me with her small eyes, her head and thorax fused together, not spinning anything. At night I thought I felt the presence of a large animal, and I sat motionless, full of fear, for some time. Eventually I fell asleep. At dawn, mist blanketed the land, and the rising sun exploded in color under my gaze. I walked around my tent, praying for a vision. I must have spent countless hours gazing into the valley. At some point, pictures flashed across my mind of our first human ancestors. I envisioned the Earth in all her pristine beauty and an image came to me: three birds of paradise—exquisite colorful creatures with long tail feathers! The birds seemed to be singing: "You can have us; you can have us." Was this a vision?

I only realized the meaning of my vision as I was writing this and setting my thoughts on paper. About four years after my first quest I was given a gorgeous bird, which has become very special to me; the person who gave it to me had no knowledge of my vision. My bird of paradise is now a part of my life. Her eyes have become windows into the natural world. Even in my office I can look into her eyes and escape into the Amazon jungle.

I recall now that during the moments that I envisioned, I was able to transcend the chatter of my mind and feel an openness to everything around me.

My day revolved around the movement of the sun; at night the moon became my focus. I could feel myself changing at sunset and becoming more introspective. As Hawk said, different life-forms come alive at night and others go into deep sleep and follow the sun in a dream state. My life was simplified to this very basic and raw state. I was stripped of all paraphernalia—there were no cars, no computers, and no cement walls here. I had come face-to-face with myself—there was nowhere to hide. All of my concerns and fears revealed themselves to me in a stark, almost harsh, manner.

On the last day of my quest, I watched the sun impatiently. When it reached its zenith, the quest would be over. At high noon the sound of drumming came from the top of the hill. Then a voice shouted: "The quest is over!" I ambled slowly up the hill. Hawk was waiting for me at the top. First she bathed me in her sweet smoke blessing. Then she held out her arms, and I fell into her embrace, weeping.

"You had a vision."

I needed to hear that. Did I ever need that confirmation!

"You are not just some sophisticated city girl. You have courage."

I smiled, wiping away my tears.

"Go get washed." She smiled tenderly.

After our quest we tried not to speak or look into anyone's eyes in order to stay focused on recording every single aspect of our experience. Hawk gave us tea, Gatorade, toast, and soup that she had made. As we lay in bunk beds on the second floor of the house, I started to feel the effects of my quest. A wonderful energy flowed through my body. I felt alive; my mind was clear and free of its usual rambling. After writing for some time, I arose and slowly made my way down the stairs. Feeling as light as a feather, I lost my balance and stumbled down the last few stairs.

"Are you okay?" Hawk asked, running out of the kitchen.

"Yes." I laughed, a little shaken but rising up from the floor.

She explained that the left side of my brain, the side that controlled logic, was disoriented. Questing had pushed me over into my intuitive side.

As we became experienced questers, we extended the length of our quests, and some Thunderbeings started to quest inside the Earth. A hole was dug about six feet deep and at least five feet wide with a tarp covering the opening in the event of rainfall.

My second quest, which was prolonged to almost four days, took place the following year in September: warm days and cool nights. I found a flat, grassy area surrounded on three sides by forest. Here birds glided and flitted about. A snail came to me, waving its antennae, symbol of higher consciousness and heightened perception. A caterpillar crawled on my tent, and I thought of the stages it would go through, turning into a chrysalis and after that into a butterfly; I smiled at the similarity of our experience. Inside my tent two spiders made their home, and one started to spin a web—symbolizing new energies coming into being? As well, a yellow butterfly danced around me. Later Hawk would tell us that a yellow butterfly symbolized divine intelligence and transformation.

During the night I paid careful attention to sounds, fearing to venture out of my tent, imagining all kinds of animals approaching. I felt a spider on my neck and jumped. My fear grew intense the next night when thunder rumbled with such ferocity that the wind whipped my tent and shook the trees; the temperature dropped sharply. This was some kind of communication—but what?

My days were taken up with studying sunrises, cloud designs, sky, trees, mist, blossoms, shadows, and insects. I experienced moments where my self seemed to vanish. Nighttime took me into other corridors of my being. The chattering of crickets, the rustling of leaves, the dainty movement of ground creatures. I peered into the luminous golden light of the moon and saw faces: a funny face, a sacred face, and the face of an extraterrestrial being. As I gazed at the forest's luxuriant foliage, images emerged of Mayan masks, African masks, Chinese masks. Was this a vision? As I crouched down at the edge of the forest, immersed in silence, something stirred inside me. Suddenly a ten-foot-tall fire deity appeared with a serpent coming out of its mouth and ferocious flaming eyes. Scenes of a lost civilization were manifested in my consciousness.

By the third day I was yearning for a shower and for an animal to come and play with me. In a very short time I got my wish. The rain came; its gentle drizzle bathed me, and I threw myself on the wet grass; it was almost as good as a shower. I looked up and saw a hawk circling and wondered what that meant. Then our group's dog leaped joyously toward me, wagging her tail, her big brown eyes seeming to say, "You asked for an animal—well, here I am!"

As the final hours of my quest approached, I became restless and frustrated. I realized I wasn't doing a pure vision quest because I was following the rigors of a structured time frame. I decided that my next quest had to be in a more isolated place and on my own time.

When it was time to leave, I struggled up the hill. As Hawk greeted me with her smoke blessing, I looked forward to the comforts of food and bathing. After rushing to take off the clothes I had lived in for four days, I stepped into a hot shower, squealing with delight.

By the following day, all eleven Thunderbeings had returned from their quest sites. After we had bathed, eaten, and written in our journals, we met with Hawk. We looked as fresh as morning dew, renewed from our encounter with nature. Hawk sat in a white wicker chair, studying us. I looked into her eyes and sensed that she already knew what each of us had personally experienced.

She spoke in a low melodic tone; her hands moved in a pronounced and expressive manner: "When you seek a vision, you have decided inside your being that you want a vision. Each time you've quested you have found a little more of yourself. But the mind is still your focus, not the heart. You are so much of the mind. When you quest you must be committed to a vision. You must spend time praying, dancing, and chanting. You can't get there on food or water. It takes courage. The next time you quest you need a greater commitment to really seek a vision."

I gathered that most of us had not come back with a vision.

"First you have to free yourself from your mind," Hawk continued. "You do that by constant ceremony and prayer, not by thinking that you're cold or hungry. Spirit doesn't think of temperature, hunger, or thirst.

"I know how powerful you are and that you were prepared to face all of your fears, endure the cold, the hunger, and all of what is going on in your lives. But you still do not believe that the bee or the bird or the ground creature can be your answer. Being a part of the elements is a new way for you. The spirit world showed itself in the mist; the Ancestors came to you in the mist, but you did not see that.

"Still, you are very courageous. The women in my grandmother's village would celebrate such courage. Still, you prayed and waited. You have much courage and much love." She spoke softly.

She asked us to talk about our experiences.

Maria, a Spanish woman who had never quested before, told us: "I began my relationship to nature with a fly. I heard the sound of the wind in the forest; I have liked the wind since I was a child. I felt alive, and I put my body on the Earth . . . but I had many fears. All the time I felt something was around me. One night I dreamed about this beautiful woman with long dark hair . . . and the next night, *la tormenta* [the storm]!"

Hawk then turned to Nora: "What happened in your quest?"

"I think it was the second night," Nora began. "I imagined that a bear was sitting on my tent! I don't know if I was dreaming or wide awake."

Hawk told her she wasn't imagining it. "You physically encountered that bear. But your fear wouldn't allow you to know that. So your mind took you into another dimension."

The sensation that Nora had was very much like waking up from a dream and wondering if it was just a dream. It felt so real that it takes a moment to realize you were dreaming; in fact, you might have found yourself in a panic to resolve the dream even though you were already awake.

After we had all shared our experiences, Hawk gave the most profound lesson on nature I had ever come across. She spoke with the eloquence of one who had an intimate relationship to the animal and insect worlds. She helped us to understand that every creature and force of nature manifested some aspect of the intelligence of the one source that lived in all things. Every creature that came to us during our quest reflected something about us.

"Why didn't we see the rain as the tears of our grandmother coming to kiss us and cleanse us and heal us? Why didn't we see that it was the power of our heart that called the wind? When we sang, the wind came." When we heard the phrase "all my relations," we still didn't feel the true meaning of it.

We are one with the trees, birds, crawling creatures, clouds, sun and moon. We think these are things that *perform* around us. But we are a part of the gears of creation. Each time we get closer to the Earth we provide an opportunity to emerge into the awesome acknowledgment that we are interconnected with the whole planet; we are coming into brief moments of this.

Hawk told us that we needed to work harder if we wanted to receive a vision. "It would have been good to come back with a profound vision," she said. "But much more commitment is necessary for that to happen. What we extend is what we get back. At the beginning you are critical and complaining about the hunger and the cold, feeling sorry for yourself.

"But who you are with out there is *you*."

She proceeded to enact a little drama, speaking all the voices of the environment and the creatures that came to visit us during our quest. It was as though she were providing a mirror for us to look into.

"For the environment, you are great entertainment. They look at you and say: 'You come to perform for us again. What is it that you want, you two-legged?' And they hear you say, 'I want everything. I want even more than abundance. I want to be a magnificent healer. I want it all!' " she said, exuberant and playful.

We chuckled.

"All of creation looks at you and says, 'Oooh, this is called a human predicament.'

"The ant people say, 'We understand organization; we build complex homes.'

"And they hear you pray, 'I want my life to come together. I want to be everything I can be. I want to construct my dreams into reality.'

"Ant says, 'I come. My human relation wants to learn.'

"Ant crawls up on you and you go, 'Oooh!'

"Ant says, 'Maybe I have not heard correctly!'

"You cry that you want to learn the medicines and work with the forces of nature. Many ants come to help you and you cry. The ant is puzzled!

"Then come the bee and the fly, and they say, 'Maybe we should help first.' The ant says to the bee, 'You go first.'

"Bee says to you: 'Be productive. Do. Become busy. Take action to make your life more fertile.' And you scream when bee buzzes around you.

"The fly says, 'Oh, maybe they are afraid. I will try now.'

The fly teaches us consistency and determination. But with a swipe of an impatient hand we shoo him away.

" 'It's not my message they want either,' the fly says to the bee.

"Then the glowworm comes to show us that life is a pattern, like breathing in and out. It teaches us tranquillity and peace of mind. We say, 'What's that? That's kind of nice.'

"The glowworm says, 'They don't know the patterns.'

"The caterpillar says, 'Life is all a matter of unfolding.' The grass-hopper jumps and then stops. In its stillness there is action. It is communicating in sign language, showing that there is action in stillness and that silence is loud. It takes a leap of faith for the grasshopper to jump into the unknown; he is showing us that it is important to get off our haunches and take a leap forward in our life.

"The slugs and the snails teach us that within the self all things are contained. Their message is 'Take courage and know that wherever you are is where you need to be.'

"When you prayed for illumination, the winged ones came. But you didn't say, 'Greetings, my relations.' "

There we were earnestly seeking proof of our oneness with creation, and we missed what was right in front of our noses: everything in the cosmos had come forward to communicate with us!

"You say that you want proof that you are part of all things," Hawk continued. "The thunder comes and rumbles in the Earth, *not* in the heavens. Creator sends you lightning and winds. The blue rays of the cosmos also come to cut away your illusory separation from the land—and you call it cold.

"Nature works only with truth—unadulterated, unbiased truth. Sometimes we can't take it. But these are the principles of life, and we have become separated from them. We don't know how to deal and harmonize with their simplicity; that is why we have illness and death. We don't hear the tree's laughter. We think the insects are there to pester us. We don't know that the sun means we have another day of life."

When we start to understand the Earth, we see that she always responds to us. She is a caring, nurturing mother.

Slowly, as our fear subsides, we begin to hear the Earth. She knows how to host us better than we've ever been hosted. You need to sleep? There is always some gentle part of the Mother—"Lay your body next to me," she says. "You would love to hear and see the beauty of the forest? That is why I have made this place near the honeysuckle bush," she says. "You need to be protected and warm? Take the branches from my trees and lay them around you."

Earth gives us everything we need. But we don't see this because we are so fixed on the illusions that our mind creates. We think we're battling nature, but it is ourselves that we're at war with.

In spite of our fears, we were determined to go through with our quest. We persevered and stayed out there when we thought the worst might happen. No, we don't hear the Earth Mother yet, but we know that we need to work harder to control our thoughts, for a single false idea can bring on fear or despair. When we catch ourselves dwelling on thoughts we don't want, we must sing a chant. We must override our habitual thoughts. We must go deep inside ourselves and maintain our focus, always remembering our ideal and being completely committed to not losing ground. That is the way of the true spiritual warrior who never quits.

Everything that happens in our quest mirrors our inner state, whether it's a bolt of lightning, a cloud formation, or a butterfly.

Why do so many ants come? Because what is missing in our life is good organization. Ants teach us the pattern of organization.

When I prayed for better relations, to have loving and trustworthy companions, the dog appeared.

Why does a spider come to us? If she spins a web, it shows us that we are the center of our own world, which we spin by our thoughts, feelings, and actions. If the spider is just sitting and not spinning, she is reminding us that we need to be more creative.

When we prayed for illumination and to rise above our obstacles and see things more clearly, the hawk came.

When we prayed for transformation and for our weakness to be lifted, the peace eagle came.

Each time we prayed for change, the winds came.

When we called out to Creator, the thunder and lightning danced around us. But we retreated into our tents!

All of nature looks at us and says, "But we give you all these things!"

And we say, in our childlike, almost whining tone, "I don't know what I am doing wrong. I have no food and no water, and still I have no vision!"

It is truly remarkable to see how distant we have become from nature. It's almost ludicrous. We have hidden behind steel and concrete and built a window to look out into the world. We have imprisoned ourselves with our own devices.

The next day I returned home. The effects of the vision quest stayed with me for some time. I felt exhilarated, for the Earth had given me new energy.

After my third quest, I realized how far I had come. It was as though the first two quests were practice sessions. I was finally able to really let go and feel connected to the Earth. I had burst from my cocoon. My wings had taken form. Nothing could hold me down. I was still the same person, but I had been transformed. Like the butterfly, I could now see the big picture; I wasn't dependent on one flower; I could go wherever I wanted and experience my life to its fullest.

I have felt the Earth respond, and I know that she will take care of me. Does that mean I will have no fear the next time I quest? No, but I will be able to control it. I will communicate with myself and understand my fears. I will trust myself. I have the courage to move forward and accept what the unknown holds for me.

Hawk was waiting for me with a big smile on her face

"What did you think of *that* weather for a winter quest?" she said, beaming from ear to ear.

"I couldn't believe how warm it was," I said, happy to see her.

Later when we all had gathered, she explained that, yes, the weather beings had been very cooperative. We prayed for warm weather, and we got it. But it was not that simple—we must first be respectful of the forces.

"Everything in nature cooperates," she said. "But understand this: we don't conjure it up or demand it or bid it to respond to our will. The elements have come in cooperation with us. Everything that is intelligent will cooperate. It is not that we have power over the elements—they came in honor of our desire to help the world."

Questing was helping us return to a balanced relationship with Earth. She is the true mother of our bodies; she is a living being with a soul. She is the one thing that we must love with all of our passion. We need three things to survive: first, air, because we can survive for only a few seconds without it; then water, because we can survive only a few days without it; and then food. All three are generously provided by Mother Earth without asking for anything in return other than our respect.

One of the greatest gifts of the vision quest is the opportunity to transcend our limitations. Without even realizing it, we have built cages around ourselves with our houses and concrete jungles. Questing forces us to tear down those bars. We step out of the monotony of the rat race and start identifying with the natural forces. We find ourselves in boundless space without barriers. We expand and become stronger; our intuitive abilities return. We realize that reality is far more vast than what our minds can comprehend. We become better equipped to handle the ups and downs of life because we understand what is really important; we feel connected to something larger. Today's concept of individualism excludes this connectedness. We have become a "me-me" generation. We are mainly concerned with what *I* can get for myself. Who cares about others? Where's the harmony and balance in that? Living like that creates movement in one direction, which goes against the laws of nature. Everything in nature happens in cycles and in an harmonious balance of give and take. If all of it is going inward, we're going to burst. We can't live like that anymore. That mentality has caused the extinction of other species around us and will lead to our own.

As the Thunderbeings continued to quest, eventually all of the luxuries, such as having a tent, except in winter, were dropped. By the fifth year, there were no more Hollywood quests.

Gradually we were becoming attuned to the Earth. We were getting in touch with Spirit, learning to live with a sense of freedom to do as Spirit does. We were on our way back to a feeling of oneness with all forms of life. In healing our separation from nature, we were breaking a genetically inherited pattern that has persisted for countless generations.

CHAPTER 13

RETURN TO ATLANTIS

Progress, man's distinctive mark alone,
Not God's, and not the beasts: God is, they are;
Man partly is, and wholly hopes to be.

—ROBERT BROWNING

HAWK PUT OUT AN urgent call that she had to be in the Azores before the end of 1993. She needed at least ten Thunderbeings to accompany her.

John, a Thunderbeing who was born in the Azores, agreed to act as our guide for the two-week journey. It was determined that we would make the trip in early fall. When the time arrived, we all traveled to Toronto from various cities and met at the airport to board a late evening flight.

When everyone had arrived, I counted fourteen Thunderbeings, including an attorney, a beautician, a business executive, an engineer, a nurse, and a secretary, ranging in age from twenty-two to forty-five. Gathered just outside the entrance to the departures level of the airport, we greeted each other with hugs, filled with anticipation of another cosmic adventure.

"Hello, hello!" Hawk embraced each of us. She had brought her son, David, along for the journey. He was a Thunderbeing, so that made fifteen of us, plus Hawk.

It felt good to be together again. On the plane, conversation and laughter kept us awake for almost the entire five-and-one-half hour flight. At some point, the topic naturally turned to Atlantis, since Hawk had described our journey as "a return to Atlantis." The Azores are the remaining peaks of that vast and highly advanced civilization. She said that these islands are one of the great power points of the planet and far older than Atlantis itself.

"Do the Portuguese believe that Atlantis still lies under the ocean?" I asked John, who was sitting behind me.

"Yes, the Azorean people pride themselves on the fact that the islands are believed to be the location of Atlantis."

Quickly some of the others joined the discussion.

"Apparently, Atlanteans used crystals to generate energy and also to increase their mental ability."

"Edgar Cayce [a well-known American psychic] believed they used large laserlike crystals to run their power plants."

It is generally accepted that Atlantis existed where there are now the Azores, the Canaries, Madeira, and in the western Atlantic, the Bahamas. These islands may be the mountain peaks of a greater island continent that existed thousands of years before Babylon. According to Charles Berlitz, author of Atlantis: The Eighth Continent, many earlier cultures throughout the world have preserved the memory of "a great island empire that sank into the sea as a result of a worldwide disaster which shook the foundations of the Earth."

One of the oldest accounts of Atlantis is given by the Greek philosopher Plato. In 355 B.C., Plato wrote about a mighty empire that dominated much of the Mediterranean; it had a carefully structured class system whose citizens enjoyed a high standard of living, magnificent harbors, lavish gardens, and immense temples covered with silver, gold, and ivory. These temples were dedicated to the gods in honor of the royal dynasty that began with Poseidon, god of the sea, who fell in love with a mortal, Cleita, who lived on a great mountain in Atlantis.

Plato described the Atlanteans as honorable people who loved virtue and were not intoxicated by luxury. "For many generations," he wrote, "as long as the divine nature lasted in them, they were obedient to the laws and well affectionate toward the gods." But somewhere something went wrong. Had limitless luxury taken its toll? As Plato wrote, "This divine portion began to fade away in them, and became diluted too often . . . and their human nature got the upper hand."

When the Atlanteans turned away from the love of wisdom and virtue, they became corrupted by lawless ambition and power. This angered the gods who brought upon them massive earthquakes and floods; Atlantis sank suddenly and violently.

It was about 6:00 A.M. and overcast when we flew over the archipelago of the Azores; the nine islands are the most isolated in the entire Atlantic Ocean. According to my in-flight magazine, the islands are located about 760 miles west of Portugal; they belong to that country but have their own local government.

"Look!" Hawk said as we approached one of the islands. "It looks like a huge breast sticking up over the clouds!"

"That's Pico Mountain," John told us, leaning closer to the window. "It's often shrouded in clouds like that."

As I looked out the window, I wondered what megalithic structures lay buried deep under the ocean. What secrets lay submerged.

Atlanteans were capable of interdimensional communication and had the ability to control sound and light as well as to transcend time-space. But they misused these powers. As Edgar Cayce pointed out, the Atlanteans had made such alterations in the affairs of the Earth as to bring destruction upon themselves, and perhaps this caused an imbalance in the collective consciousness upon the Earth and the Earth itself.

Our plane landed on São Miguel, the largest island in the archipelago. When we had collected our baggage, John hailed some cabs for us. It was a ten-minute drive into Ponta Delgada, through a labyrinth of one-way cobblestone streets lined with trees, through which we could see the ocean. We stopped in front of the hotel John had booked for us.

"Somebody told me that this is a nice hotel," he said as we looked up at an imposing whitewashed structure with black stone arches. But after we'd carried our baggage up several flights of stairs to our rooms, we were surprised to find that our five-star hotel was missing four stars.

We found broken shower heads, peeling paint, and mismatched bedspreads. While we were deciding what to do, three of our group went out to rent two cars and a minivan.

"Whoever told you about this hotel has a different set of standards," Hawk said. "We need to get away from here. Where can we go that is a little more quaint?" she asked John.

"The closest place," he replied, "is the lakes."

With that decision made, we regrouped on the street and hurried off in our rental vehicles. A winding two-lane road cut a path through gently sloping pastures and rows of cone-shaped hills that had been created by volcanoes. Dark patches of forest were interspersed with fields accented with vibrantly colored wildflowers. John informed us that the island is even more vibrant when the hydrangeas are in full bloom. The very road seemed to disappear into the lush, luxuriant carpet of greenery that envelops this enchanting island. I sensed the isolation of the land, like a little world set off on its own—a dreamy place suspended in time, where the winds of the ocean meet. Perhaps these islands, once fiery craters and cinder cones, had emerged from the very core of the Earth, from her soul?

We could hardly contain our excitement as we came upon a most exquisite view. Parking our vehicles, we scrambled out at a lookout point. Before us lay two lakes in the crater of an extinct volcano having a perimeter of about twelve kilometers. The lakes, which are separated by a narrow land bridge, look like huge craters just touching each other. The one closer to us was emerald green while the one farther away was a deep vibrant blue. Shimmering transparent waters were framed by low, lush vegetation rising up steep slopes. Huge ancient faces stared back at us, carved into the mountain that hugged the entire edge of the blue lake. Some of us said they felt as if we had walked into the mythical, lost land of Shangri-la. I turned around and noticed, just above us on a higher elevation, a hotel that seemed to appear out of nowhere. On first glance, it looked closed, for there were no vehicles or any sign of people. "Look!" I said excitedly. We walked a little closer up a steep gravel road. Hawk suggested that we find out if it was open and asked five of us to check it out. Looking up, I noticed a stand of tall cedars cloaking the hill that towered above the hotel.

We discovered that indeed the hotel was empty. The manager

was only too happy to have our business and offered us half-price on the usual rates. The modern four-story structure was going to place us in the lap of five-star luxury: canopy beds and bathrooms as large as a Manhattan apartment, appointed with huge sunken tubs. It looked as if we would have the entire hotel to ourselves!

It was some time past 5:00 P.M. when, after having settled into our rooms, we met in the lobby. Bursting with excitement and eager to explore our new surroundings, we hurried into our vehicles and ventured toward the bottom of the crater. Descending a steep, winding road past tree-covered hills, we drove over the bridge and into the village of Sete Cidades, named after the seven cities of Atlantis. We arrived at the lakes and parked near the edge of the blue lake. Legend has it that great palaces and monuments of Atlantis lie under the bottom of these lakes.

"Look at that! Isn't that gorgeous?" Hawk exclaimed. We made our offerings and drew close, huddled around her. The luminous green and blue of two bodies of water existing side by side created a beguiling scene. John told us that the lakes were the subject of many myths. In one myth, the lakes were supposedly formed by tears shed over a broken love affair, one by a green-eyed princess and the other by the blue-eyed peasant boy she loved.

The soft and radiant energy of the lakes had a powerful impact on us. We were feeling some strong emotions that were difficult to express—there was something here that spilled forth the essence of ancient times and other dimensions.

Then Hawk said that this was where celestial beings arrived and departed; this was some kind of doorway for them into the Earth. This was where they lived out the legends that we now talk about, legends based on real historical events. Indeed, there are some—such as Ignatius Donnelly, who published a book about Atlantis in 1882—who claim that "the gods and goddesses of the ancient Greeks, the Phoenicians, the Hindus, and the Scandinavians were simply the kings, queens, and heroes of Atlantis"!

We spent some time enjoying the solitude, for the winds seemed to come to a halt. As we sat at the very edge of the blue lake, excitement arose in us as we became aware of the spirit beings in the environment.

"The nature spirits are alive here," Hawk said with obvious delight. "They would not live here unless people communicated with them." By now I understood that spirits are often absent because of our indifference. Unless we respond to them, the spirits of a place exist in suspended animation until they're recognized and appreciated again.

"The people in the villages practice Catholicism," Hawk went on, "but many in the valley still follow the old religion and work closely with the natural elements."

John mentioned that while religious festivals honoring the saints are very popular both on the islands and on the mainland of Portugal—with the more important festivals including an elaborate procession through the streets—old ancestral rites are still observed. He told us about some of the pagan practices in honor of gods and goddesses that personify natural phenomena that "take place under the guise of Catholic saints." On Saint John's feast day, for example, many of the locals get together to celebrate the return of the sun god. As part of their celebration, they leap over bonfires because originally it was thought that the higher they jumped the higher their crops would grow.

We had been there for some time when we noticed, in the pale light of the moon, something at the center of the lake. Hawk asked us what we saw.

"We're not sure," some of us stuttered, while John, one of the first to overcome his doubts, said slowly: "I see two pillars of light dancing with each other. They're moving in harmony with each other."

Hawk asked him to point to them, and he did. She confirmed that indeed there were two columns of light hovering and gliding above the water. I looked around and observed everyone's eyes focused on the same spot above the water. The longer we looked the more we realized that we were not imagining them.

"Beloveds, this is the fountain of youth, where time stops," Hawk said in a soothing, gentle tone. "The water in this lake runs through into the other universes. There is no bottom here. This water runs through into the center of the Earth." I knew by now that she was referring to vibratory energies, for she always saw beyond the physical. Indeed, I could feel my energy shift into a physical sensation of lightness. And when Hawk whispered that there was a vortex here that was connected to the inner earth and that all of us lived in the inner earth 650 million years ago, it seemed fantastic, but why not? We are ancient souls from ancient places that we can't even begin to fathom. We *are* magical beings, and our origins *are* fantastic.

She went on to tell us that at an earlier time twin pillars of solid crystal stood here in this very spot, on the surface. They contained passageways that permitted entrance into their interior: they were the original towers of crystal that are referred to in many of the myths and legends about Atlantis, that have been passed all the way down to modern times.

The crystal structures buried beneath the ocean floor symbolized for me the powers we could have as Atlanteans returning to Earth, illumined beings who have learned the lesson not to destroy.

As we made a spiritual offering of cornmeal at the edge of the lake, the mist became so thick that it engulfed us. The nature spirits were welcoming and embracing us. Hawk took out a smudge bowl, lit the cedar and sage, and passed it around. We watched the smoke carry our prayers of thanksgiving for the blessings that this day had brought.

We returned to the hotel. Hawk asked us to meet her in fifteen minutes at the entrance to the dining hall. Once seated at a long, lavishly decorated table, she broke bread and passed it around as an expression of gratitude.

I looked around and noticed there was nobody else here, just us. We were pampered by five or six staff members, who brought us swordfish steak and rolled in carts of desserts. Each time we took a sip of mineral water, they would be there, poised, ready to fill our glasses to the brim again. Each crumb that fell on the table was swept up by a handheld gadget with a silver handle.

The conversation zigzagged between the sacred and the profane. Phillip said that when we arrived on the island he'd developed a serious headache that subsided only after we had visited the lakes.

"The top of my head was pulsing . . . but being near the waters seemed to take the headache away," he told us.

Hawk shared recent incidents in her life and we laughed uproariously while the staff, who understood a smattering of English looked on with straight faces. Toward the end of our meal, Hawk asked us to come to her room on the second floor. It was about 11:00 P.M. when we gathered. We reviewed some of the day's events, talking about everything from the weather to the food to the hotel and how long we might stay in São Miguel.

At this time we also dispensed with our watches. As before, we did this to escape the prison of our schedules and the constraints of mechanical time. It was the way back into the ocean of superconsciousness. José Argüelles has said that we are the only species on this planet that wear watches; we are the only ones who do not live according to our natural timing frequency. We have been following a timing device that is mechanistic and speeded up, and that is what has happened to our minds.

We also started our practice of silence; when we were in our rooms we did not talk or engage in chatter. The silence and "being off the clock" shifts us into an alternate reality, into a vision place, that magical place deep inside ourselves. We become aware of what was there all the time but which we can't see because we're so caught up in our monotonous, synthetic everyday lives.

It was very late when I returned to my room, yet I tried to meticulously record the day's events in my journal; soon I found myself falling asleep. In the morning the phone rang: it was our wake-up call from Hawk. We slipped outside to greet the first light of dawn, seated on the rocky slopes around the hotel. As we have done before, we meditated in appreciation of the rising sun, which has given us another day of life.

Then we gathered in the formal breakfast area to share our first meal of the day. This time we were seated at a number of small tables that had been arranged near a large window offering a view of the blue and green lakes. Looking over, I noticed Hawk sitting with David and John. It was especially beautiful this morning as the mist rolled up the side of the mountain and above the lakes.

"You could get drunk on the scenery here," we heard Hawk say. We ate breakfast totally absorbed with the view, just like children watching our first Disney movie.

We returned to our rooms and gathered what we needed. When we regrouped in the lobby, Hawk invited us to go back into town to do some shopping. It was important for us to move together, for that was how we became one consciousness and magnified our Thunder-being energies.

When we stepped outside, the air was cool but comfortable. We seemed to arrive in Ponta Delgada unusually fast, although I knew it was at least a thirty-minute drive. We walked around the cozy narrow streets enjoying the Baroque structures of this flat, rectangular town built of volcanic basalt. We sampled pastries and café au lait and examined wickerware, hand-painted pottery, and embroidered linen. We all purchased colorful blankets, which would help us fuse with the energy of the land.

In the early afternoon it started to drizzle and we headed back to our hotel. As we drove past views of the sea and luxuriant vegetation, I realized I was feeling extremely calm, not trying to control the outcome of anything. At this point I noticed segments of time passing by in no clear sequential order. Suddenly I looked out the car window and realized we were driving up the steep winding road that led to our hotel. It seemed that just a moment ago we were in town.

In our discussions we agreed that not having to observe a time-piece is a delightful experience that allowed us to move between the worlds. We became less attached to form and our focus turned to the present moment. We stopped analyzing and judging our experience, and just let it happen. Our vision expanded; we became like the eagle. We had the sensation that we were gliding slowly and silently. So much more was revealed to us when we let go of our attachment to a clock or a Gregorian calendar.

When we arrived at the hotel, Hawk invited us to her room and out on the balcony. A cool breeze caressed our faces. Down below, the mystical waters of the green lake beckoned us. It was magical. We sang to the spirit of the lake, and she responded to our offering of love. She expressed her emotion through a display of ripples, like sign language, in a constant repetitive pattern on the surface of the water.

The spirit of the lake had come up and was singing to us. We called her the Green Lady of the Inner Earth. The surface of the lake was her divination tool. In the silence we could hear the voice singing to us; it was an audible and true sound. Josephine, a talented song-writer, later wrote a song from the melody that the lake gave us.

We had not been standing there long when the mist rolled in and thickened. The Ancestors were visiting us; thousands of Ancestors were dancing around us! The presence of mist and moisture enabled them to come to be with us—the negative ions helped them walk into our three-dimensional physical world. When we sensed their presence in the distance or felt something walking beside us, we acknowledged the Spirits, for if we dismissed them they would come less often; they would take it as rejection.

This was a tantalizing moment for Hawk to reveal why we had come to the Azores.

In a whisper, she said that humankind had lost its sixth and seventh senses. The sixth was our vision sense: "We used to be able to see through everything and talk to everything, including the stones, the birds, the four-leggeds, the trees, the winds, and the mountains." The seventh was our sense of integration, which enabled us to transform ourselves into light. She went on to say that at one time, fourteen temples of quartz crystal surrounded the Earth and that crystals were formed from the love of how we reflected God.

When all was said, I had a thousand questions. But Hawk, being the wise shaman that she is, does not always give away answers too easily. Instead, she encourages us to find them on our own. Did the Atlanteans develop those crystal chambers? And did the energies they worked with interfere with the natural energy flows of the Earth? My mind raced ahead trying to piece it all together.

Some believe that the inner Earth contains a powerful crystal whose energies radiate out and form an etheric geomagnetic grid. The Earth is just like us: a global grid system forms her circulatory and nervous systems; she has an etheric body that contains energy centers and acupuncture-type points. The grid carries communications between all living beings—indeed, our consciousness is interconnected with the consciousness of the planet. If the energies are not moving freely within the grid lines, we as humans likewise experience blockages, and we lose our higher senses. All beings who are attuned to the grid—including migratory birds who have followed it for millions of years—are affected.

Hawk said that the Azores area is a vital connection in the Earth's grid and that if the energies in this area are destroyed, humankind will lose another energy center.

So that was why we were in the Azores—to connect the Earth's grids! I was flooded with apprehension as I realized the magnitude of what was expected of me. I could not fathom how I could cure what ailed something as immense as Mother Earth.

It became clear to me that activities such as mining and construction had affected the grid. And what about man-made grids? Transportation grids, telecommunications grids, and power supply grids had obscured the pulsations coming from the Earth's core. I wondered if our Atlantean ancestors had altered the vibrations of the planet. While the use of crystals for energy is a more natural technology, possibly even that was misused. In their arrogance perhaps they came to believe that they, rather than the Creator, were the source of their powers. As Hawk put it, "They chose the exploitation of the ego over the wisdom of the heart." And since that time, humanity had wandered far from being truly awakened.

At this point the mist had become as thick as a cloud and obscured our view. We could no longer see beyond the balcony. I could feel the presence of the Ancients around us in a way I had not felt before. I could feel their caress letting us know that we were loved.

Hawk took a moment to remind us why the Thunderbeings had returned to Earth. "You are here to raise the consciousness. That can be done only by being here in form. Your true essence is light, but you're more important to evolution by being in a physical form at this time. You are recognized in places of consciousness that you can't even begin to comprehend."

Some time later we ventured down into the valley near the twin lakes, to Sete Cidades. We stopped at a row of houses next to an old parish church. Inside the house was a small tavern and a cozy living-room-style restaurant. Speaking in Portuguese, John ordered fish, bread, and cheese. Our meals had become an important social time for us; it was as though we'd become one big family. Sitting down at the table together brought out conversation and even turmoil, but it was always resolved in a respectful way.

As we ate, I noticed a vibrant glow on our faces. We had started to move and breathe as one consciousness, bonded in our mission to heal the wounds left by the destruction of Atlantis. Traveling in sacred time and space, there are no rules, no expectations, and no restrictions.

Another segment of time passed in the twinkle of an eye until the evening when Hawk announced that we were going to disco the night away. . . . *What?* Weren't we supposed to be on an intense inner journey? But I knew better than to question her—it was evident by now that she never said or did anything without purpose.

We strolled down to the discotheque in the hotel. The whole disco was ours in which to play and dance under strobe lights. Hawk had another lesson up her sleeve, but what? The evening passed and we danced without too much thought to mostly 1980s music. I watched Hawk, who was a good dancer, get up for songs with a gentler message, though I realized this only later. Every moment of her life was lived purposefully; even in a discotheque she moved with purpose.

It felt very late when we left the disco and gathered in the lobby. Oh-oh, something was wrong; Hawk had a grim expression on her face. She proceeded to chastise us for dancing to songs that had negative or destructive messages. She reminded us that dancing was a state of meditation that must be accompanied by good thoughts; that was why she danced only to songs that contained positive or life-enhancing lyrics. Because of the power of our Thunderbeing energies, we must be careful—we move energies when we dance!

When I got back to my room, the plush carpeting and rich Mediterranean wood furniture was warm and inviting. The silence was so great that it soon overshadowed the physical forms around me and drew me deep into myself. My life on the other side of the ocean seemed to fade away like some former lifetime, and I contemplated the way I used to be. I had always been too serious, too ready to crawl into my protective shell like a snail carrying its house on its back. I had so many layers of emotion around myself that I had to probe deep to find what lay underneath—but I was getting through them one by one. On these journeys with Hawk we were healing at such an accelerated pace: we were shedding parts of ourselves that didn't fit in with who we really were. Few could understand why we needed that healing, but Thunderbeings always felt uncomfortable in an environment where there was malice and imbalance.

I walked into the bathroom, turned on the water, and watched as it filled the luxuriously deep tub. Climbing in, I breathed a huge sigh of contentment. I found myself floating upon a sea of timeless boundaries on cushions of soft blue, my gaze sinking into specks of sunlight dancing around me on silky waters. For all I knew, I could've been soaking for hours. I didn't have a clue what time it was when I got into bed.

That night I had a strange dream, that Hawk had left her body and was moving among us in a subtler form. All of us in the group traveled with her through a black hole into the center of the Earth. We landed in a sacred temple, having become evolved beings who could use our sixth and seventh senses. In this temple we were surrounded by inner earth beings with huge almond-shaped eyes emanating so much love.

My dream turned out to be a foreshadowing of the next day's events.

By the third day of our visit we had fallen into a nice, relaxed rhythm. I felt blissfully connected to the cosmos, like a big contented cat lazing in tall grasses, yet tuned into the subtle energies around me. The mist was mesmerizing as were the deep blues and greens of a landscape which was largely untouched by technology. The pace here was determined by small herds of cows that occasionally blocked the road. We felt keenly alive as the vibrations of the land drew us into the fullness of each moment. The sense of a lost paradise and a mythical past felt very real. Indeed, there are some who believe that Atlantis was produced by fire and love—in the words of Mauricio Abreu, an Azorean poet, "the awesome power of this passion still makes itself felt erupting violently and disgorging molten lava into the peaceful valleys."

Hawk announced that today we would go to the hot springs, one of São Miguel's tourist attractions. On our way there we stopped to purchase ice cream and pottery and to explore one of the beaches.

It was early afternoon when we arrived at Furnas. The mineral-rich spas in the Furnas valley draw people from all over Europe. From our vehicles we could see clouds of steam rising to more than twenty feet in height. John informed us of a traditional dish that is buried in the soil and cooked for nine or ten hours by the volcanic heat. Furnas, we learned, had erupted five times since A.D. 850, the last eruption being in 1630.

We walked across the smooth black rock and stood near the pits of boiling water and mud. A light sulfur fog floated among us. As the hot smoke and gases permeated my senses, I could feel little tremors shoot up through my body. The Earth seemed to be reaching out to me and embracing me, like a child asking for help.

I could sense that something momentous was going to happen— I could feel it coming.

One of the hot springs in particular, Hawk told us, was an opening of the Earth Mother's heart. She pointed to another and said it was one of the openings of the Earth's pulse whereas the many little springs were her nerve endings: "Every time we open our mouths we let off steam. The Earth is just like us; she lets off steam when she speaks or sings."

We walked down one of the stone walkways toward the biggest hot spring, which was framed by boulders. The waters boiled furiously, leaping up. Vapors poured forth into the atmosphere, creating the appearance of a huge white cloud. Hawk moved over to stand on the rim of heat and invited us to join her. "Take your shoes off and put your feet in," she told us.

Jim was the first to take his shoes off. "I have a feeling that if we do this, like our fire walk—if we put our feet in, we won't get burned. Is that right?"

"Yes!" Hawk answered.

I decided I wanted to be a part of this initiation and sat down to remove my shoes. "Ohh, is that hot!" I shouted, dipping my feet in quickly. After a few of us had braved the ordeal, Hawk told us there was a fire in that hot spring that would purify and cleanse all of the negative emotions that had lodged in our organs. She said that those of us who had put our feet in the water now had "thunder feet." She meant that we would always walk the red path of the heart with thunder in our feet, and when we danced, we would bring the Thunderbeings out. "You're now wearing the red moccasins," Hawk told us later. "You will walk the red road of the earthkeepers and bring the message of the heart wherever you go."

As we gathered around the rim of the hot spring, Hawk started to sing what she called her "heart song," a beautiful melody that came from a deep inner feeling, the same sound that resonated from the soul of a gospel singer. Whenever she sang it, the emotion gripped us. As we joined in, I looked down to see if the hot spring was responding to our song—and, yes, the Earth Mother was accepting our offering of love.

At this point everything started to happen so fast that boundaries became blurred; light, color, and sound faded into the distance.

Hawk ordered us to move away from the hot spring. "Stay on the walkways."

Our anxiety level hit a boiling point as we rushed out to the walkways. Hawk instructed us to make sure no one came up to the hot spring where she stood. We all took our places on the walkways. It was time for her to deliver the ancient tablet, which had been faithfully protected and passed on through the generations of her clan. She had been given the stone tablet, which contains sacred writings, and had been its caretaker, having been instructed to deliver the tablet at this particular time and place. It was important also that she bring at least ten Thunderbeings with her. "Ten shall bear witness," she was told. Ten reflecting parts of the crystal.

I stood on one of the pathways near the road, pacing back and forth anxiously. I turned around to see what Hawk was doing. She was no longer on the edge of the hot spring—where had she gone? Suddenly I felt a rush of clarity. I could vividly sense Hawk stepping into the hot spring. I could see the spring boiling faster and faster. Indeed, the steam from all of the surrounding openings became so thick that it engulfed us and limited our range of vision, leaving us with the feeling that we were no longer in control of the situation. The steam billowing from the Earth was now the director of this scene.

At this point we moved farther along the pathways and waited. Great clouds of mist became even more intense, creating the effect of a curtain that we could draw and obscure the view from the curious eyes of tourists.

Then a tourist bus appeared out of nowhere. I mean it materialized out of thin air! It almost floated into our presence! We looked nervously to one another. Oh, my God, how were we going to stop all of these people? On second glance we saw that it wasn't a tourist bus but rather a school bus! Two children, a boy and a girl, emerged from the bus, smiling and laughing. I watched closely, fascinated; they looked like angels. Their expression was beatific, the kind I had seen in Renaissance paintings of angels. Later we learned that the children were light beings from another dimension and that the bus was not of this physical dimension!

I turned around to what is now a vague picture in my mind. It was the entranceway to the tourist office at the hot springs. A man was standing there watching us. How odd! Eventually we learned that he too is from an ancient world: a galactic being who travels in all dimensions of time and space and is helping Earth in her evolutionary path. We called him the Traveler. The Traveler had the ability to appear in a third-dimensional form, and he occasionally met with Hawk. While at the hot spring, he appeared in a physical form that was lean, about five feet six inches tall, and attired in brown pants and a yellow shirt, or was it a yellow raincoat? I thought it interesting that Hawk was also wearing yellow that day.

Then I watched as both the bus and the Traveler vanished.

I could sense that Hawk was now up over her knees in the hot spring. At this point she made a sound and we were all with her in an instant. We were traveling to the inner earth, spinning through the ocean depths deeper and deeper. Only the shells of our physical bodies remained. I felt light-headed and lost awareness of the space around me. The spiritual vapors of the mist took me away. I was spinning on currents of energy through the vortex into the inner earth. I knew no emotion, no fear, no desperation . . . just blank. In my vision Hawk had descended into the bottom of the hot spring and stayed submerged for approximately ten minutes of linear time. We were *with* her for this period of time. When we returned to our bodies, I felt a jolt and regained my footing. Ooohh!

We noticed that although Hawk had emerged out of the boiling pit, her clothes were completely dry! Lynn, who stood closest to Hawk at the hot spring, was the first to notice her clothes. "I realized she'd been in the water, but her shirt didn't get wet!" she told us, astonished.

We were all in an altered state after this, and we got into our vehicles and found a restaurant in the center of the village of Furnas. I was in a complete daze and had absolutely no appetite. As I sat back and watched everyone eat and talk, I had the sensation of floating inside a huge bubble; everything around me appeared nebulous and unreal.

After we left the restaurant we stopped at several places looking for a mineral bath; the largest one was closed.

"Okay, we'll stop here," Hawk said, and we parked at the edge of the road. We waited while John walked down several steps to a stone wall near the water. In a few minutes we saw him run back up, looking frightened.

"I felt a sensation so real that it reminded me of a big cat leaping onto my back and clinging to me," he said, shaking.

Hawk suggested there might be some lower-world energies here. "Let's get going!" she said. As the cars rushed on, she worked her medicines to clear the imbalanced energies on John.

Back at the hotel we gathered to review the day's events. Hawk took us through a meditation. "Allow yourself to go beyond your five senses. Recall that moment at the hot springs when you were in the nucleus of inner earth for ten minutes. Slow it down enough so that your mind can catch it.

"Allow your seventh sense . . . The Traveler was there with us. Let yourself remember what happened as we entered the heart of the Mother. It is your fear that wouldn't allow you to see what was happening."

I slowed down my breathing. Within moments I was taken back. I saw myself going down into a whirlpool of energy, down, doown, dooown. A swirling, cyclonic feeling of traveling into a center. I entered the inner chamber of a shimmering solid crystal mountain. I was kneeling at a sacred altar, a magnificent slab of square stone embedded with amethyst, emerald, and ruby. Many beings of light were here, including representatives of vanished races, such as the Anasazi. The Traveler was there as well, looking on. Winged creatures—Pegasus and the ancient griffin and the unicorn—were present. Even Bigfoot was there, but the ten-foot tall creature didn't want any part of our civilization and communicated telepathically. It was such a pristine and healing environment.

All of us in the group were standing in front of the altar. We were participating in a sacred ceremony in which the tablet with the writings was being placed in its rightful place. The inner earth beings, whose vibrations are so subtle that they can exist only at this level, rejoiced in the fact that Hawk had fulfilled her duty.

My experience was confirmed by the others. We all had a swirling, cyclonic feeling of going into a center and entering an inner chamber, as if we had spiraled in on the same energy current. Jim told us that in his vision he was carrying a gift on a pillow: "a big shiny ruby-like gem that glowed and gave off light."

When Jim looked at his ring, which was supposed to contain nine stones, he realized that one of the stones—the ruby—was missing!

"Hawk, did I really give the stone to the inner earth altar?" he asked, astounded.

With her eternal tenderness she replied, "Beloved, your gift was received with great joy."

When I asked Hawk about the meaning of the unicorn in my meditation, she said that it represented my desire to be free of the Earth to travel to other dimensions because of my intolerance of an environment that had become coarse and uninhabitable.

We asked her why the ancient tablet had to be deposited in the hot spring at this time. She said it was to communicate and give permission to the Earth Mother to heal herself at her own pace. Having devoted herself to taking care of her children for so long and being weakened by pollution, toxic wastes, and many environmental disasters, the time had come when she must consider her own needs for both her preservation and our own. We can no longer hold the devoted Mother to our original covenant with her, which stipulated that she was to take care of us, her children.

"In the seal I gave her back with the writing, we're saying that we understand that she must start her changes," Hawk explained. "We're breaking our ties with her that hold back her quakes. We're saying that we've done everything we can, that you must do what you have to do to heal yourself. We're telling the devoted Mother not to take the abuses of her children . . . because they have chosen greed and destruction over respect.

"We are no longer holding her in agreement to think of us before she thinks of herself, for we know that her preservation is our preservation. We must now look after her as she has looked after us."

The tablet had been kept for a predetermined time when it was to be put back in the Earth—and this was the pristine moment. Hawk had now fulfilled her prophecy. Returning the tablet was like reconnecting a vital link; it was like replacing a missing piece of a giant puzzle.

"The fact that we're here in the Azores reconnecting the Earth's grids means there is hope for humanity," Hawk added.

The fact that we were here also fulfilled a prophecy made by Pope John XXIII and preserved in a book he wrote in the 1940s. He stated that "the roll of parchment will be found in the Azores" and "it will speak of ancient civilizations that will teach men unknown ancient things about themselves." I believe that the parchment represented the stone tablet with the sacred writings and that returning it to the Azores signified that the time had come when the whole world would know the ancient truths.

We had completed our mission on São Miguel, and it was time now to leave. The next day at dawn Hawk awoke us as usual by telephone. After we had settled our account at the hotel, we gathered in the parking lot, the pervasive mist curling around us.

"I'm sure going to miss this place," I said as I placed my suitcase inside the van.

"Yeah, what a hotel. It was perfect, like a dream!" Phillip answered.

"We had the whole staff to ourselves. They lined up for us whenever we needed them, and they'd disappear when we needed our privacy. We were pampered silly," Jim concurred.

"It's almost as if this place manifested itself out of nowhere," Hawk laughed.

We did indeed wonder if we had conjured up the hotel out of our sheer desire for a secluded place in a beautiful setting. Certainly it was odd that we were the only guests and that it was so mystically perfect!

It was now time to head for the airport to catch our Air Açores flight to the next island.

CHAPTER 14

TIME STOPPED

The transcendental state of Being lies beyond all seeing, hearing, touching, smelling, and tasting—beyond all thinking and beyond all feeling.

—MAHARISHI MAHESH YOGI

BY LATE MORNING WE had arrived at the tiny turtle-shaped island of Faial. John hurried off to get us two cars and a van. As we followed the road that circled the island, beams of sunlight bathed the fields and hillsides, coves and islets, creating an almost ethereal glow. John told us that Faial was called the "blue island" because for most of the year masses of blue hydrangeas framed the houses and bordered the roads.

Cultivated fields separated by hedges gave the island the look of a huge grandmother's quilt sewn with many hues of green. Here and there were splashes of color as clusters of white buildings and bright red windmills adorned the landscape.

And there were wonderful views of the ocean; but best of all was the view of nearby Pico Island where a mysterious, cloud-shrouded mountain rose to almost 8,000 feet, the highest point in the Atlantic Ocean. A winding hilly road took us into a big courtyard. We had arrived at our hotel, which consisted of several two-story buildings surrounded by gardens. John had reserved one of the buildings for us. We checked in and began the routine of settling into our rooms and balancing the energies.

There was a knock on the door and I heard David shout: "We're meeting outside in about ten minutes."

"How are the rooms?" Hawk asked when we gathered outside. "It's nice to have a whole building to ourselves, isn't it?" We strolled across the way to the lobby and paused in the gift shop to look at books and embroidery. I picked up a book and read out loud the short description on the back flap: "It says here, 'When all questions of space, time, matter and the nature of being have been resolved, only one question remains—Where shall we have dinner?'" I was trying to inject some humor into our serious mission here when I pointed out that that had become one of our scenarios.

"That's kinda what we did in São Miguel after our experience at the hot springs," Charles mused.

"Yeah." Hawk laughed.

This search for the restaurant at the end of the universe became our inside joke for the duration of our journey: we were cosmic travelers who had come to Earth to help awaken the consciousness, but we had other lofty purposes too, such as eating well!

We managed to locate two tables in the restaurant that were long enough to seat all of us.

Looking at the menu, Hawk turned to John: "Well, I'm in a spirit place. So no matter how long I look at the menu all I see are dots. Order me some salad."

"I'm going to have salad and fish."

"Umm, I'll have the same."

"I think I'll have . . ."

John scribbled down our orders and then conversed with the waiter in Portuguese.

We were *all* in a spirit place. Our journey had become as magical and adventuresome as charting new exotic land. We felt bonded by the intensity of our purpose here, collectively living out our dream of a higher order of reality.

I continued to float in and out of that haze between waking and dreaming. And I could now feel the presence of the Ancients—they were always with us. My awareness had become so lucid that everything appeared mystically beautiful, and yet at the same time I felt detached from the forms around me. During lunch, Hawk asked John if there was a beach in the area.

"There's one not too far from here, in town," he replied.

Then three of our group brought the cars around to the front of the building. And we took off, through the tourist port town of Horta where transatlantic yachts lined the harbor. We approached a hill attached to the island by a narrow strip of land. John pointed out that some of the buildings along the side of the hill were abandoned whaling factories. We parked and walked down the ramp to the beach, which was situated on a bay. We met up with a few curious glances from passersby and John offered a friendly *"Bom dia."*

The beach was set against a background of steep black cliffs. We arranged our blankets and towels while Hawk lit sage and cedar in her smudge bowl. As she passed it around, the sacred smoke quickly established an introspective mood; and we received more attention from onlookers.

She then lifted her head as if testing the energies here. "There are real strong meridians here," she said in an undertone. She told us that during the time of Atlantis there was a sun temple and a moon temple on these islands—and that Faial was a kind of passageway between them.

While the day had started off overcast, the sun was now breaking through. I stretched out on the sand, basking in the warmth.

At this point Hawk reminded us how important it was for us to expand our awareness. When we identified with the divine essence within, instead of the body and the ego, we felt connected, we felt a sense of oneness. The spirit of Atlantis remembers that oneness is the key to the power of creation. By getting into harmony with the universe, one has much more power because the universe is where all power comes from.

"What kind of power do you think you have of yourself, on your own?" Hawk asked us. "How can you make yourselves something separate from Creator? Even to be a mere cell on the body of Creator is exciting. Until you realize that you are part of the divine mandala, you will never have any power on your own."

And she added that we really don't have to try so hard because of who we are: "You are like the elusive butterfly . . . and it frightens you to feel special."

She then directed our attention to the cluster of buildings that clung to the side of a mountain. "My grandmother taught me that man's memory is infinite. No matter how many times the Earth has had to renew herself, men have always had a tendency to build their homes on the sides of mountains. In Atlantis the mountaintop symbolized an altar. The original altars on Earth were the mountains."

We spent the afternoon on the beach, immersing ourselves in the water and looking for symbols in the landscape for drawings that would later be incorporated on our shields.

As the day wore on, I found myself disappearing into the weavings of time. While staring at the mountain, I could see the forms of altars and dazzling candelabra within its structure. With my eyes closed, it seemed that I was winging high and walking straight through the side of the mountain. Once inside the mountain, I levitated to the top and encountered some inner earth beings. Their shimmering presence inspired me to thoughts of the primitive soul, which has been ignorantly ignored.

At some point we returned to the hotel, had dinner, got dressed for cooler weather, and set off to explore more of the island. Along the way we stopped to photograph the awesome cloud-capped mountain that emerges from neighboring Pico Island.

"It's fabulous," I muttered to Jim, who had also scrambled out of the car, his camera poised. "There is something special about that mountain. I can't express it. For all we know, it could have been one of the most sublime altars in all of Atlantis."

"Yeah, it has a mysterious presence," he sighed.

We continued on, past green meadows and tilled fields that clothe the island's rolling hills. John led the way into the center of the island until we arrived at an enormous crater known as Caldeira. Our vehicles labored up a hill to an isolated stretch of unpaved road surrounded by moss and shrubbery. It was foggy; as we emerged from our cars, we wondered if this was the right place.

Hawk grew silent as she gathered data about the area. "There comes the Traveler and the grandfathers," she said peering into the fog. "Turn off your cars."

I guessed we were going to be in good company here!

We walked through a little tunnel carved into the land. As we came out of the tunnel we looked, astonished, into the bowl of an enormous crater covered with vegetation—cedars, junipers, ferns, and moss. It felt like a twilight zone or the way the Earth must have looked in prehistoric times. Standing near a makeshift fence constructed of twisted branches, we made our cornmeal offerings. The light mist that cloaked the crater suddenly intensified—the Ancients were responding to our offerings.

"I think every grandmother and every diva within a five-hundred mile radius has come to be with us!" John joked, as the mist rolled in so thick you could cut it with a knife.

We stood huddled together for warmth. Some of us raised the collars on our parkas and others who had brought blankets raised them over their heads.

At this point, we heard our car doors slam shut. We looked wide-eyed at Hawk, and she smiled, "That was you shutting your doors." We just looked at each other, stunned. We were caught in a cycle of vivid déjà vu, knowing we'd already done it before. It was dizzying to the senses.

And as we stood there, I could feel the presence of something in the crater but to this day I'm unable to describe it with words. All I know is that I felt taken out of my normal reality; my old beliefs were crumbling; the perpetual struggle within ceased; only the wind moved through me. What I had thought was reality was disappearing. What I thought was unreal and illusory was now becoming the true focus of my being, my real identity. It carved a new path before me, one that I found much easier to travel.

"Oh, look!" Patty said excitedly, whispering that she could see the female guardian of the crater.

She and Hawk were having the same vision; they started to kneel, and the rest of us followed. Patty described the vision in a quavering, breathless voice.

"It's a beautiful lady. I can see the astral form of bright lights filling the whole sky. Like an angel, with wings, there is no end to her. Blue and white and hovering like a cloud. There is so much love emanating from her."

While we lingered, the fog became so thick that we could no longer see into the crater. The Ancients were dancing us—and we felt loved! Within minutes, rain began to pour down on us and we returned to our vehicles, overwhelmed with appreciation for the blessings we had received.

When we arrived at our hotel, we worked late into the night crafting our shields. As I painted symbols and pictures on my shield, I felt such a great satisfaction, as if something trapped inside me had escaped. Shield work had become one of my passions.

I returned to my room and fell into a deep, deep sleep. I dreamed about the crater and that we had developed our higher senses and could communicate with the nature spirits. The feeling of oneness was becoming a reality.

The next morning Hawk announced that we were going to visit the site of an active volcano that had erupted in 1957–1958 and demolished houses and farmland, leaving much of the island covered in ash.

After breakfast we ventured out of the hotel across meadows and pastures and along a jagged coastline. We pulled off the road at a deserted, desolate section of the island, covered with black lava.

"It's beautiful, isn't it?" Hawk muttered as we gazed at a volcanic mountain that curved gracefully into an enormous rocky cliff jutting out into the sea. "There is still boiling lava here," she said.

It was awesome. It was primordial, as if we had stepped into a prehistoric warp. And it was easy to imagine the heaving and outpouring of lava, the blasting and breaking up of land.

"This volcano is a sacred altar," Hawk said softly, adding that communication was going on between the cloud beings and the top of the mountain.

We fell silent as she chanted an ancient greeting and spoke to the spirit of the volcano. Immediately the wind spirits picked up and blew their essence across the sand in response to her call. Hawk continued to pray and sing to the volcano with a passion that made our hearts throb. Her hands gesticulated in a symbolic language that spoke of her feeling of oneness with Great Spirit. As she chanted, we could feel the ground vibrate beneath our feet.

Two eagles soared across the side of the lava hill.

"Look, we have two eagles!" Alison said in a shrill voice.

"The eagles are welcoming us," Hawk said, pleased. We watched as they circled the volcano.

The wind was strong now; it swept across the sandy surface of the volcano's flank. When it ceased, there were huge letters in the sand. The surface, which had been completely black, was marked up with huge swirls as though a galactic being had tried to communicate with us. We interpreted them as sacred symbols that contained a message for all humankind: we must extend ourselves beyond our present limitations and return to harmony. We must free ourselves of the old paradigms in which we experience ourselves as separate from the perfection of the universe. Once we realize our oneness with everything, the separation will dissolve.

"This volcano is a living altar," Hawk told us, her voice filled with quiet passion. "It has birthed itself for our generation. The volcano is so sacred and new. You can almost see it breathing and observing us."

She called the volcano the child of Thunder Bird, a spirit creature that could make tornadoes and hurricanes. Thunder Bird's dance is the dance of Shiva. When he flaps his wings the land begins to churn to the momentum of his wings. He destroys all that is not pure; he restores the wholeness.

"Thunder Bird," Hawk told us, "is getting ready to erase the ignorance that exists on these islands."

My soul leaped at the sight of the volcano; he spoke to my spirit—I felt as though I were looking into a portion of eternity. He held the promise of a realm where no limits existed. He had power yet also purity, softness, and grace.

We climbed over a stone wall and down the steep, sandy slope to the foot of the volcano. I struggled to maintain my balance and slid part of the way. As I trod across the lava sand, my pulse quickened; I felt something stir beyond the visible. I glanced around at the others who were scattered about. Jim and Brian were climbing up one side of the mountain, and I watched to see how high they would go. Hawk had told us not to climb above the height that the eagles had flown. "Follow the path that the eagle has shown," she had said before we started our descent.

I took several steps and decided to stop. I turned toward the sea and watched the waves shatter upon the black rocks. All of a sudden I felt the presence of something so sacred that I had to avert my eyes. It was a palpable sensation, and it compelled me to come close to the ground. As I lay down, my body crumpled involuntarily. The environment around me faded away. With my face in the sand, I found myself being lifted as though in the palm of a huge hand. I was trembling— I could feel gentle tremors in my body. The sea and the sky and the mountain were fused. I was surrounded by whirlwinds of sea and sky and mountain until I was indistinguishable from them. I was being lifted higher and higher, far from any sense of composure or thought. An energy was bursting inside me, unlike anything I had ever experienced. How can I describe it?

I felt as though I were astride a magnificent white stallion galloping through a forest, with shafts of golden sunlight from above breaking through the thick green canopy. I could feel the vibration of the stallion in my body and the wind across my face. The shafts of light were dancing all around me, glistening like diamonds. The horse moved upward, thrusting its body into the air, riding the shafts of light and breaking through the canopy into pure white light. My excitement intensified by the moment as I became one with this magical horse. The thundering hooves pounding the ground reverberated through my body; its heaving breath was in unison with mine. I was a part of the horse; we were as one, flying among the clouds in total freedom and exhilaration, rising higher and higher, riding beams of white light.

All of my past burdens disappeared; I was free of the weight I had been carrying around, the weight of expectations continually added to by everyone, including myself, as though I had been dragging around a heavy suitcase. I tossed it away with one easy gesture. I could do anything and be anything! I was not moving toward a particular point or away from it, yet I experienced both movement and stillness, past and future, all in one instant. I was outside of time, free of all the paraphernalia I had been carrying as if it had never existed.

I started to weep because of the intensity of what I was feeling. It was like being bathed with the waters of pure energy, and the experience was almost too much for me. It was so intense that for a moment I felt as though I might drown in it. This experience changed me; I would never be the same again. I felt truly alive and connected;

my separate "identity" did not exist or had blended in with a much bigger whole.

Afterward I realized that the potential for awakening is within us and can happen in an instant. It became clear to me that we need this feeling of ecstasy in our lives. Nothing—not food, not sexual pleasure, and not wealth—can give us such a high on life as even a mere moment of spiritual bliss. Without it we will never feel complete and whole.

I don't know how long I remained in this transcendent state. Minutes? Hours? But at some point I slowly raised myself off the ground. Hawk had helped me to understand that being in the presence of an altar, such as this volcano, is a heart medicine that touches and changes us. It connects us back to the source of our being. We realize that we have been experiencing only a small fraction of the totality of life. It's like looking at the surface of the ocean and thinking that's all there is; but then as we dive into the depths we find an immense shimmering world opening up before our very eyes.

It was time for everyone to reunite at the top of the hill; I staggered back up the sandy slope. When I asked the others in the group, everyone had felt the intensity of the energy here in some way. Jim told me the experience was "awesome," and Brian said that when he was climbing up the side of the volcano he had to sit down and he dozed off into another dimension. Before we left, Hawk sent out prayers in a sacred smoke ceremony. As she sang to the grandmothers and grandfathers of our ancestors, immediately the eagles appeared and flew around her.

On the way back to the hotel, I felt intoxicated with the emotion of my experience, and yet my mind was crystal clear. As I peered out the car window, I saw the world through new eyes. The island shimmered with color and light, as if it had just been painted with a brush dipped in fresh paint: mesmerizing hazy blues, wondrous green tints, splashes of bright red.

Later that night, after we had all gone to sleep, Hawk returned to the volcano. She did so in the middle of the night so as not to attract attention. She worked her medicines and spoke with Thunder Bird. She sent out a voice for change, that Thunder Bird might purge and purify that which is not wholesome.

Hawk did not return to the hotel until morning. She had called Patty in the middle of the night to tell the rest of us to go ahead and have breakfast without her.

On the last evening of our stay on this island, we gathered and talked about the volcano. We joked and laughed, shared our dreams and felt such a strong bond, as if some greater force had drawn us closer together. We realized we had raised ourselves one step higher toward our goal. Then some of us began to notice something strange.

"Hawk, there is someone in our building," Patty whispered.

"Yes, I sense something too," Lynn said slowly, her eyes wide.

As we grew silent and stared into the hallway, we realized that we did indeed have company!

Some of us could see silhouettes of tall figures in flowing robes with hoods that concealed their heads and faces. They floated gracefully through the walls and doors without touching the floor.

"I see a tall, lean man with an ebony-black braid and he has a sharp-featured face," Hawk whispered as she looked into the hallway.

She said they were ancient Lemurians who had come through in the mist in recognition of who we were and our work here. (Some say that Atlantis was a subculture of Lemuria, one of the greatest of all Earth civilizations—a gigantic continent that occupied most of the southern hemisphere.) They were circling our building and coming in from the back!

"The Lemurians are here to take care of the islands," Hawk said quietly. "They have such elevated thoughts that they cannot live in a physical form for very long."

One of the people in our group mentioned he had read a story about a Los Angeles newspaper reporter who, in 1932, discovered that a colony of Lemurians lived on the slopes of Mount Shasta and possessed the power of Tibetan masters: they could vanish at will and surround their village with an invisible protective boundary.

And that led to a discussion of the lost continent of Mu, which Hawk believes was the Garden of Eden and the motherland of man.

There is some documented speculation that Mu was the fountain-head of civilization, predating even Atlantis. According to *The Lost Continent of Mu*, by James Churchward, Mu was a beautiful tropical country with vast plains, an earthly paradise, with great temples and palaces of stone—and was comprised of ten separate kingdoms or tribes, distinct from each other but all under one government.

"The Lemurians were the original sages of Mu," Hawk told us. "They are the remnants of the first peoples who lived in perfect peace and harmony. They were the medicine people. They lived and breathed the original breath of life." She said that Lemurians had little admiration for technology; they rejected it, for they knew that machines would turn them away from their strong spiritual structure. In their unconditional love, if struck on the cheek they would remain passive and offer the other cheek.

She said that the Atlanteans were adversaries of Lemuria and that they "began rumors" which led to the murder of these peace-loving people. "The maliciousness of the tongue is what started the destruction of Atlantis," she told us.

After almost four days on this island, it was time to move on. On our last day, windy and overcast, we drove down to the harbor and boarded a ferry for Pico Island. During the thirty-minute ride, the lofty mountain wrapped in clouds loomed closer and closer, seeming to represent a pivotal point for all of the Azores—and perhaps beyond. It made me think that there was a time when Earth was closer to heaven and the gulf between cosmic zones could more easily be traversed.

As we neared Pico Island, mysterious formations of massive lava rock emerged out of the water.

"A friend of my aunt's will meet us at the dock," John told us as the boat slowed down. When we stepped onto the cement dock, we saw a small, thin man and a red pickup truck waiting for us. The man, whom John introduced as Emanuel, didn't speak English; he just nodded. After he and John exchanged some words in Portuguese, we tossed our luggage into the back of the truck. John, Brian, and Jim, who had gone to get some rental cars, brought them around. We followed each other along a cobblestone street, past fields and vineyards dotted with cedar and laurel trees as well as some indigenous species of trees. There was lava everywhere! The orchards and vineyards, which had grown in the lava-enriched soil, were riddled with a chaotic maze of tiny walls made of stone on top of stone. Even the houses were constructed of lava stone, a material that became abundant after volcanic eruptions rocked this island.

We stopped at a large white two-story house perched on the curve of the road. The simple rectangular structure with green shutters and terra-cotta tile roof, surrounded by vineyards, was within steps of the ocean.

"Bring your luggage and leave it here on the porch for now," John shouted from the porch. As we hauled our suitcases up a stone stairway of about a dozen steps, the resident's dog, a German shepherd, came out to the front of the house; we remarked how badly flea-bitten he was. Hawk would work her medicines on him later.

We removed our shoes and stepped inside the house. As John led us down a long, dimly lit hallway to the kitchen, I couldn't help but notice how dark and gloomy the house was. Maybe it was the poor lighting, but something didn't quite feel right. A sweet aroma of the local culinary delights wafted from the kitchen. John's aunt, who lived a few houses away, had very kindly offered to make dinner for us. As we entered the kitchen, she greeted us with a warm smile. It was obvious that she'd been cooking all afternoon. We offered to help set the table and brought in some extra chairs from the other room; in the midst of all this, we heard a baby cry.

We learned that Emanuel was the caretaker of the house and lived here with his wife and children. As we lingered in the kitchen, I tossed a quizzical look at Patty, who concurred; she too had noticed that something about this house made her uneasy.

Dinner was ready. We sat down around a huge wooden table laden with pots of chicken, tuna, fish, and stew. John's uncle had arrived and greeted us. By now Emanuel had also come into the kitchen. Since I was sitting directly across from Hawk I noticed that she was unusually quiet amid all the hubbub. That was not like her at all! She was being humorous and gracious, but her eyes were heavy with worry.

She turned to John and said, "This is delicious. Tell your aunt that she's a good cook."

I knew then that Hawk was responding to the energies in the house. You didn't have to be overly sensitive to feel the dark cloud that hung over this house. As we would soon find out, something was awry.

Emanuel had taken a plate of food and was eating while he walked to and fro. A smallish man, with salt-and-pepper hair, probably in his thirties, he watched us with an expression of fascination, trying to size us up. We must have appeared odd to him.

"Mmm, this is good," Brian commented as he tasted the stew.

At this point Emanuel brought out a video of a pig being slaughtered. A small television set was positioned above the table in the corner of the kitchen in such a way that it was difficult for some of us to see the screen.

We learned that in the remote villages, Azoreans still get together when the pig is fat and ready to be killed. Family and friends are invited to help clean the pig; then it's cooked, seasoned, and smoked. John said that at one time "the slaughter," as it was called, used to be a major event of celebration and feasting.

Emanuel inserted the tape into the VCR and while it played, I couldn't see it.

"I don't know if I can eat any more," Patty gulped under her breath.

I could see that Hawk's uneasiness was growing.

The topic turned to some of the pagan festivals on the island; John told us of a popular festival in which the people of the fishermen's village honor their sea goddess by making offerings and having processions of boats.

After we finished eating, we washed the dishes and congregated in the living room at the front of the house. Several of us managed to squeeze onto a long brown couch positioned in front of a mirror that spanned the length of the couch. As I studied the room, which was modestly furnished with a dark brown carpet, a coffee table, and a stereo, something didn't feel right. I found myself feeling sullen and melancholy, as if I were having a bad dream.

When we were all in the room alone with the door closed, Hawk asked John to find us a hotel for the night. "Tell your aunt we appreciate her hospitality but that there are too many of us," she said wearily. "There are not enough beds."

John called all the hotels on the island, but they were booked for the night.

At this point Emanuel entered the room and Brian graciously offered his chair. Emanuel sat down and didn't say a word. He just watched us.

With him in the room, we stiffened. We were on our guard but continued our discussion, sharing our dreams, which had become a daily routine with us.

Josephine started to describe her dream about traveling on a road and finding a dead black bird that gave off a stench.

"The dead bird is a messenger that has been sent," Hawk explained.

We talked about the islands and how magical they were, comparing our reactions so far.

Meanwhile, I noticed that Hawk's eyes were constantly focused above our heads; I turned around to see what she was looking at and realized it was the mirror. What was she seeing in the mirror?

After Emanuel left the room, she told us that the house was infested with lower world entities. She described these entities as grotesque beings that were the product of destructive thought-forms—people's anger and fear, an emotional garbage bin.

"The mirror is a gateway for these entities to come through," she said, her eyes fixed on the mirror because the entities were still coming through. While we had been sitting there talking, Hawk was busy sending these lower world entities into the light as they crept in through the mirror.

"I exorcise them toward the light because electricity burns and destroys them," she told us.

"I knew there was something coming out of that mirror!" Patty exclaimed. "They were coming out over our heads."

These underworld energies were threatened by our presence. Part of the reason for our journey was to disperse the unhappiness that still hung over these islands because of the wounds inflicted by the fall of Atlantis.

Well, it looked as if we would have to stay here for the night. It wasn't a place that I wanted to stay; it was cold and damp and flea-infested (fleas are associated with lower world energies). I felt as though I had dug a hole and buried myself in it. My journey had been so wonderful up until now that it made the present moment seem worse than it actually was.

"The women can sleep in this room, and the men will sleep in the bedrooms," Hawk said, getting up. "How many bedrooms do we have?"

"Four," replied John, obviously perturbed.

"It looks as if some of you will have to sleep on the floor," she told the women.

We stepped out to the porch to get our luggage and sleeping bags. John brought some sheets to cover the floor, and we divided the floor up as to who was going to sleep where.

As I slipped into my sleeping bag, I realized my feet were almost touching Jackie's head. We were squeezed in like sardines. As the commotion died down, Hawk tiptoed into the room and sprinkled gardenia powder on our pillows and sleeping bags; she also slipped fragrant sticks of sage inside our sleeping bags: protection against the underworld spirits.

As I lay on the hard floor in the dark, I tossed and turned in discomfort. I slid deep into my sleeping bag. It was some time before I fell asleep, and even then it was a shallow, disturbing sleep. I dozed on and off throughout the night.

When morning came, most of us complained of having headaches; none of us had slept soundly throughout the night. We felt drained and washed out. The lower world energies had been feeding off our light from the moment we stepped into the house. While Hawk was up most of the night exorcising them, I had a sense that we had been assisting her in our dream state: I could see her sealing the mirrors and electrical plugs, smudging and calling in her whole line of ancestors. I had seen shadows disappearing into cracks in the ceiling.

After we had taken our showers and gulped down some coffee and bread, we started to gather our belongings.

Finally we were ready to leave. John's aunt had come back to the house to say good-bye; she, Emanuel, and Emanuel's wife waved as our cars sped away. We drove about a mile to the hotel, dropped off our luggage (it was too early to check in), and headed for the waterfront. We had planned to charter a boat to take us out to a place where we could swim with the dolphins, but John told us it was unlikely that we would encounter them now; summer, he said, would be a more auspicious time.

We boarded a large passenger boat, but even the fresh air and deep blue sea did not alleviate my headache. I still felt drained because of the psychic work we had done during the night.

The boat circled the island and provided various profiles of Pico Mountain, which was covered with dense forest and crowned with a cone of naked lava. Not far from shore, rock formations with intriguing shapes rose out of the water like mysterious shape-shifters. "The rocks are the oldest sages on Earth. We think they are a heavy mass, but they are moving faster than light," Hawk said as we passed one of these formations. It occurred to me that they could very well be Atlanteans observing us.

Vigorous cooling breezes tousled my hair, but still I wished my headache would go away. "I have a horrible headache," I told Hawk.

"I know," she said gently, and invited me to come sit down beside her in the bow of the boat. As she wrapped her arm around me, I smiled, feeling the magnitude of her warmth and loving every minute of it; I felt safe beside her.

At this point, she confirmed that during the night she had worked her medicines to close and seal the portal under the house that allowed the underworld spirits to come through.

"Did your parents get along when they were in that house?" she asked John, who had lived there at one time with his parents and sister.

"As soon as we moved into the house, my parents started to argue for the first time," he recalled. "And now that I think about it," he went on slowly, his face darkening, "my sister had the same nightmare over and over. She heard steps coming down the hall toward her bedroom, and the presence would open the door and walk to her bedside. It would pull her hair, and she would scream."

John said that many people on the island had reported hearing voices and encountering spirits and that these stories were part of the local folklore.

When the boat had traveled quite a distance from Pico and reached a particular place, Hawk remarked that there were still freshwater springs in the vicinity that bubbled up from the bowels of the

Earth. She told us that deep under the ocean's waters lay spectacular golden temples and other structures of Atlantis.

She said that a Soviet submarine had carried out underwater research in these waters some time ago and discovered steps and a gateway and a stone pillar. It was some time later that I read *Atlantis: The Eighth Continent*, by Charles Berlitz, who described the Soviet expedition of 1974: using advanced devices they had probed the ocean depths and obtained photographs of massive stone ruins.

John directed the boat's driver to a place where we might see dolphins—but they weren't there—and so we motored around the north side of Faial Island. Two or three hours later we returned to shore and checked into our hotel.

"I can hardly wait to step into a nice hot shower," I mumbled to Lynn as we dragged our luggage to the end of the hallway. We were both exhausted and anxious to wash off the negative energies.

As I stepped into the shower and felt the impact of the water, my whole body heaved in relief. I turned the faucet to steaming hot. Oooooh, this was wonderful. The ultimate satisfaction! I could feel my inner balance being restored. As I came out of the washroom, the phone rang.

It was Hawk. "Come down whenever you're dressed."

"Okay, we'll be down in a few minutes."

After an informal dinner on the carpeted floor of Hawk's room, she started to explain what a medicine person does, revealing more of her own fathomless being: "A medicine person lives *in tune* and *attuned* to all levels of intelligence in the Earth. This involves an enormous state of conscious awareness and working for the harmony of the whole, which includes the mineral, plant, and animal kingdoms."

And this led to a discussion of the significance of our journey and what we had accomplished.

"Since you've come to these islands you've experienced a tremendous elevation of your perception," Hawk said. "You're remembering a lot. . . . These islands will never be the same again because of our presence here." She was full of tenderhearted passion as she sat on the bed. "You are here to reestablish the pattern of wholeness and health. You are creating a new Earth." She said that we had initiated a movement of change that would purge and purify the unwholesomeness of these islands. "We have put a big thing in motion here," she said quietly.

That evening we talked about everything from tornadoes and hurricanes (a force that destroys and at the same time purges what is sick and impure) to Haitian witch doctors, to prophecies about religion and politics (religion is very politically motivated).

Our time here was cut short; we spent only two or three days on this island. On the last day it was very late in the afternoon when we started to prepare for our climb up Pico Mountain.

We had dressed in two layers of clothing and packed our vehicles with plastic tarps and blankets. John's cousin and two of his friends arrived at the hotel; they were to be our guides. It was not advisable to climb the mountain alone because of the huge cavelike openings concealed by grass.

Although it was dark and overcast as we drove through the rugged countryside, I could still sense the raw energy that had molded and shaped the contours of this island. Within about fifteen minutes we arrived at the foot of the mountain and proceeded up a steep, winding road. We climbed higher and higher up the side of the mountain. After we parked, John's cousin and two friends led the way up in the fog, helping to carry our tarps and firewood.

"Be careful," they cautioned. "As we get higher there are some very deep holes." And John told us that a person could fall into the holes and never be found. "People here say that the openings are connected to the ocean." A tourist guidebook I had picked up described these cavities as long corridors that stretched into the very depths of the Earth.

It was a difficult climb, with our heavy backpacks as well as our shields, which were some twenty-seven inches in diameter. Soon we were panting. Hawk reminded us to make cornmeal offerings along the way. She said that the sacred way to climb a mountain would take an entire day: we would have to stop many times to pray and erect little shrines of stones.

After fifteen or twenty minutes of struggling up the grassy, shrub-covered slope and breathing the thin, pure air, we were out of breath. We decided to stop and make our camp in a flat meadow just off to one side of the trail. John's cousin and two friends said their goodbyes and turned around. We placed our plastic tarps on the ground and built a fire.

It was dark and misty and difficult to see much of anything beyond a few feet.

"Be careful," Hawk cautioned. "Don't go too far. There are caverns all over the mountain." We climbed over to a cavern whose opening was covered with grass. As we stood around it, we could see a black emptiness beneath the grasses. I shuddered, imagining long tunnels connecting to the inner earth.

As the mist and drizzle blanketed us, I experienced a strange transformation. Could it have had something to do with being on one of the last peaks of a greater land mass, with Atlantis reposing deep beneath us? Could it have been that we were on one of the most powerful energy centers of the planet? And I remembered a dream I'd had long time ago that prophesied this very moment.

The silence wove its spell on me; I could feel the door opening between our world and the spirit world. I sensed distant voices from other galaxies upon the wind.

We built a fire and snuggled together under our tarps; we laughed uproariously. Everything around me started to take on a magical significance; everyone looked larger than life, as though I were looking through a camera lens that revealed a world where there was no contradiction between real and imaginary, past and future, high and low. Perhaps this romantic view of life was a truer state of being?

We removed our shoes and started to dance around the fire with our shields. We passed them over the fire in a sort of rite of consecration. The energy we felt was electrifying and intense. We were filled with hope that we would regain lost information about Atlantis that would reconnect us with our true origins.

"When you walk the fire, walk for those who have forgotten that they are the fire of God," Hawk said fervently. "The original flame was one of love and hope."

We had entered into the realm of the truly transcendental when Hawk turned her gaze toward the mountain just above us: the mist had come in as thick as a London fog.

"The warrior chiefs are here," she said quietly, obviously very pleased. "They have come in on the wind. Four chiefs are on horseback, and one is walking." Had an etheric door opened, allowing the chiefs to come through? We stayed near the fire while Hawk went over to pray with them.

At this point the entire side of the mountain became illuminated as though a column of energy had pierced the surface. The vividness of everything around me increased a hundredfold. I was diving again into the ocean of superconsciousness. As the mist bathed my face, I felt vertigo, my mind dreamy, a sense that nothing could hold me down, reality and the dream were now the same.

My reality was expanding to include other dimensions that I had thought didn't exist or that other people had told me were imaginary. I realized again that I had been experiencing only a fraction of life and never had the opportunity to perceive the depth of my existence.

Most of us lingered by the fire, now reduced to embers. When I turned around, I saw that Hawk was standing near the grotto where we had stood earlier and was chanting. And in the next moment I couldn't see her. Did she go inside the cavern? The grottoes could not be entered on foot. Several minutes passed, and she seemed to have climbed higher up the mountain—or had she?

"Hawk went into one of the caverns, and now she is ascending on the wind," Patty whispered, her eyes wide with awe. Indeed as I looked, I did a double take—Hawk looked enormous! She had risen ten feet into the air and was speaking to us from that elevation.

This was the first time that I had seen Hawk move with the light and wind spirits. It was truly wondrous.

While we had planned to quest at this site for the entire night, she told us that we had accomplished what we'd come for. "We have received our blessings. We can go down now," she said from her elevated position.

We were pleased about that, for it was getting cold and the rain was coming down hard. We packed our belongings and started the slow, treacherous hike down in the darkness with just one flashlight.

Hawk also started to come down behind us, and when I turned around I saw that her feet weren't touching the ground.

"Did you see that?" I turned to Lynn, breathless with excitement. "Yes!"

As we drove down the steep winding path and I turned to look through the back window of the car, instead of seeing Pico Mountain, I found myself looking at the fringes of the universe, as though the heavens were chasing our car. It was a vision that no doubt was the product of my heightened awareness.

The last island we visited was Terceira, one of the largest in the archipelago. Our taxis took us through green hilly countryside which, as on the other islands, was divided into walled fields and dotted with volcanic cones known locally as mouths of fire.

We arrived in the heart of the main town, a bustling street of shops, restaurants, and hotels, where traditional bullfights take place. Our hotel was set back from a charming circular plaza studded with trees. Terceira, we learned, was the site of an American air base and an international airport. It was also one of the most commercial islands we had seen, having an eighteen-hole golf course, football fields, cinemas, and nightclubs.

"Where shall we eat lunch?" Hawk asked John after we had settled into rooms and reassembled in the lobby. Just around the corner was a crowded restaurant with a battalion of waiters serving an array of fish, shellfish, and chicken. We sat down at one of the larger tables. As I studied the people in the restaurant carrying on with their lives, it made me realize just how far we had moved outside of any schedule or program of time. Indeed the people around me seemed stuck in a life made of illusions. In my heightened awareness I didn't know if it was six o'clock, seven o'clock, or eight o'clock—and it really didn't matter. I had managed to step outside of linear time and what a blissfully transcendent state it was! The space around me unfolded—I was spiraling and ascending in a larger sphere. I had escaped the gilded cage of time that modern civilization had gifted me with. Before freeing myself, I had no idea of the great truths that lay outside that cage—how could I have fathomed the boundlessness of the world?

After we ate, we browsed through nearby shops and purchased souvenirs. When we returned to the hotel, we were fortunate to procure the privacy of a huge room on the top floor overlooking a terrace.

"As your dreams continue to unfold, I want you to keep writing,"

Hawk said after we had arranged couches and chairs close together. "I want you to write a song about your experiences here. Your song starts with the blue and green lakes and the hot spring on the first island. It continues with the volcano and the crater we visited, and it concludes on a war base."

We called it our sacred fire song because fire in these islands signified inevitable and constant change—and because through trials of fire new pathways were opened.

"Your first dance with fire was fear," Hawk said softly, referring to our experience of walking across a bed of hot coals.

"As you write, ask yourselves who has sung to you here? Hum the song of the lakes and the voice in the winds and the feeling of the Earth when you sat on her."

As Hawk spoke, war planes flew overhead at a steady pace. The enormous reverberating noise of the supersonic jet fighters invaded our very thoughts, reminding us how much work we still faced to create a new Earth. Just three years earlier, American troops had been in the early stages of mobilization in the Persian Gulf following the Iraqi invasion of Kuwait.

I looked around at the others, and our eyes met with the intimacy of knowing that we had all been profoundly changed. We had experienced a reality beyond ego and separation. Each of us had discovered the sense of oneness that came with unifying ourselves through time and outside of mechanized time. Many deep memories had been stirred.

And as our journey came to a close, Hawk said a "tremendous healing" had taken place on these islands. "We are the oracles of that healing," she said in a hushed voice, her eyes glowing with appreciation and love.

She told us about a dream she'd had the night before, which suggested we could still restore the sacredness to this troubled Earth and recover our natural abilities.

We were all in her dream, dressed in "brilliantly colored" ceremonial clothes, signifying "pure and true light," and red moccasins that were "like velvety suede." Our eyes, highlighted with gold eyeliner, were "as big and liquid as those of baby seals." We looked like ancient gods, and the men had medicine totems dangling from their braided hair. The scene consisted of a large mountain—"our church"—and views of lowlands, deserts, and valleys that extended to the ends of the Earth. Thick and puffy clouds rolled and tumbled over each other, and the sunset was so pervasive "you could almost reach up and touch it." Huge columns, reminiscent of the Parthenon, lined the path into the mountain. The columns were exquisitely bedecked with crystals, amethysts, rubies, diamonds, emeralds, and opals. Every column had an alcove and inside it was an altar with symbols written in stone; these symbols contained the keys to open our consciousness to the highest and purest of thoughts. Each of us in the group guarded an alcove that had a waterfall illuminated by shafts of light.

Hawk told us that "a deep rumbling and distant thunder came from the mountain" followed by a thunderous rendition of "Nights in White Satin." Some of us knew this powerful and hypnotic tune by the Moody Blues and started to sing it.

And as she continued to describe her dream, her voice became choked with emotion: "We were all climbing the mountain. And as I turned around there were hundreds of thousands of people from all of the world's religions coming forward. Children were held up by carpets being moved through the air by light beings. And a thundering voice, the voice of God, said: 'Thus the prophecies are fulfilled and the seven seals are delivered. The Earth shall rejoice and the children of happiness shall lead them from the desert to the mountain. All will come to pass, and again the Earth shall be right and man shall live in right relationship.' "

Tears streamed down her face as she told us that "the sweet sound of flutes played in the distance while thousands of voices sang 'I love you, I love you, I love you, oh, how I love you.' Inside the mountain all the people had gathered and were moving toward an altar. All of you moved up the side of the mountain where the Ark of the Covenant was, and you were ignited into light. The doors of the mountain folded like wings, and all was silent."

It was a beautiful and prophetic dream. We were overcome with emotion, unable to hold back the tears.

The shields we had crafted during our time here contained a message that came from our hearts: "We are the Atlanteans returning home—not those who destroyed this great and ancient civilization but illumined beings who can transcend our physical senses and experience our oneness with the universe."

"Feel the fear and heartbreak when these islands went down into the ocean," Hawk said, asking us to recall the memory of the devastating planetary upheaval when the knowledge and records of our human history were lost. "Don't walk away from Atlantis this time," was her impassioned plea. (Many Thunderbeings who were incarnate at the time of Atlantis had fled from their responsibility to maintain harmony and peace on that continent.)

When we left these islands we would focus our thoughts on the energy of love and light, which was the true spirit of Atlantis. We would focus on the visual beauty we had seen. We would hold on to our focus even while the world played out its drama of turmoil and destructive rage. We would pray for the continuation of these islands and for the reactivation of Atlantean energy for the entire planet.

Slowly and in a very low tone, Hawk told us that we would lose another chakra if the Azores were destroyed. (Our body is made up of several chakras or energy centers: most people now believe we have twelve major chakras; Hawk says we have fourteen.)

I cringed at the thought of losing these islands, which were so important in nurturing our consciousness.

At this point we went to the restaurant for dinner and then returned to the hotel for our last evening together.

Where had the time gone? We were in a transcendent state, filled with the beautiful images of these islands, having escaped the prison of mechanical time. We had no idea of the extent to which our timing devices controlled us—until Hawk quizzed us about our two weeks here.

"Can you account for the time?" She smiled half mischievously. "Think about it. When you were in the shower or on the toilet, time went by . . . but you didn't know just how much time."

And slowly it started to dawn on us that we really hadn't done all that much. Where *had* the time gone?

Just to illustrate how little we had actually done, Hawk asked us to write on a sheet of paper everything we had done over the past fourteen days.

There was a silence as we scribbled. I wrote down some thirty things, including eating, driving (to the twin lakes on the first island, to the crater and the volcano on the second, to the house and the mountain on the third island), packing and unpacking, crafting my shield, and taking a boat ride.

Then she revealed that we'd had an average of two hours sleep a night!

What?

"Some nights you had six hours; other nights you had twenty minutes of sleep."

We were flabbergasted.

"Most of your waking awareness was equivalent to nighttime awareness, which is the place of the shaman."

We were stunned.

"Explain what you did twenty-two hours each day. What you did wouldn't even take four days! Feel the intimacy we felt and the dreams we had and the stories we shared."

And finally she revealed: "We have been functioning in a time warp. *Time stopped.*"

She explained how that had happened: we were accelerated beyond our physical ability to handle such an experience. "Can you even count the days you were here?" she asked.

And we couldn't; we had completely lost track of time until it didn't even exist! When we compared our experiences, it became obvious that we had all been functioning on a higher plane of existence. For a fleeting moment we experienced the life of an illumined body. We had made a quantum leap into an expanded reality that would never let us be the same again.

Hawk warned that when we got home this sensibility would stay with us for some time.

"You are going to be preoccupied. You will have days when you wonder where your time went."

And that is exactly what happened: when I returned to my daily routine, I often found myself staring into space and forgetting what I was supposed to be doing.

We had initiated a major movement here that would play a part in purging the planet of the harmful vibrations that were preventing Mother Earth from being elevated to a higher level of existence.

"The eyes of the Ancients will be watching you," Hawk said. "Stay focused on the land and the visual beauty of these islands rather than on the outer drama of the world." If we could stay focused when the winds of change blew across this land, they would have to blow past us first. Our focus would form a protective wall against the impact of destructive emotions raging across the nations of the world.

The next morning we arrived at the airport to catch a transatlantic flight, but our adventure was not yet over. While waiting at the airport, Hawk was overcome with a profound (sixth?) sense that the plane we were about to board had engine trouble. "Oh-oh," she said nervously after we checked in with our baggage; her face practically turned white. "I don't know if this will be a safe flight. This is not a healthy plane." And we all became quite nervous and agitated.

When we were inside the plane, we arranged ourselves in a particular order in the last few rows. As the plane sped down the runway, Hawk took us through a meditation: "Close your eyes. Pull down the invisible rays around the plane and pull down the light beings from the clouds to surround and carry us." And we chanted and prayed with all our might. It must have worked, because we all made it home.

Our journey had transformed us; we felt totally different in mind and spirit.

Spirituality was now becoming a real feeling for me. I had experienced fleeting glimpses into a larger realm where the contradictions of dreams and realities are resolved. I had transcended the opposites within my own being. I had discovered the bliss of nonlinear time. I felt connected to a multidimensional reality and realized I didn't have to look far; that reality was inside me. My return to Atlantis is part of what I am today; these islands continue to live inside me.

We are the Atlanteans returning home; the spirit of Atlantis is alive in us. We had gone through a portal in time and space. We had been adjusted physically and psychologically, and our Thunderbeing energies had been amplified! We had come here to address the imbalance in the galactic grid, recognizing that the Atlanteans played a part in the breaking of that sacred grid because they chose the experience of ego over the experience of the heart.

We are the Atlanteans returning home, synchronized in mind, heart, and will.

CHAPTER 15

THE FIRE IN THE SKY

Thus, when the lamp that lighted
The traveller at first goes out,
He feels awhile benighted,
And looks around in fear and doubt.
But soon, the prospect clearing,
By cloudless starlight on he treads,
And thinks no lamp so cheering
As that light which Heaven sheds
  —THOMAS MOORE

THE SOLAR ECLIPSE ON May 10, 1994, cast an eerie blue light across our planet. In astronomical circles the event was referred to as a "ring of fire." It signified the birth of galactic winds of change. Some people will move ahead because of these winds while others will be blown by them and forced to look within to release outworn restrictive patterns and ways of being.

The ring of fire created by the eclipse marked the arrival of the last Thunderbeings on Earth.

At this time Hawk and the Thunderbeings were busy preparing for their greatest assignment, the success of which would have great reverberations for our planet. Our preparation included celestial studies, which involved exploring the skies and ancient astrology. We recognized that the heavens are relatives who abide by the same law of cause and effect as we do. They are our ancestors; we are part of the same cosmic metabolism. There is constant interaction between celestial and terrestrial life-forms. As Hawk put it: "The universe is a network of wheels called cycles, and our being is the combination of it all. Our form and all of its inner galaxies are connected to that which is above, including the planets, stars, comets, dust, and fires."

The great cosmic wheels create the huge gears of our existence. The rotation of one of the celestial bodies turns many others. All of the planets rotate; they are interconnected, performing the movements of a huge clock, and we are one of the gears in that clock.

During the eighteen months leading up to our assignment, we studied the sun and the moon; we familiarized ourselves with the vibrational forces of the planets: Jupiter, Saturn, Venus, Uranus, Neptune, Mars, Mercury, and Pluto. We became *emotionally attached* to them.

We did our own charts—each one a replica of our solar system—to determine the position of the planets at the moment we were born and how our personality relates to that. Every person is motivated strongly by one particular planet. Mercury people are quick-tempered and impatient, with strong communication skills; they are the trusted messengers with a message of wisdom to deliver (I have a Mercury temperament). Jupiter people are gentle and refined with an unquenchable thirst for inner knowledge; they love solitude and tend to be hermits. Venusians are the decorators of the world; they're devoted to good taste and etiquette as well as material comfort and wealth; they have given the world beautiful colognes and perfumes. Martians are the pioneers and adventurers who are always seeking to explore new universes; they are very intense, full of fire and spontaneity; they have exotic appetites and are socially inclined.

Pluto people are unsurpassable in their nobility and dignity. No man can live up to the expectations of a Pluto woman, and she can be deadly when betrayed. Movie star Elizabeth Taylor is a manifestation of Pluto's energy; indeed, no man has been able to hold on to her!

Those with Uranian traits are the lawmakers, nurturers, and providers. While very opinionated, they are the ones who initiate change and are capable of going the full distance when something needs to be done. Neptune people are the public speakers and philosophers who work from a base of profound principles. They are a powerful spiritual resource who call forth the forces of the whales and dolphins; Leo Buscaglia, author and public speaker, is a Neptunian.

Saturn types are extremely private and powerful; they can find beauty in the most barren of places. They are the magicians and keepers of knowledge who are also capable of being assassins because life and death have the same significance for them.

We realized that Neptune and Saturn types are rare because our society had been structured along functional and mechanistic lines, rather than spiritual lines. According to some astrologers, Neptune and Saturn link us to a more transcendent consciousness.

Exploring the planets helped us to gain a more objective view of our lives; we saw our interconnection with another dimension of beings dancing in the stars. We acknowledged the planets as people who had feelings and thoughts. We worked at connecting with their energies. Every morning, we greeted Mars and Saturn; in the evening, Venus and Jupiter. We paid careful attention to the phases of the moon; we made a special effort to be outside during the full moon. We also stopped following the Gregorian calendar, replacing it with a Mayan calendar. The way we felt about the planets was the way we felt about our lives. They were our family; they had a life on a different scale. Our form would die, but our energy would continue; similarly, the planets would be transformed.

At the same time I was becoming increasingly aware of the power of my thoughts. I had to constantly review my thoughts, for they manifested themselves almost as soon as they came into my mind. I had freed myself to a great extent of old patterns of behaviors—although I still had to work at it. I realized that the biggest hurdle I faced was overcoming my own habits and compulsions.

Our reality had changed so much from the time of the Harmonic Convergence in 1987. We had started to appreciate and love every part of ourselves. Hawk had been a great catalyst in helping us understand that wisdom is beyond being Eastern or Western, Buddhist or Christian. Rather, it is individual and a function of the heart.

We knew that the process of expanding our awareness didn't have to be fraught with struggle—Earthlings were the ones who originally made that restriction. We were seeing the potential of ourselves and understanding how much more fun it was to go through life in an awakened state. At this point we would not let anything stop us from realizing our personal dreams along with our desire for a transformed Earth. We were graduating from a limited human perspective and becoming galactic beings.

Hawk encouraged us to dream *big* and work toward our highest ideals. "Exercise faith," she advised us again and again.

As I focused constantly with a clear vision of what I wanted, my life started to come together in a way that was beyond my wildest dreams. Oh, there were still intense times, but I was happier than I had ever been.

I knew that anything could be created. I had gained access to other dimensions and realized that the bridge of the soul stretched beyond the limitations of body and brain. I had experienced freedom from being stuck in linear time. Earth is the ultimate place where anything can be manifested. It is a magnificent theater that offers endless stories and colorful characters. We can choose our part: do we want to be in a comedy, a love story, or a musical? Or do we want our life to be a melodrama?

The Thunderbeings, myself included, were exhausted from theatrical productions that involved destruction, murder, and abuse. We saw how desensitized people had become. We were also concerned that some of the leading players who formed the phalanx of the world's social, political, and economic forces continued to ignore the plight of Mother Earth.

In spite of this, we continued to focus on connecting with the Earth as a place of beauty. Nothing could make us give up our vision of a new world of peace and harmony.

And now we were ready to tackle the biggest challenge of our mission as Thunderbeings.

It was an event that had been prophesied and discussed for 5,500 years. Ancient and indigenous peoples call it "the fire in the sky" and "the light in the heavens."

This was the Second Coming we had all been waiting for. We were about to become part of a really major solar system event.

This prophecy, which is as old as Atlantis, states that: "When the flash of light is seen in the heavens, man's mind will begin its transformation and enlightenment."

That flash of light was none other than the celestial fireworks of the comet that smashed into Jupiter in July 1994, creating the biggest explosion ever seen in our solar system!

Jupiter has long been described as "the sleeping sun" because its atmosphere consists mostly of hydrogen. All that is required is a spark, such as the comet, to ignite it.

Astronomers estimated that the comet had the impact of six million megatons of TNT—100,000 times the power of the largest nuclear bomb ever detonated on Earth.

Nearly two dozen mountain-size chunks of the comet slammed into Jupiter, creating 2,000-mile-high fireballs above the planet's cloud tops. The fireworks associated with several of the larger fragments emitted enough light to allow large telescopes on Earth to record the faint entry flashes. The biggest fragment produced a 5,000-mile-wide plume that towered above the planet's surface.

Astronomers had feared that they might see only a momentary brightening of some of the inner moons. What they actually did see exceeded their wildest dreams. Said one astronomer at California's Jet Propulsion Laboratory: "It was like God striking the planet."[1]

The crash took place on the surface of Jupiter facing away from Earth, but the fireball rose so high that its tip peeked over Jupiter's rim and became visible to Earth-based sensors.

Astrogeologist Eugene Shoemaker, codiscoverer of the comet, said that it was a rare event. He expressed it as a bloody miracle and that a collision of this sort occurs less than once every few thousand years.

Time magazine noted that comets are "extremely delicate" and that "it is amazing that the solar system could create an object so fragile that would stay together for so long."[2]

Even more amazing, this comet was formed by the Thunderbeings! It derived its impact and power from the presence of 144,000 Thunderbeings on Earth. It was the Thunderbeings who formed the body of that speeding comet that crashed into Jupiter with an energy greater than all the nuclear weapons on Earth!

This was possible because the Thunderbeings are made of the

same intensity as a comet. Comets tend to be a mixture of ice, rock, and dust, along with substances like carbon monoxide, that evaporate easily to form a halo and a tail. They are objects that look like fuzzy stars with tails. The Thunderbeings are made of both fire and ice.

This was the grand moment we had been preparing for. It was part of the divine plan that we would be here at this precise time. We had been invited to the greatest event of all history

During months of preparation, we talked to the planets, we romanced them, and we made offerings. We learned how to draw upon their energies. "They are eager to come forward," Hawk told us.

As we started to plug in to planetary frequencies, we experienced vertigo, hypertension, and sluggish circulation. Planetary travel buzzed us into new places within ourselves, which gave us a sensation of spinning; we were walking between the worlds.

I spent many evenings journeying to the planets. Often I would go outside. After making an offering of sacred smoke, I would lie down on my blanket and use my rattle to get into a meditative state. Once I had succeeded in getting within the very depth of my self, I would travel to the planets.

In the months preceding the summer of 1994, we focused exclusively on Jupiter. Every evening I would go outside and locate him. I lay down under the night sky, covered my eyes, and found my focus. I attached my consciousness to Jupiter. I journeyed with him.

I began to understand that the planets in our solar system also live in a village just like our villages on Earth. The planets interact with one another, and some take more than they give.

Some time ago a great crime was committed among the planets; power was seized, causing a great imbalance to the solar system. One planet was destroyed in the process; Maldek, the fifth planet from the sun, is now an asteroid belt. Mars was rendered uninhabitable.

The problems began with Jupiter and Saturn, who had conspired to take over the star system.

Jupiter, the solar system's largest planet, was named after the king of the Olympian gods, who was also called Jove. He was usually depicted sitting on an ivory throne and holding a sheaf of thunderbolts.

Jupiter represents our subconscious and secret nature. Jupiter creates shadows that keep us unaware of our true nature. A lot of New

Age teachings and philosophies advise that we suppress or try to transcend our shadow self. Rather, we must acknowledge and understand its existence so that we may decide whether we want what it has to offer; then we will be in a position to follow a different path in our lives.

Jupiter could hold more than a thousand planets the size of Earth. The Jovian system is almost a mini–solar system in its own right; it rules at least sixteen moons! Jupiter is a major player in the solar system, with more mass than all the other planets and moons combined.

Astronomers say that it is rare for comets to collide with Jupiter. Comets, they say, may be drawn toward the planet and then fractured and flung into the space. They have found evidence of this on Ganymede and Callisto, two of Jupiter's moons. This suggests that millions of comets may have broken up the giant planet. Jupiter's gravitational pull is so great that it distorts the orbits of all other bodies and flings countless stray comets out into the solar system.

It is an enormous planet—maybe even overbearing—that almost seems to be in competition with the Sun, creating struggle and turmoil amongst the planets. In fact, it radiates twice as much heat as it receives from the sun. But like everything in nature, including unpleasant experiences—such as the wolf that hunts the beautiful deer—it has a purpose.

Jupiter wanted to be like the Creator. "What if I could be of myself?" was its thought. It took Saturn into the conspiracy, spitting out debris and meteorites. When it fired out at Earth, Maldek took the impact.

Meanwhile, Venus aligned herself with Earth. She deflected all of the radiation and meteorites hurtling toward our planet.

The bands and swirls of red, orange, yellow, and blue in Jupiter's atmosphere, created by counterflowing winds, are quite beautiful to behold. He has a dazzling prominent feature: the great red spot, a giant counterclockwise cyclone, sandwiched between two jet streams of wind that flow in opposite directions. Jupiter's surface is riddled with storms, and the great red spot, which is larger than Earth itself, is the eye of the storm. Hawk and the Thunderbeings call it the medicine eye. Scientists believe it has existed for more than three hundred years, but they don't fully understand the causes of its formation.

Jupiter has built its power around this magnificent red spot. But how did he get it? According to indigenous peoples, Jupiter took the red spot from Earth. It had been a gift to Earth of purity, beauty, and grace from the Pleiades. It held the vibration of love and beauty like no other form. Earth was a duplication of what existed within the Mother Universe; when that chemistry entered into our planet, pure intelligence was seeded. The medicine eye gave Earth the status of a gem in the universe; it was part of her electrical field and her frequency. She has wobbled in her rotation ever since it was torn from her. All of the beautiful and gentle creatures, including the unicorn and the dragon, saw the impending darkness and escaped into Earth's inner core.

Jupiter caused the time tunnel between Earth and Uranus to be closed. He blocked the passage between these two planets, which hold the third and the eighth orbits—they hold the orbital balance of the solar system. When Jupiter fired at Earth, she tilted on her axis and was changed; our evolution was affected. Since that time, the earthkeepers and peacekeepers have rattled, drummed, and chanted to act as Earth's crutch; their drumbeats keep her going. If it had not been for them she might have fallen apart sooner.

As this planetary drama unfolded, I felt like a child watching its parents argue and break up. As children of the planets, we felt hurt and traumatized that Jupiter and Earth were not getting along. We didn't want to believe that Jupiter was trying to take over the solar system and destroy Earth.

Our mission was to reclaim the forces that belonged to Earth without causing devastation to the solar system. The fulfillment of this prophecy called for every Thunderbeing to be present on Earth.

The Thunderbeings faced a great battle. The Ancients called it a battle to reclaim the forces and bring the solar system back into balance. This is a reckoning! Our mission was to return the great red spot to its rightful place on Earth where it was always meant to be. The giant of our solar system had built all its power around this spot!

And so the moment of our great battle arrived; the moment that the Ancients had always waited for was here. In June 1994, some thirty

Thunderbeings gathered on the hill where Hawk had sung her sacred chant eight years earlier. All of our years of preparation would now be put to the test.

It was a warm and sunny day. The sky was exceptionally vibrant, lightly accented with puffs of clouds. We arranged ourselves in several rows, facing north, as nervous as mountain climbers preparing to meet the challenge of the highest summit ever, filled with anticipation and fear; we would soon find out if we were up to the task.

We sat on the ground and concentrated on clearing our minds of rambling extraneous thoughts. It was important to clear our minds, to feel focused. We had to direct our thoughts to one single purpose; everything else must disappear. We had to transcend the pull of our emotions and find a clear conviction as to what we were doing. Every Thunderbeing present understood this.

"Make sure your mind-set is very clear," Hawk warned. "This is no time for emotionalism."

As we prepared ourselves for our ceremony, you could feel the anxiety in our breathing and our movements.

"This is a warrior's altar," Hawk said, her voice booming and powerful. "You *can't* be wishy-washy. You have to have a clear focus and a clear conviction. We're in opposition to Jupiter, to the imbalance to all the life-forms."

I took a deep breath; my heart was pounding, as though it would burst from my chest. I felt both panic and excitement. Everything I had ever done and worked toward had led me to this ultimate moment. The adrenaline was rushing through my veins; it was as though I were preparing myself for a battle that would only permit one victor; it could only go one way.

This much we knew: we had to stop Jupiter or there would be no Earth. We had been born for this purpose. The imbalance had to be corrected. Earth must become illumined or all of the planets would become moons to Jupiter!

"Pick up the picture of Jupiter. See him as a thing of beauty. See him as a magnificent being," Hawk said, full of passion.

As I focused on Jupiter's beauty and the great red spot, I wanted to laugh and cry at the same time. He evoked such strong emotions in me; even though he was our enemy, I loved this Cyclops. He too was part of creation.

Hawk told us that we had no reason to pursue our goal with hatred or prejudgment. That was not our way; it was more powerful to focus on Jupiter's beauty.

"Jupiter has something that never belonged to it. Without the great red spot—the medicine eye—Earth cannot be a place of tolerance and compassion."

As I looked up at Hawk, I felt gripped in the hands of tension.

We started to chant.

We prayed in unison for balance between my mother the Earth and Jupiter, that all things might live equally in harmony and joy as was originally given. We were powerfully focused, like one breath heaving together. We chanted and prayed with all of the fire and thunder within us.

"What we put into our ceremony is clear conviction," Hawk emphasized. "We're part of the fuel of that spearhead that is moving toward Jupiter." She noted that all of her elders had sent their support and that we were all moving in synchronization.

This was it! This was the moment!

In our ceremony we sent our message and our voices upon the sacred smoke. Our pleas were carried by the smoke. We became flames and whirling forces and thunder. We became the dance of Shiva that tears down the destructive and the weak. We resounded with the most powerful forces on Earth. Our thoughts resonated past the clouds and into many dimensions of time and space.

The Thunderbeings became one consciousness, traveling through tunnels and parallel universes. We ignited the space around us; we rode a wave and moved inside a huge spiral. We projected our thoughts, which became a thousand times more powerful than an atomic bomb. We created an enormous pulsation.

This much we knew: the imbalance must fall to the wayside. Where there was balance and harmony, there was no limit as to what could be done. We were part of that force that was moving more powerfully than we could fathom, moving to do what it knew it had to do.

We *formed* the icy comet that smashed into Jupiter: a massive chunk of rock and ice that hurtled through the Jovian heavens at 134,000 miles per hour—the most spectacular bombardment ever recorded by humanity! The comet *was* the consciousness and thought processes of all of the Thunderbeings and peacekeepers on Earth.

"We're going to send some parts of Jupiter back into the great mystery and other parts where they are meant to go—[to Earth]," Hawk said as she stood before us.

Just as we completed our ceremony, the winds got very still; a great stillness descended upon the hill and the valley. There was a haze all around, almost a whiteness and dryness in the air.

We had been involved in a major event, and yet it reminded me of my childhood, one day in the playground, when I picked up my marble and, with all of my ability and strength, hurled it at a larger marble, forcing it to move!

"Look, a hawk, an eagle, a vulture, and a raven are dancing in the south!" Hawk said exuberantly, pointing to the area behind us.

We turned around and saw them circling. They had come in response to our work. It was a propitious sign—four powerful messengers!

Immediately we heard shouts from the valley below. Hawk's medicine room, which holds many of her ceremonial objects, was on fire! We dropped everything and ran down the steep path to the bottom of the valley. Smoke was coming out of one corner of our building. Jupiter was fighting back with his own fireball! We filled buckets with water and passed them along until we had the fire under control. We were fortunate—while the walls, ceiling, and carpeting were charred, we were able to salvage most of the objects.

"I really expected more clout from Jupiter!" Hawk laughed as she examined the room. "If that's the worst that we can expect, we're blessed. I was expecting a better fight. If that's the size of your fireball, wait until you see ours! It's bigger than your planet!"

"How could it happen so fast?" I asked astonished.

"We're lucky the building is still here," David said.

We were flabbergasted.

"You have been effective," Hawk confirmed, obviously delighted with our work.

The rest is history. A few weeks later, in mid-July, the comet struck Jupiter. Headlines around the world confirmed our success: "The abrupt appearance of fresh wounds on Jupiter's colorful face is cause for celebration, proving that Shoemaker-Levy 9 is not a dud." "The comet tore huge holes in Jupiter's atmosphere." "The fragments of the comet plowed into Jupiter, leaving behind a necklace of dark bruises on the planet's gaseous atmosphere." "Some of the impact bruises were larger than Earth!" "Jupiter is taking a beating!"

The Galileo spacecraft had a full view of the fireworks. It was in the right position to directly observe the collisions, which occurred on the back side of the planet just out of sight of ground-based and Earth-orbiting telescopes. The swirling black clouds that remained in the comet's wake surprised scientists, who had expected them to be white and cloudlike. One planetary science professor said these clouds looked "like Gettysburg after the battle."[3]

After the comet slammed into Jupiter's nucleus, waves from the impact were sent out to the sun and to our planet. Every dimension in the galaxy was experiencing repercussions.

The Thunderbeings corrected a huge imbalance that was beyond time and space. The imbalance had existed for so long that people didn't even acknowledge its existence. They didn't even know that they'd distorted the natural cycles of time. (How could they say there were thirty-one days in a lunar cycle when there were only twenty-eight days?)

Most people don't live as part of nature. They hardly pay attention to the moon and the planets. They've been disconnected; something in them has broken. Their spirit has become sick, and their bodies are riddled with illness. The Old Ones say the spirit is diseased.

Less than a month after the comet crash, NASA scientists reported receiving radioed distress signals from the devastated planet! They were able to tell from the mathematical pattern of these signals that Jupiter was pleading for help. Using state-of-the-art computerized sensors, they picked up sounds similar to those made by dolphins and whales, and then decoded them.

There were three sentences, each one consisting of two or more words: "Help me!" "I surrender!" "I seek forgiveness!"

Jupiter was asking for forgiveness. He agreed to be part of the harmonic balance of our solar system, knowing that he would be saved from total annihilation if he let go of the red spot that he held in the nucleus of his being.

Hawk said we had succeeded in totally dismantling Jupiter's frequency that allowed him to cause so much destruction to the other planets. The Thunderbeings were the comet. Each messenger we sent out made an impact on Jupiter's surface.

"I want you to have conscious awareness of what you did," she told us. "You moved as warriors that day. This is your ability and your power as galactic beings."

In forming the comet, we dismantled Jupiter's power, which had been a huge influence in our lives. As Hawk said, "It has been one of opposition . . . but we also have to look at our participation in this. We have to have appreciation for our opponent; otherwise we would not have had the experiences that came out of that. We would not have the experience of sorrow and suffering. We need sorrow. Without it, how would we know joy?"

Immediately after the comet battered Jupiter, many of us felt a great sadness, similar to separation anxiety. But now we could more easily free ourselves of the negativism that had run deep in our consciousness.

It occurred to me that people on Earth had experienced battles similar to those of the planets. While Jupiter had acted like an aggressive bully, similarly, individuals had been suppressed by larger, more powerful individuals, as in the struggle between parents and children, husbands and wives, nations and citizens. The red spot that we dislocated from Jupiter could almost symbolize what had been taken from the weak and the innocent—their dignity, self-control, and ability to decide their own future. Freedom from all abusive relationships could be attained only when the red spot was returned to its rightful owner.

But even after leaving an abusive relationship, an individual remembered loving the other person and that there were good times, and now the person was ready to forgive.

When we gathered again, we sang a chant to celebrate our breakthrough.

"If you feel melancholy, that's okay," Hawk told us. "Allow the grieving to take place. Appreciate what Jupiter has been in your life, even though it was pain and suffering. The Tibetans appreciate Jupiter as a teacher of opposition that tests our skills."

The impact of the comet initiated a new stage in Jupiter's evolution. The giant planet would now be a little smaller in size. The time tunnel between Uranus and Earth would be opened. Maldek would return and would become even bigger and more glorious.

When the comet hit Jupiter it sent a wave to the sun, which in turn sent out an energy that would alter the way the Earth moved. This would also result in changes to our planet's life-forms. The great red spot would return to being a part of the electrical field of Earth—it would be our second moon. As the prophecy stated, there would come a time when we would have two moons and we would stand between two suns. We would be the generation of the new sun. We would have full consciousness.

Hawk said, "When you see this big thing hurtling at you in a few years, you'll wonder if Hawk made a mistake. You'll wonder if maybe we went a little too far." She laughed.

She added that the effects of the comet's impact would continue until the year 2000. Jupiter's enlightenment would have major reverberations on people and institutions. It would herald a five-year period that would be one of humanity's most challenging times. "All governments and religions will fall," Hawk told us. "Many things will pass. It's a lot more than what we can comprehend right now."

By the year 2000 we'll have shorter days and the Earth's wobble will disappear.

Scientists have predicted that the comet's impact will cause a great upheaval on Earth. Because our solar system is very tightly connected, what happens in one part of it affects all the other parts.

NOTES

1. *U.S. News & World Report*, Aug. 1, 1994, Science & Society Section; cover story by Traci Watson.
2. *Time*, May 23, 1984, p. 47, by James Reston Jr.
3. MIT professor Tim Dowling, quoted in the *Montreal Gazette*, March 1995, by Reuters, Washington.

CHAPTER 16

WHO WILL MAKE IT TO THE NEW WORLD?

The world is being carried to the brink of ecological disaster not by a single fault which some clever scheme can correct, but by the phalanx of powerful economic, political, and social forces that constitute the march of history. Anyone who proposes to cure the environmental crisis undertakes thereby to change the course of history.

—BARRY COMMONER[1]

AFTER THAT FATEFUL DAY with Jupiter, time seemed to race ahead faster than ever before, like an overwound clock. The world was in a state of accelerating crisis. But there were also heartwarming signs and wonders in the skies—beautiful rainbows and cloud designs; sunsets containing brilliant magentas, pinks, blues, and golds; and convergences of celestial bodies. As well, new planets were being discovered. One of the Thunderbeings said that he hoped this meant that Creator was letting us know that the new world was coming. Out of crisis and pain would come the birthing of a new world, a new human.

And, yes, there are now signs that the new world is coming. The Mayans, who had a much more universal and spiritual culture than ours, have waited five hundred years for this time. According to their calendars, a synchronization took place on March 21, 1995, that blasted the planet into real people time.

On that day Mayans and Tibetans gathered at the ancient site of Chichén-Itzá in the Yucatán. Hawk and eight Thunderbeings attended the event. Thousands of people filled the square at the base of a pyramid known as Kukulcan, which was built according to strict astronomical guidelines. The temple has four sides of ninety-one steps; on the faces of these steps are fifty-two notches on either side of the stairway: fifty-two years is the synchronization of Earth with the Pleiades. Four stairways each having ninety-one steps add up to a total of 364, which is the number of days in the solar year. On March 21–22 and September 21–22, which are equinox days, between noon and 5:00 P.M., the sun casts a shadow that gives the appearance of a serpent slithering up or down the north-facing steps of the pyramid.

The crowd became quiet as the shadow started to undulate up the stone stairs of the pyramid. It created seven triangular shapes that gradually leveled out into the silhouette of a serpent. This was and is a sacred moment to the Mayans. It celebrates the arrival of Kukulcan, which imbues us with cosmic energy. I sat in awe at the base of the pyramid as the spirit of the serpent emerged, seeming to beckon us to awaken to the powers of our mind and spirit.

Kukulcan is the god-man-bird serpent, the all-knowing divinity that preceded all things on Earth. The energies of the serpent are aligned with the galactic energies of the Pleiades. According to the prophecies, a new human is now emerging from the mouth of the serpent, a galactically aware human, and Kukulcan is returning to protect the pure and the innocent beings on this Earth.

The ceremony continued. Three Tibetan lamas, wearing yellow-gold and dark maroon robes, along with a handful of Mayans, stood facing the pyramid. A long procession of people queued up to greet and shake hands with them. The lamas chanted in a low tone and sounded their bells. There was a great deal of commotion amid the huge crowd of onlookers. Some people were climbing up the steps of the pyramid while others were clicking away at their cameras and camcorders. A potpourri of people were singing their own chants. Three small Mexican women were bellowing with heartfelt intent at the top of their lungs. Conch horns were blaring. Standing behind the lamas, a woman dressed all in white held up a sign that phonetically spelled out their chant: "Om ma ni pa me hom." With all of this going on, Hunbatz Men, a Mayan elder who had been trying to control the crowd, directed a group into another chant.

Meanwhile the Thunderbeings were chanting quietly, observing all of the craziness going on. It was a great moment. It had much significance for me and the others. But that doesn't mean there wasn't a feeling of a circus taking place. Hordes of people were there as gawkers; they were not respectful of what was taking place. They were behaving as if they were at a rock concert; they didn't understand what was being done, and their behavior diminished the whole ceremony. Such behavior is not an isolated phenomenon; it's the underlying truth of all religions. They all started with pure intentions but somewhere along the way they lost their innocence. Where did they go wrong? Religion is like a lighthouse; it was erected to help guide the ship to its destination. The lighthouse itself is not the destination but merely a beacon and companion to us, the ship. When the lighthouse presents itself as the destination, it draws the ship into raging waters and jagged rocks. Instead of guiding it through the fog and as it leads us through times of turmoil, giving comfort and easing the passage, it entraps. When the lighthouse, or the church, becomes self-serving to the point where it thinks of itself as more important than what it represents, it does more harm than good. As Alexander Pope put it: "Who builds a church to God and not to fame, Will never mark the marble with his name."

Later, as the ceremony came to a close, when most of the crowd had departed, the Mexican police were shooing us out of there. We were shocked to learn that while tourists could climb up the pyramid, the Mayans were forbidden to do so; they could not perform their own ceremony on their own altar! I have yet to understand all of the reasons behind this, except that it's the result of political control in that country.

When we arrived back at our hotel in Mérida, we gathered outside around the pool. It was dark by now, and we had complete privacy. As we reviewed the day's events, we were dismayed at how little understanding was shown for the Mayans' place of worship. This is their church; the pyramid is their altar. It just happens to be under the sky. You don't walk into someone's church and perform your own ceremony; you don't go up and sit on top of the altar.

We continued our discussion until well after midnight, seated under a starry sky. At one point we all stood up to gaze at the half-moon, which was shaped like a cup. Mars, Jupiter, and Venus converged in the shape of a triangle that enclosed the moon. I was in my place of worship—this was my church. My real altar, greater than anything I could ever create on my own, had been given to me. I realized at this point that I had always had a church to go to: the stars, the moon, the sun, the Milky Way, all of this was my church. I had visited beautiful churches and synagogues but they had not stirred me spiritually. I knew that if I allowed myself to be anchored by one structure, I would create a limit, but if I regarded the universe as my church, there was no limit; it was endless. The doors to my church were always open—no one could close them, no one could control this church or take it away from me. Why would I need stained-glass windows when I had the stars? Why would I need a golden altar when I had the sun? Why would I need silver chalices when I had the moon?

"The wind seems to be breathing a sigh of relief," Irving whispered.

"There's the moon sitting on Venus," Hawk said excitedly. "She's beautiful. That's part of the prophecy. The cup is starting to tip and pour into Venus. Those who are open to receive will receive the love that's being offered, and those who are not . . ."

Our discussions took us into the meaning of this prophecy. As we approach the millennium there will be great joy for those who are open to receive the new wisdom and energy and love that is being made available to all humans. If ever there has existed an opportunity to make a quantum leap into a new way of being, this is it! We are headed for the most important spiritual adventure ever! A new consciousness is being birthed. To the Christians it's the Second Coming of Christ; to the Hopi it's the beginning of the new world of peace and harmony.

All human beings will now have the opportunity to experience their true potential. The transition has begun—we are in the death throes of our civilization and the birth pangs of a new era in our evolution. We have entered the perilous space between two world ages, a time of maximum danger and limitless opportunity. We are experiencing a great acceleration of spiritual energies; we are being purified of all the sludge that smothers our full potential. We will go through things that are presently inconceivable.

Millions of people have embarked on a search for the sacred in their lives. It is as though the entire planet is suffering with PMS—pre-millennial syndrome. People are hungrier than ever for spiritual illumination, but they are turning away from traditional institutions. The universal longing to be whole, to be healed, to have a greater connection, is not being answered by them.

In spite of modernization and mass communication systems, we live in a dark and violent age; we are still *very* spiritually backward. Our atmosphere is filled with destructive thought-forms—fear, ignorance, laziness, denial, judgment, and reactive habits—that have a negative impact on all of the life-forms around us. Stress, anxiety, and psychological disorders have become commonplace. We are still plagued with a polluted environment and other problems too numerous to mention. Most people are too busily involved in the struggle of living to even think about changing the march of events, let alone to believe they can. The way things are going, humanity may be working on its own extinction.

Even more disturbing is the lack of an adequate response from society's leaders, who already possess the ability and the technology to redirect the course of history. Government and industry have played a major role in shaping our reality, which has become a theatrical performance with smoke and mirrors hidden behind a curtain; the illusion is so good that all we do is sit passively and gawk at it. Those who have the inner strength to stand up from their assigned seats and look behind the curtain will be able to find the true reality.

Unfortunately a lot of people feel helpless and desperately alienated from themselves. They find themselves buried in a hole and have abandoned any hope of freedom. They've been put in that hole by the power structure, which has made it very hard for them to get out.

People must take back the control they've given to their governments; they must participate and make changes that will create a future that reflects what is deep in their hearts. All that most people really want is to be alive, to laugh and cry, to love and be loved, to have a home and a family. Yet they're being manipulated and herded like a flock of sheep being taken to the slaughter, walking behind one another with glassy-eyed stares. And by their inaction, they've empowered the one who takes them to the slaughter. They've forfeited the right to decide their own fate. Unless the flock of humanity breaks this almost trancelike state of mindlessness and takes an active role in governing itself—*with wisdom*—it is headed for a disastrous future.

President John F. Kennedy once expressed this very thought: "The credit belongs to the man who is actually in the arena, whose face is marred by dust and sweat and blood, who knows the great enthusiasms, the great devotions, and spends himself in a worthy cause; who at best, if he wins, knows the thrills of high achievement, and if he fails, at least fails daring greatly, so that his place shall never be with those cold and timid souls who know neither victory nor defeat."

The Thunderbeings are trying to encourage people to have this kind of direct effect on their society. We are trying to demonstrate that being more spiritual and harmonious with the planet is to their own and their children's benefit. We are trying to show that we are all part of the same family on this planet—the *human* family—we are all members of the same community of interdependent beings. By pursuing spiritual development, people will be performing the greatest service for themselves and for the planet.

Our vision is that of a global community in which tolerance and understanding are shown for all the different religions of the world. We know how religious dogmatism turns people against each other and creates hatred and prejudice. As Mayan elder Hunbatz Men so rightly pointed out: many believe that they are the possessors of the real truth, and they attempt to impose their personal morals on others. Humanity must take a giant leap forward and look beyond differences in race, nationality, culture, and religion. They must start to follow the example of the Tibetan monks by practicing real kindness and loving compassion every day.

The path that humans are traveling is taking them nowhere; it's leading them to the edge of a cliff. As a collective energy of souls they have to step off this path. It takes courage to burn new paths, but sometimes it is the only way to happiness. Artists, sages, and shamans throughout the ages have had to pull away from society in order to achieve their goals and live truly passionate lives. Even if they experienced loneliness, at least they truly lived. Helen Keller wisely observed that life is either a daring adventure or nothing at all. I know that I had to step off the beaten path for my life to open up and become meaningful. All of the Thunderbeings did. We know that people must follow their deepest yearnings and that they can't continue to give themselves to the dangerous illusions that have led us to the brink of ecological oblivion. The philosophy of progress at any cost is not the answer to our most cherished dreams.

Our survival and the well-being of the planet depend on our returning to nature. In the search for security and comfort we have cut ourselves off from the very forces that nourish and sustain us. Social researchers have found that North Americans, on the average, spend over 80 percent of their lives indoors using various technological gadgets to discern what is going on around them rather than using their own senses and mental processes to experience the world. Our sheltered existence has become a disorder and an illness. When we return to the natural cycles of time, we will live as part of the whole. An old teaching from the Chandogya Upanishad says, "That which is Whole is joy. There is no joy in fractioned existence. Only the Whole is joy. But one must desire to understand the Whole." The destruction on this planet is a cry for a sense of this larger vision of life which celebrates nature and the source of our being, our creativity, and the deep dream. People *want* to believe in celestial gods and angels, imps, unicorns, and elves. They do exist, but our disbelief has driven them away to the other realms. As the Santa Claus character in a recent movie says indignantly when the existence of his toy workshop is denied by an army colonel who has explored the North Pole: "There is no way that the gentleman could have seen my workshop. It doesn't exist in the physical world. It is in the dream world. I always thought that was completely understood!"

You can take your first steps toward your awakening by spending time with nature. Start with the trees. Adopt a tree, visit it, sit down beside it. Just *be* with the tree; you can do this during the day or at night. Close your eyes and listen to its spirit. The tree will love the attention; it possesses life sensibilities, and its reactions are similar to ours. Try clearing its roots, pull out the weeds, make it comfortable. Hang ornaments instead of lights during the Christmas season—the electrical charge is harmful to them. The trees are our relatives. If they perish, so will we.

It's important also to take your children to be with real living things, not superficial, mechanical contraptions. Children love animals and nature. It's necessary for them to have this larger experience of life; nature is the best teacher they will ever have.

The changes that mankind will experience will bring immense joy and happiness to some, but this will be a time of incredible pain and anguish for others. Those who accept the changes with open arms will be greeted with heavenly bliss they have never before experienced. Those who are ill prepared to meet the challenge of enlightenment will suffer pain and distress the likes of which the world has never experienced. For them, the magnitude of light that is coming to Earth will feel more like a harsh glare than a wondrous illumination. The greatest hardship will be felt by those whose consciousness contains anger, resentment, frustration, despair, stress, disbelief, and distrust, as well as those who are indifferent to the Earth, self-centred, or arrogant, and the list goes on.

The Great Awakening has begun; there is no place, no cave or thick-walled dwelling to which we can escape. We will not be able to run from ourselves. We cannot fight the cosmic energies; powerful vibrations are coming to our planet; we cannot hide from the intensity of the light. We will be forced to look within and confront ourselves; we will all have to come into the light. Perceived worthiness will have no merit. For those who have embraced the deeper values and are truly worthy, this transition will be easy to accept. Others will fight it but eventually will come to the realization that they have only one choice. And still others will perish; they will oppose and resist it to the very end, but they are no match for the collective universal energies that will be thrust upon them.

When we finally arrive at the new world, we will feel as if we're coming home. It will be a place where we feel safe and nurtured and can be our true selves. We won't have to pretend or perform; we can do anything we want.

With this quantum leap will come physical changes to our bodies; we will become lighter and of a higher vibration, which is our natural state. We will be less affected by gravity, giving us the ability to levitate and move freely upon the wind. As we move to a path of light, we will be capable of many things that we now consider impossible or phenomenal.

The forces of evolution are drawing us together. We are all formed from the same mass of clay, the same energy; we've just taken different forms. There is nothing but consciousness—we are one consciousness. We will realize this. We will realize that we *are* the trees, the rocks, the water, and the animals; it's a feeling that has been trapped inside us. We are coming back together again; we have been going outward and have gone as far as we can go. As quantum physics has shown, energy goes outward, becomes scattered and random, and then it needs to become exact and pure again; it has to return to the one point. We're returning to that point of oneness; it's going to be a great union. How can I explain what it will feel like in mere words? How do you describe absolute love? I'm struggling to find the words. Nothing comes as close to this feeling as the experience of two lovers embraced in each other's arms. They have different bodies and different goals, they are moving in different directions, but in the moment of climax, they are moving toward a common point. They no longer exist as separate entities; they are no longer limited by their bodies but have expanded into the sensation of pure energy. Imagine everyone on the planet having this kind of experience at the same time, becoming one huge mass of pure energy, one being. Imagine having that exalted feeling all the time. It's constant and never goes away—you're free and you're happy. Has Mother Nature teased us with a glimpse of how wonderful this new consciousness will be with the experience of two lovers who, although they're from different walks of life and have dissimilar desires and thoughts, are nevertheless able to become one entity?

As we approach the new cycle of civilization, we will return to this subtler realm of being. But gaining entrance into this paradise requires that we have the right keys or we will be barred by the gates. If we do not understand that the kingdom of heaven is *within*, we will surely be left standing outside. Only the spiritually strong will survive the journey into this new world. There will be no room for an ego-centered life or for fear, distrust, and control; the rarefied atmosphere will not allow that. To be spiritually strong is to embrace the principles of generosity, compassion, and beauty. It means respecting every part of ourselves as sacred. It means seeing ourselves in all of the life-forms around us. If we see ourselves in the animals and in the trees, we might not destroy them so matter-of-factly. We might be more compassionate and selective.

To gain entrance into the new world, we must be willing to give up our misery and our suffering. We have been burdened with the belief that suffering ennobles the soul and that we have to struggle to make our lives work, but does nature struggle to sustain itself? If we are miserable, it means we're in the wrong place—we're doing something that's contrary to our nature. Self-perpetuated suffering has no purpose; none of Mother Nature's creatures will continue to dwell in a place that causes them anguish. Humans, on the other hand, have created this false notion that suffering is a measure of one's determination, but the only thing they've determined is their own extinction. As Lord Byron once eloquently wrote: "In hope to merit heaven by making earth a hell."

Only love and harmony are real and worth pursuing; that's why we're naturally drawn to this state of being. There is nothing spiritual about suffering. Suffering breeds nothing but sorrow and pain. Neither does poverty bring you closer to the forces that have created you— why would it? To have less does not automatically make you pious and good. It certainly does not make you one with the creative forces, which have no limitations. When you aspire to that which has no limitations, there is nothing that you don't have. The whole concept of poverty was created by people who sought to control and manipulate, such as those who wore the cloak of religion. Who singled them out to be God's representatives on Earth?

In the same vein, celibacy does not make you spiritual. It is a denial of a natural need and a means of creative expression of what drives you. To allow others to control you in this way is to give them complete control over your life so that you are forced to fill the ensuing void with their "God" and their "church."

Love and compassion are our vouchers into the new world; they are the coupon that will take us in. Without them we will not be allowed to pass through the gate.

The Thunderbeings continue to pray for the human race to

awaken. To be awakened is to be in the light, to be fully conscious and not allow fear or the shadows of the unconscious mind to control us. An ancient Mayan prophecy states that our sacred destiny is to awaken and be the true sons and daughters of the cosmic light: "The time of knowledge approaches, the light in the center of the pyramidal house of Hunab Ku will flash like lightning that will pierce through the shadows that envelop the human race. Let us prepare to receive the light of knowledge that comes from Hunab Ku and transcend into the memory of the creator and become beings of eternal luminosity."

The Thunderbeings have come from the Pleiades to be of service here. Our presence makes a difference; our thunder is heard in the distance. When we came into our bodily forms, we picked up their genetic histories. We are *in* the Earth but we are not *of* the Earth. We come from a place where life is peaceful and harmonious, where people are far more advanced in technology and spiritual understanding. We know that humans must change or they will perish and that as long as they live a material existence of consumerism set solely within the third dimension, they'll consume themselves.

We know that they have the potential to create a world free of pollution, disease, and destruction. But they must first awaken from the illusion of separation. Separation and individualistic forms of thinking are unnatural to other species. The birds and the animals don't question their identity. Only the two-legged asks "Who am I?" Such puzzling existential questions are the product of a mind that clings to separate ego identity. The mind that is interconnected and experiences the oneness of everything does not ask such questions but bathes in the glory of being.

I have learned that the pure spiritual road is neither drab nor hard. It involves controlling my own destiny and making myself happy. It's about adventure, joy, and movement. Spirituality is about being open and receptive. It's about ceremony, for ceremony is a recognition of the divine order of the universe. It's about being willing to face new challenges that are fearful and difficult—and sometimes leaving behind what is comfortable and secure. It's about assisting the balance of the whole and caring about others; we don't have to like or approve of them. It's recognizing that I have no deficiencies or broken parts. It's means staying in touch with my own thoughts and desires and not allowing someone else to determine my life. Spirituality is not difficult; it's the discipline that's difficult, the work we must do to go beyond the snare of the mind and the senses. It's realizing that our true self is the soul, not the body and the mind.

In our quest for spirituality, we can't always expect the waters of the ocean to part for us and say, "Come on in!" When we go into a forest we can't always expect the trees to sway back and forth and lower their branches to touch us and say, "I love you." We've become so mesmerized by phenomenal events and catastrophes that when something meaningful happens we don't give it any value. A sudden gust of wind or the appearance of a particular bird or animal in our immediate surroundings is telling us something. The voice of Spirit speaks to us through all the manifestations of nature, but we miss what's being said because we're so busy in our minds; we're so full of ourselves and our expectations.

In the quest to attain our spiritual goals, we do not have to leave society and live in the wilderness—although it would certainly help once in a while! Instead, why don't we bring the wilderness back into our lives? When there's a raccoon in our backyard, we don't have to go berserk trying to get rid of it; we don't need to snuff out the spider's life just because it wanders into our home. Let's welcome wild creatures back into our lives—make them feel wanted! If this means having more trees and wildflowers and creatures around us—and fewer manicured lawns—our lives will be immeasurably improved.

Spirituality doesn't come from any organization. We don't have to wait for spiritual times—all time is spiritual. It's our everyday thoughts, words, and actions; it's the totality of our being. Spirituality is measured by subtle things. It's the tingling sensation of gaining the wider perspective when we climb a mountain and attain a bird's-eye view. It's an intensity of consciousness, feeling alive and blissful and connected. It's what we feel when someone we love looks deeply and tenderly into our eyes. It's discovering that the wind and the trees do respond to us. It's the sacred silence beyond thought and language. It's the sensation of being aligned with the flow of movement in the universe, as in my experience of the vortex in the Azores.

I know that I have come a long way in my journey—I have made quantum leaps. Do I know all the answers? No. But I feel more comfortable with who I am; I feel more connected with nature. I take time every day to acknowledge and appreciate the life force that is within me and all around me. I can truly say that I am in love with life and more capable of handling the difficulties and challenges that naturally arise in the course of anyone's life. My goal is to live as fully as possible, and I often remind myself not to get too serious. Humor and playfulness are very important.

My life has truly reached a point of contentment. Ever since childhood, I always felt there was a place I had to go to. I now realize it wasn't so much a place as a state of mind, and I have arrived there. It was as though I were a river born on a mountaintop, and as I started to move down the mountain, I encountered many obstacles and attempted to plow through them. I tried to move huge boulders and flow uphill, which caused me grief. My upbringing taught me to be tenacious in the face of obstacles, but that is not the way a river flows. The river seeks a more harmonious path, which in turn brings it to its destination more effortlessly and more swiftly, and this causes less harm to its surroundings.

Once I put myself on my true path, I was quickly rewarded by the sound of my ultimate goal, the ocean. I could hear the ocean up ahead calling me—that timeless, spaceless, eternal mass from which I was created. Now my life has this incredible meaning to it. I feel that I will be embraced by the power that created me; I feel complete again.

As I look ahead to the next millennium, I foresee that many human-made systems and institutions will surely collapse. The atmosphere of our planet is in transformation and we will continue to have earthquakes, floods, droughts, hurricanes, and erratic weather. I think that as we enter into this very troubling period, there will be a terrible fear of "the end," and it will prompt people to change, just as a serious illness or near-death experience compels them to re-examine their lives. It will be very important to forgive and release judgments, grudges, and hatred, to clear old patterns and past experiences. Calamity will bring humanity back together in a spirit of community; faced with extinction humans will band together. As Hawk said, "We are in for a real awakening as to what it will take to pull us together as a family of humans. We are going to see how much the Earth is truly the mother of us all."

Many prophets have foreseen a time of great tribulation and the establishment of a more spiritual civilization, with a return to the instinctual divinity which was originally expected of us. They believe this will happen some time between 1995 and 2025 and that the human race will be able to advance tremendously within this period of time. Nostradamus, one of the most widely recognized prophets in history, who wrote his predictions in hundreds of four-line poems, described a series of dramatic cataclysmic events, including pestilence, famine, and war, "a terrible time for men," but one that will be short, followed by a time of great happiness and peace. Most existing faiths, as well as people of various disciplines and walks of life, have predicted in one form or another this very same scenario happening roughly at the same time.

We can expect major upheavals to the extent that many parts of the world will be changed beyond recognition. American psychic Edgar Cayce foresaw many geological changes, including a breakup of land in North America, the loss of much of Japan, the upper portion of Europe being changed in the twinkling of an eye, and upheavals in both polar regions.

This is a good time to get out of large cities and away from coastal areas, and to keep a year's supply of water, food, and other necessities—or become self-sufficient: grow your own food and harness your own energy source.

The Bible describes Saint John's vision of a many-horned lamb that opens the seven seals of a book: God's wrath is released upon humanity with the opening of each seal, decimating a large portion of the population. Only those protected with "the seal of God" will be spared.

Astrologers have predicted that on August 18, 1999, the sun and the planets will take a particular alignment, a phenomenon they claim is associated with the destruction of human society on Earth.

Does that mean that all this is inevitable? No, but that's the course we're on. It can be altered if the majority of people take action to move into a more positive avenue of consciousness. Then the prophecy need not come about, for its purpose, to generate change in people's minds, will be accomplished.

Possibly through some of the Thunderbeings' actions we have

managed to eliminate or delay some of the cleansings, and as more people choose a path of light we may be able to circumvent more of the prophesied scenes of destruction. If not, we can expect much upheaval and maybe a breakdown in our supersystems, which would create pandemonium in modern cities.

There may be fewer people left on Earth, but when all this has come to pass we will enter the most amazing period in history: a thousand years of peace. All existing political and economic structures will be done away with. As Nostradamus predicted, there will be painful readjustments, but wars will cease and the world's people will live in a true brotherhood; conflicts will be settled by words of understanding, not with arms.

Our reborn spirituality will assist in the discovery and invention of forms of science and technology having humanitarian goals. We will uncover the true scope of our abilities. The Tibetan prophets, for example, believe that science will finally realize and discover the mystical powers that are inherent in the human race, such as our latent ability to visualize the higher reaches of the light spectrum.

Some scientists who are currently exploring new views of reality are beginning to believe that the universe itself is a kind of giant hologram. As Michael Talbot states in *The Holographic Universe*, there is evidence to suggest that our world, along with everything in it, is a projection from a level of reality so far beyond our own that it is literally beyond both space and time. I believe that in the near future the holographic model will confirm the existence of a wide range of phenomena, including telepathy, precognition, and psychokinesis.

We have come to the threshold of a very different era. Now more than ever before we're at a point where science has an opportunity to prove itself as a friend of mankind. Science can enhance every aspect of human society, from controlling the population to producing nontoxic consumer goods to developing ecologically harmonious technologies. Science can help broaden our horizons, as demonstrated by Fritjof Capra and Gary Zukav, whose pioneering research has opened our minds to the similarities between quantum physics and Eastern mysticism.

In *The Tao of Physics*, Capra advocates a more compassionate and caring science; we need more scientists to take the "path with a heart" instead of wasting their ingenuity in developing ever more sophisticated means of destruction.

As we head into a new cycle of civilization, we will see the complete transformation of the human spirit. We will expand into fantastic and unexpected dimensions of being. Feelings and the mind will come into harmony, and we will function more completely on the intuitive plane. We will increase the focus on the soul and its power in our life here on Earth. As Hawk has said, we have experienced five evolutions of five worlds; we have five layers to our brain and we will begin our sixth as the Earth and the sun begin their next cycles of evolution. The creative mind will become part of the conscious mind, and we will remember who we really are and what we can do as untethered beings. We will open to the radiance of being itself; the creative power within us will burst forth like a river bursting through the dam that has held it back. We will tap into the full range of our senses, not just our sixth sense but also the seventh and eighth and so on, right through to the fourteenth! We will be clairvoyant and telepathic. We will enjoy natural teleportation and full spiritual awareness. The Earth will release all of her hidden secrets of paradise past, and we will emerge into the dawn of harmony. The Thunderbeings will have completed their mission. Some of us will return to our home in the Pleiades and others will find a wormhole to another universe calling for our assistance.

As you cross over into the millennium, things will move very fast; nothing will feel stable or secure anymore. Don't give in to the dark forces. Focus on beauty; focus on compassion. Go with an open heart and you will find the answers within. Awakening will be like coming out of the stupor of a deep sleep. You'll feel a sense of relief and euphoria when you realize that none of it was real; it was a game, an illusion. You are finally awakening to reality. Your long-dormant senses will be revived and you'll experience exciting, vivid sensations as you regain control of your destiny. There is a love waiting for you that is unlike anything you have ever experienced.

I leave you now with this thought, as stated by Thomas Moore:

As Half in shade and half in sun
This world along its path advances,
May that side the sun's upon
Be all that e'er shall meet thy glances!

NOTES

1. Barry Commoner, *The Closing Circle* (Alfred A. Knopf, Inc., New York, New York: 1972).